5-19-09

Kathy
Thank you for
all your help.
Enjoy
Renée

MEMORABLE RECIPES

MEMORABLE RECIPES

TO SHARE WITH FAMILY AND FRIENDS

Renée Behnke

with Cynthia Nims

Foreword by Joanne Weir

Photography by Angie Norwood Browne

Andrews McMeel
Publishing, LLC

Kansas City

09 10 11 12 13 SDB 10 9 8 7 6 5 4 3 2 1

Library of Congress Cataloging-in-Publication Data
Behnke, Renée.
  Memorable recipes : to share with family and friends / Renée Behnke with Cynthia
Nims ;
foreword by Joanne Weir ; photography by Angie Norwood Browne.—1st ed.
    p. cm.
  ISBN-13: 978-0-7407-7393-8
  ISBN-10: 0-7407-7393-3
  1. Entertaining. 2. Cookery. 3. Menus. I. Nims, Cynthia C. II. Title.
  TX731.B3875 2009
  642'.4—dc22
                                                          2008035113

www.andrewsmcmeel.com
Designer: Gretchen Scoble
Food Stylists: Patty Wittmann, Charlotte Omnes

ATTENTION: SCHOOLS AND BUSINESSES
Andrews McMeel books are available at quantity discounts with bulk purchase for
educational, business, or sales promotional use. For information, please write to:
Special Sales Department, Andrews McMeel Publishing, LLC, 1130 Walnut Street,
Kansas City, Missouri 64106.

To my grandmother, Mom, and my wonderful mother
for always letting me help stir.

CONTENTS

Acknowledgments

Now that all the recipes have been written, tested, and retested, I want to take the time to acknowledge the people who inspired me to cook, eat, and share so many wonderful meals.

First, I want to thank my grandmother and mother for always encouraging my interest in cooking and expanding my horizons when it came to new food. That old saying "Just try it" has always stayed with me and guided my adventures of new tastes.

Through the years, I have realized my friends and I spend so much time working that sharing a meal was the best time we could give each other. To my friends, I can't thank you enough for all the meals you have been willing to share with me. I have had the opportunity to travel and meet so many people who share a passion for the next great meal. It has made me realize that when I eat something special, whether a perfect peach or a grand five-course meal, it is always better when enjoyed with others.

A special thank-you to Joe McDonnal, who came to Seattle over thirty years ago. Joe creates simple meals and grand parties that inspire all of us. Every dish he serves is perfect, from easy deviled eggs to Paul's Death Cake.

To my husband, Carl, for the way he always supports and encourages me to follow my passions. He cheers me on with every new project even though it takes time away from each other. I also want to thank the children in my life who are always willing to eat the many meals I prepare for them.

Thank you to Pat Cunningham and Joanne Ellis, who came to my kitchen for months on end to help create and test every recipe. Your undying dedication to always assist me made this journey much easier.

Thank you to all of our employees at Sur La Table, who together help create a wonderful, unique company.

To the many great chefs, such as Julia Child, Marcella Hazan, Joanne Weir, Alice Waters, Mario Batali, Martha Stewart, and Christopher Kimball, who have all been an inspiration to me. You have taught us new techniques and styles, and graced our stores with your books; you support our growth and give us the energy to cook better and learn more.

To Cynthia Nims, who is a professional in every sense of the word. Thank you for your support, and for your ability to create, cook, and analyze every recipe; your honest feedback helped me through many tough decisions. The cook always loves every creation; the guest is the best critic.

To Dan McCarthy, for sharing your wonderful wine expertise with me, not only for this book but for our own wine cellar; your contributions to the Seattle-area wine community are much appreciated.

To the team at Andrews McMeel Publishing, who believed in my ability to create a book with broad appeal and exciting recipes that anyone can master.

Finally to Angie Norwood Browne, Gretchen Scoble, and Patty Wittmann. Angie is a wonderful photographer who treated each dish as though she was photographing my child. Gretchen's calm, organized approach took each page of this book and brought the written words to life with her design. Patty's cooking and styling talents gave life to every recipe.

To all of you—for making every day of my life special, I am most thankful and appreciative.

Foreword

Imagine this lunch. I'm bundled up in my ski gear and having a great day on the mountain skiing. The sky is clear and the sun is bright—one of those perfect spring ski days. "I'm hungry; let's meet on the top of the mountain!" she says. "Fine," I say, "count me in!" And when I arrive there's a table set all in white. And here she comes, our hostess, carrying a platter of grilled lamb chops and a winter potato salad! I guess the Côte-Rôtie will keep us warm! And for dessert, she's buried containers of vanilla ice cream in the snow. I help her scoop it into bowls and from a thermos, she pours warm bittersweet hot fudge sauce over the top. She sprinkles each bowl with toasted pecans. I still remember the steam as the warmth hits the cold ice cream! Now that's a picnic!

Or what about this one: She invites seventy of her closest friends to her annual Fourth of July barbecue at her summer house in the mountains. She says it will be fun and the menu is "easy." "Easy," I say as we find ourselves behind the stove for four hours cooking her famous recipe for fried chicken. That's after chopping red onions and shucking fresh butter-and-sugar corn for the black bean salad; chopping celery, green onions, basil, and mint for a summer potato salad; and slicing perfect heirloom tomatoes for a third salad. She said that we were let off the hook for dessert; the "ice cream man" would be stopping by later. I had visions of the "ding-dong man" as we called him when we were kids, riding up in his bicycle with the little refrigerated wagon on the back, ringing his bicycle bell to let us know he'd arrived. Her idea was a semi-trailer ice cream truck filled with a hundred different kinds of frozen ice cream treats the guests lined up for hours to taste.

And I will never forget the night she invited me for paella. I was thinking that she'd make a little pan of paella and call it a night. That's not how she thinks. Tango music spilled out the front door as I entered. The table was set impeccably with colored glass horses riding down the center and candles all around to set them aglow. I closed my eyes and for a few minutes I was dancing in Spain. I remember everything so clearly. The paella pan was so large, about three feet across, she needed me to help her carry it from the grill to the table inside. Once again, the food was delicious and the ambience divine, and she was painting memories for all of us.

She's my friend Renée, born with a whisk in one hand and a dinner bell in the other, and she has this special way of transporting you to this magical place where she lives. She loves to plan, to cook, to invite, to share—and she does it all so well, so effortlessly. It's her gift! It's the herb garden that greets you even before you enter her front door, it's the warmth of her extraordinary kitchen, it's the fun of cooking next to her at her stove, it's how she sets the table, it's the room off her kitchen totally devoted to her collection of dozens of sets of dinnerware, glassware, linens, candles, and flatware. This is how she sets her stage. She takes the ordinary and makes it extraordinary, whether it's the food, the company, the table, or the evening. . . . It's the smile on her face, the twinkle in her eye, and the heart that aims to please. I am delighted that Renée has written this book to share with all of us what comes so naturally to her.

—Joanne Weir, *cookbook author, cooking teacher, and television host*

INTRODUCTION

Nothing is more fun than bringing friends and family together for dinner. I've been throwing dinner parties of every size and style for many years now. From two to two hundred guests, denim casual to tux-and-tie formal, long-planned to last-minute, intimate conversation to dynamic celebration, comfort-food favorites to exotic international fare—it's all part of my entertaining repertoire today. Along the way, I've discovered countless tools to help make these dinner parties, luncheons, barbecues, and cocktail gatherings successful. These are the tools that I'll be sharing with you in these pages. My favorite recipes, my shortcut tips, my do-ahead suggestions, even a few menus that offer detailed game plans for pulling off a special dinner. You'll be entertaining with style and ease in no time.

I grew up in a family that made it natural for me to fall in love with food. We harvested vegetables and fruits from our huge garden, dug for razor clams at my grandparents' weekend home on the Oregon coast, and gathered wild mushrooms in the foothills of Mount Hood each fall. My grandmother, of German descent, made pickles and sauerkraut that held a place of honor in the basement as they cured. She also made stuffed cabbage, goulash, and great soups that remain in my recipe collection. My mother was a great baker, so we always had homemade breads. I can still smell the aroma of her cinnamon rolls; she managed to time things just right so that they came from the oven the moment we got home from school.

We didn't eat out very often, a family with five children and not a lot of money. Instead, we created good food at home. When it was someone's birthday or a special occasion to celebrate, my family threw their energy into cooking a great meal to be shared at our dinner table. I would stand in the kitchen and practice my ballet steps, helping stir, chop, and clean up while asking my mother or grandmother questions about what they were doing.

On school holidays or Saturday mornings, I often took the bus into Portland with my grandmother. We would do a little shopping, have lunch at the Meier & Frank tea room or Manning's lunch counter downtown, then head to the farmers' market to see what was fresh. I'd use my babysitting money to buy a perfect eggplant, maybe some chipped beef at the German meat counter, an artichoke or two if they were in season. These were things we didn't see in our neighborhood grocery store, a treat to share with my family.

As you can tell, good food and cooking were an important part of my life from an early age. Every family meal and food-related excursion left a deep and lasting impression on me.

When I moved out on my own, gathering friends together to share a meal was a highlight of my week. As our lives got busier, families grew, and jobs became more demanding, it was harder to keep up with everyone. Sunday became something of a standing date for many of us, a relaxed day to get together, often with children joining us at the table. I had the day to cook, set a great table, and prepare to share precious time with family and friends. It was not only a way to stay connected, but these meals also nourished my passion to cook and gave me the chance to create new dishes or try a recipe I'd seen in a magazine. Those Sunday dinners fed me in many ways.

In my twenties, I worked as a buyer for Nordstrom, a job that took me frequently to New York and Los Angeles. The exposure to new food, new people, and different cultures from around the world motivated me to try new dishes at home and share those experiences with family and friends. Travel opportunities only grew over the years, particularly when our family bought Sur La Table and began building the business, which has taken me literally around the globe.

Cooking today is becoming increasingly global. As we all travel to new destinations and more and more exotic new products show up on store shelves, we're enthusiastic about exploring new territory in the kitchen. But sometimes it may seem daunting, the prospect of re-creating the paella or samosas or sauerkraut you've had on your travels. Among the dishes in this book are many with an international focus; I've honed and developed these recipes by taking classes abroad, learning tips from the locals, and experimenting once I got home. It's a little "armchair travel" for you in your own kitchen.

I've had my fair share of amazing experiences in life, but I believe that the food I've eaten and the people I've shared meals with have created my fondest memories by far.

Throwing a Great Dinner Party

The most important lesson I've learned about entertaining is that it's about creating an experience for your guests, creating a memory for all to share. It does not have to involve the most elaborate dishes, expensive ingredients, hippest table setting, or most highly rated wines. All those elements may embellish your dinner party or luncheon with panache—and it is fun to splurge now and again—but they are not the starting points for creating a memorable time together.

While there certainly is some "fancy" food among the recipes that follow, you'll find a wealth of dishes that have stood the test of time, whether in my own family's recipe archives or because they are among traditional American favorites. It is a decidedly eclectic collection of recipes that reflects the many and varied influences that contribute to my cooking. I love to surprise my guests with dishes that lean toward the retro and traditional—clam dip, fried chicken, braised brisket—but always with a modern touch that fits today's approach to eating. Comfort food served even at an elegant gathering has a way of putting guests at ease. I watch them unwind and relax a bit more when familiar foods are served.

But don't worry. When you want to "wow" your guests with something stylish and striking for a special occasion, you'll find plenty here to fill out your menu. I just find that I don't always reach first for the most lavish recipes to cook for most of my dinner parties. It can be freeing to realize that you don't have to rely on the fancy factor all the time.

The more relaxed you are, the more relaxed your guests will be and the more welcomed they'll feel when you can chat with them as they arrive, handing them a glass of wine or savory nibble. I'd rather serve my guests a simple but delicious ice cream sundae for dessert than take on a more elaborate recipe that I cannot realistically accomplish with the time I have available. Be good to yourself, and to your guests, by budgeting your time and energy carefully as you plan out the evening's menu.

Planning Tips

To help you put on a wonderful party with minimal stress, I provide with every recipe two important tools that will help in your planning.

First is Menu Ideas. Here I'll prompt you with some recommended dishes that will partner well with the dish, either an item to serve alongside, or recipes to consider serving before or after to form a full menu. Most often, these recommendations will be other recipes in the book. But sometimes I'll just prod you in the direction of "a simple grilled steak" or "your favorite homemade cookie," so that you can keep things simple by preparing a recipe from your own collection.

The other tool you'll find with each recipe is the Do-Ahead Tips. These are key resources for you to help economize your time, particularly for a larger dinner party with multiple courses to prepare. One of the best lessons to learn about entertaining is that by no means should you try to do all the cooking in one fell swoop. Almost every recipe has at least an element or two—a sauce, dressing, pastry dough—that can be prepared in advance. And some dishes can be prepared fully in advance, so you have no more than to scoop, slice, or garnish just before serving. These are recipes that you will want to put to the top of your "dinner party" recipe list.

What I want most to accomplish with this book is to give you the confidence, the building blocks, the tools to help you pull together great dinner parties, celebratory luncheons, or any other delicious gathering of friends. With the recipes and ideas you'll find in the following pages, you'll be able to pull it all together with ease. After all, ease and enjoyment are the name of the game when it comes to entertaining.

The Menu

The format for dinner parties can vary greatly. In fact, it should vary from time to time. While the sit-down, three-course dinner party is certainly a reliable plan, it's also fun to mix things up for your guests. Consider throwing a tapas party with a dozen different appetizers for nibbling, followed by a main-course salad and light dessert. Or treat your guests to an elegant buffet dinner where they can suit their own tastes and appetite by serving themselves from the sideboard. I love the buffet setting, too, because it creates a particularly convivial setting by encouraging more guest interaction, such as mingling while plucking avocado and blue cheese from a grand platter of Grand

Cobb Salad (page 60) or scooping up a bowl of aromatic Chili with Fire-Roasted Peppers (page 94).

Sometimes I'll even switch format in the course of the evening, serving salad, soup, and main course seated at the dinner table and then serving dessert from a buffet arranged in the living room where guests can relax and continue the dinner conversation.

Especially for larger groups, I often make a few different desserts and invite guests to serve themselves from the buffet, also offering coffee, tea, and a chilled ice wine. A few cheeses or fruits are usually welcome, to complement the sweets. This gives guests a chance to stretch their legs after dinner and the conversation, energy, and appetites will be renewed.

When it comes to selecting the specific dishes you'll be serving, you want to play both with complementary and contrasting elements. The first place to start is usually the main-course selection, then build your meal around that. While it certainly can be fun to throw a dinner party with a distinct theme that plays out through all the dishes and décor—whether Italian, Mardi Gras, or Moroccan—don't feel that you always need to remain geographically focused as the menu builds. A dinner of lamb tagine may just as well begin with clam dip as with Moroccan meatballs.

What you do want to think about is flavor and texture. Too much of one flavor tone, such as spiciness, tart citrus, or gentle mellow flavors, can be overkill. I'll instead choose contrast and counterpoint, partnering a richer entrée with a bright, crisp salad, or a spicier entrée with a soup that has gentle sweet tones. Plenty of pairing and menu ideas are to be found throughout this book, to give you some starting points.

If you are doing a seated dinner, limit the hors d'oeuvres served early on. Light finger food, such as Cheese Crackers (page 39), Olive Pecan Bites (page 10), or Crudités with one or both dips (page 28), might be plenty. Then draw your guests to the table with a plated appetizer to launch the dinner. Nothing gets the conversation going more than the delicate, lovely Cheese-Stuffed Zucchini Blossoms (page 25) with a dusting of sea salt and a crisp white wine, or aromatic Mussels à l'Escargot (page 35) with a glass of bubbly.

Planning the Evening

When it comes to the cook's workload, making things easy and efficient not only makes your life easier, it helps make you a better host or hostess. There's nothing worse than the dinner party at which the host is a yo-yo, racing in and out of the kitchen and barely sitting at the table, let alone relaxing and engaging with guests.

Be realistic about the amount of time and energy you'll have and tailor your menu plan to follow suit. It is fully acceptable to focus on a delicious appetizer, salad, and main course that you make yourself, then serve a wonderful seasonal tart or cake picked up from your favorite bakery. Or let your guests in on the fun and ask a few of them to bring their tried-and-true appetizer while you devote attention to the main course and dessert selections. You don't have to do it all. Remember—your guests are going to be thrilled with whatever you do make, and spending time together is the most important gift you're giving them.

It does not matter if there are six or sixteen people coming for dinner, if you're serving a buffet or formal multi-course dinner, the steps are the same, though specific time allotments and tasks will vary based on the individual recipes you choose.

1. A few weeks ahead, organize your guest list. Make sure you have at least one person in the group who is a good conversationalist. He or she could have an interesting career, be a great storyteller, or know how to generate interesting topics or icebreakers. If you are hosting a family gathering, you will find that inviting a few non-family guests helps energize the evening's dynamic. The same may be true of your old college friends, your close colleagues—any niche group in your life. A dinner party guest list that crosses over or between these groups can make for a wonderful, engaging night.

2. Three to four days out, plan your menu and review the recipes. Check if any ingredients need to be special-ordered or if you need to budget early prep time to marinating or some other advance step in the recipe. Start working on your shopping list, taking stock of what you have on hand and what needs to be purchased. Think about the wine options and other beverages as well. Try to group your shopping lists by store or neighborhood, so you can be efficient about your shopping time. Consider what you may want to use for décor elements: candles, flowers, fun tabletop accents that will suit the theme or focus of the gathering.

3. Read the recipes carefully a few days in advance, particularly the Do-Ahead Tips, to determine what parts can be prepared (or perhaps fully cooked) in advance. This will be important to lessen the demands on your time the day of the meal. Have a look at the sample menu plans that begin on page 194 to get an idea of how I plot out menu preparation tasks. It helps to create a detailed list that guides you through the tasks, checking things off as you work your way to the dinner itself.

4. Two days out, plan how you will set the table, which linens you'll use (do they need ironing?), dishes, silverware (a little polish?), and of course what you'll use for your centerpiece and other decorations. If you won't be eating at the big dinner table between now and the party, you should consider setting your table a day or two ahead, then simply add fresh flowers or other last-minute additions the day of the party. If you're planning a buffet dinner, get out the serving dishes you plan to use for each item, making sure you have enough dishes of the correct size; borrow from a friend or neighbor if needed. I like to write on a slip of paper the name of the dish and put it in/on the serving dish itself, so I don't have to rethink later what was meant to go where. It also makes things easier on kitchen helpers, so they won't have to ask you in the height of final dinner prep.

5. Do as much of your shopping the day before as possible. Have a quick look back through the recipes before you head out, making sure you haven't overlooked an item you assume you have on your shelf but actually don't: cornstarch, walnuts, baking powder, white rice. While you will have already reviewed the Do-Ahead Tips for each recipe and have some advance prep on your checklist, there are often other ingredient preparations that may be done a day in advance. Read the recipe ingredient lists carefully to look for items like garlic or bell peppers to be roasted, nuts to be toasted, spinach or lettuce greens to be rinsed, and other items of this nature.

6. The day of the meal, begin by working on the most complicated dish first, then continue with day-of preparation for the other recipes. Don't be tempted to start doing last-minute errands too early in the day. It's important to get some of the cooking prep checked off the list, and along the way you may find another item (crème fraîche for garnish?) that needs to be picked up as well. While you're cooking, be sure to wash and put away all your tools, bowls, and pans as you go. Not only does this keep your work space tidy and avoid having a huge mess to clean up later, but it ensures that when you next need to peel something or need another medium bowl, you won't have to stop everything to do some cleaning. Make sure that white wine and any other beverages that need chilling get chilled. Make the place cards, if you'll be using them.

For a large or more complex dinner party, I usually hire someone to help serve and clean up—a local culinary student, a neighborhood teen, a friend of the family, a staff person from a nearby catering company. Ask them to arrive 1½ hours before your guests are scheduled to begin showing up. Take a good half hour to go over the menu with them, the dishes to be used, the schedule for the evening. Make sure they understand exactly what you'll need them to be doing for the next few hours. You may then turn your attention to final table settings, filling ice buckets, setting up the bar. Be sure to schedule in a bit of "down time" for yourself just before guests arrive, time to change clothes, freshen up, put your feet up for a few minutes. It does wonders to have this little break before the evening's festivities begin.

People will always gravitate to the kitchen while the evening gets started. I enjoy this very much. Our kitchen is large and open, so everyone can mingle and I still have plenty of room to move about. If you find you're getting cramped, though, and don't have the space to take care of your last-minute prep, you can gently nudge people toward the dining room or living room so you can finish your work in ease.

One thing that often throws off a home cook is when someone arrives with an armload of flowers that need attention. Excuse yourself, find a vessel to get them in water, but don't feel obligated to create an arrangement and display the flowers immediately.

Also, if a guest brings wine that you weren't expecting, you should not feel obligated to serve it that evening. However, if it's a special dessert wine, you may decide to share it with your guests. We usually add a note to the wine label reminding us who gave us the bottle and when, so that we can remember the source when we enjoy the wine later. It is always fun to thank them after we have had a chance to savor the wine.

The bottom line is to keep things easy on yourself and try not to get derailed by little surprises that come along the way. Entertaining is about the time shared together. That's what matters the most. The time, energy, and love that you put into cooking for your friends and family are fuel for those wonderful gatherings.

Wine Notes

Once you've got your menu plan in place, planning the wine element of the meal can stop even the most experienced host in his tracks: How much wine to serve? Which wines to serve and when? As a wine merchant, I try to reassure folks that although wine pairing is not a science, there are ways to navigate toward easy answers to these common questions.

First, the question of how much. Make note of the following: How many people will you be hosting? How many hours will the event last? During what season does the meal take place? With these in hand, you can calculate the quantity of wine needed fairly closely. Take the number of hours and multiply by 2.5 to get the predictable average number of ounces needed per person. A 2-hour party is the minimum, requiring 5 ounces of wine per person. A 3-hour party yields, 7.5 ounces, and so on. Somewhere it all stops. To avoid planning too much wine, don't let the number exceed a bottle per person.

So, if you're having 16 people to dinner for about 3 hours, you calculate 7.5 ounces per person, or 120 total ounces of wine needed. Divide this by 25.4 (the ounce equivalent of a 750 ml bottle of wine) and you get 4.7 bottles. In this case, I would round up to 5 bottles, maybe 6 to add a buffer.

If the attire is casual, more red will be consumed, usually about 65 percent red. As the event becomes more formal, a higher proportion of white wine will be consumed. Even those who swear that their friends prefer red wine will discover that this is a real phenomenon.

As to season, consider that cooler climes result in more red wine being drunk, so plan accordingly. As the temperature rises, white wine consumption increases dramatically. And when it is downright hot, the higher alcohol of red wines makes their flavors almost unpleasant to drink, with rosés and white wines to the rescue.

Now to consider which wines you'll be serving. You've probably heard and read many wine-pairing rules—serve white before red, sweet wines with dessert, white wine with fish, red wine with meat—often as if they are set in stone. Instead, I think it's time to realize that the choices of what wine to serve when can be as varied as your choices of what ingredients to include in a dish. You can forget those rules and serve a heavily peppered, boldly flavored seafood dish with a Syrah or red Grenache instead of white wine. I only serve Pinot Noir with salmon, as well. Mix things up and serve a game dish like duck, pheasant, or Guinea fowl with a white Burgundy, a surprisingly delicious pairing. Rosé with ham, Champagne with red meat, Cabernet Sauvignon with chocolate, there are many wonderful food and wine pairings that seem counterintuitive but work beautifully.

Here are a couple of pairing principles that will be helpful. The acidity of a dish is a great starting point to help choose the accompanying wine. High acidity in a dish should be complemented by a higher acidity in the wine, so that neither becomes overwhelmed. As the fat content of a dish soars—such as rich rib eye steak—so should the levels of tannin in the wine poured. Heavily tannic reds are easily tamed by fatty meats. Salty foods require crisp, dry white wines and rosés to find balance.

These are some starting points for your explorations of wine and food pairings. Experiment a bit on your own, as everyone's palate is different. Taste a couple of different wines with a dish to understand how differently each will complement (or not) the food. You will soon gravitate to some combinations that you prefer and can employ again and again as you entertain. Rules don't need to apply. Making enjoyment of food and wine easy and fun is the ultimate goal.

—Dan McCarthy, *co-owner, McCarthy & Schiering Wine Merchants, Seattle*

APPETIZERS AND STARTERS In the following pages you'll find recipes that help set the stage for a wide variety of occasions, whether it's the Sunday game, a casual cocktail party that is all about nibbling, or a more formal multi-course dinner treating your guests to a splashy first course. Inspiration for these recipes comes from around the world, with flavors that touch on the Mediterranean, Asia, and South America, but also include plenty of selections from across the United States.

This chapter encompasses both appetizers—finger food that's ideal paired with a cocktail or glass of wine—as well as dishes that may be the starter to a formal meal, plated for a sit-down dinner. Many of these recipes are versatile and are easily adapted to both scenarios.

You definitely should not feel obligated to serve appetizers or a starter course at every dinner party. For a casual gathering, there's no reason you can't launch right in to your entrée with salad and a side dish, then finish with a simple dessert—your guests will be satisfied. Or simply have a few bowls of salted nuts, olives, and fancy crackers to snack on as guests gather, adding no more work to your load. But on those occasions when you want to begin the evening with a little extra panache, you'll find dozens of options here from which to choose.

CARAMELIZED ONION TART
WITH NIÇOISE OLIVES

My friend Lydie Marshall, who owns a cooking school in the south of France, is the inspiration behind this recipe. It's reminiscent of the pissaladière from that region, a distinctive savory onion tart accented with anchovies.

I like to use both Gruyère and Appenzeller cheeses in this recipe. Appenzeller, from Switzerland, has a slightly stronger, tangier flavor than Gruyère. You can use Jarlsberg in place of the Appenzeller (which can be a little hard to find), or simply use all Gruyère if you prefer.
MAKES 8 TO 12 SERVINGS

2 tablespoons vegetable oil

2 tablespoons unsalted butter

4 large yellow onions, thinly sliced

2 cloves garlic, pressed or minced

1 tablespoon sugar

Pinch of cayenne pepper

Salt and freshly ground black pepper

1 egg

2 tablespoons Dijon or green peppercorn mustard

½ cup grated Gruyère cheese

½ cup grated Appenzeller cheese

24 Niçoise olives or pitted dry-cured olives

6 anchovy fillets, halved lengthwise (optional)

PASTRY DOUGH

½ cup unsalted butter

1 cup all-purpose flour

¼ teaspoon salt

3 to 4 tablespoons cold water

1. For the pastry dough, cut the butter into small cubes and freeze for 5 minutes. In the bowl of a food processor, combine the butter, flour, and salt. Process for 10 to 15 seconds, until the butter is finely chopped. Add 3 tablespoons water and pulse for another 10 seconds, or until the mixture looks like cornmeal. Pinch some of the dough in your fingers; it should hold together, not feel crumbly or dusty. If necessary, add more water, a teaspoon at a time, pulsing once or twice after each addition.

2. Turn the dough out onto a clean work surface. Gather about one-quarter of the dough into a small pile and use the heel of your hand to push the dough away from you 2 or 3 times, which helps thoroughly blend the butter and flour, producing a flakier dough. Don't overwork the dough or it will become tough. Repeat with the remaining dough, then use a pastry scraper to gather the dough, forming it into a disk about 6 inches across. Wrap the dough in plastic wrap and refrigerate for at least 30 minutes.

3. Preheat the oven to 425°F.

4. Heat the vegetable oil and butter in a large skillet or sauté pan over medium heat. Add the onions and garlic and cook for about 20 minutes, stirring occasionally, until tender. Stir in the sugar and cayenne and cook for 10 to 15 minutes longer, stirring occasionally, until the onions are very tender and take on a deep caramel color. Season to taste with salt and pepper. Whisk together the egg and mustard in a small bowl; set aside.

5. Roll the pastry dough out on a lightly floured work surface to a 12-inch circle about ⅛ inch thick. Use the dough to line a 10-inch tart pan with a removable base. Brush the bottom and side of the tart shell with the egg/mustard mixture. Cover the bottom of the tart pan with the grated cheeses, top with the caramelized onions in an even layer, and scatter the olives over. Arrange the anchovy halves lengthwise over the tart.

Menu Ideas: This savory tart will be an ideal first course of a Mediterranean-style menu that could include Ratatouille with Fresh Rosemary (page 152) and Osso Buco with Sage Gremolata (page 113). Cut into smaller finger-food portions, the tart also makes a great option for a cocktail party spread.

Do-Ahead Tips: The pastry can be made up to 3 days in advance and refrigerated, or frozen (well-wrapped) for a month. The caramelized onions can be made up to 1 day in advance and refrigerated. The tart will be at its best enjoyed right after it is baked, preferably warm. Reheat in a low oven if needed.

6. Set the tart pan on a baking sheet and bake for about 30 minutes, until the pastry is nicely browned. Let cool on a wire rack for 10 to 15 minutes, then remove the sides and cut the tart into wedges to serve warm.

LINING A TART PAN: Here are a few tips to make easy work of lining a tart pan: First, roll the dough out into a relatively even circle so it'll be easier to work with. To transfer it to the pan, I loosely roll the dough around my rolling pin, then unroll the dough over the pan. Press the dough out evenly across the base and be sure the dough fits snugly into the corners for a tidy edge. Lay excess dough over the rim of the pan and roll the rolling pin over the top to evenly trim away the excess. Use your fingers to neaten the edge, pressing to flute the dough, following the pattern of the tart pan.

FRIED OYSTERS WITH RÉMOULADE

Although I sometimes shuck fresh oysters for this dish, jarred oysters make the recipe a snap. Check that the liquid surrounding the oysters in the jar is clear, rather than cloudy, to ensure they're good and fresh. These fried oysters are an element in the wonderful Spinach and Hearts of Palm Salad (page 44). **MAKES 6 TO 8 SERVINGS**

24 small shucked oysters

1 cup buttermilk

¾ cup all-purpose flour, plus more for sprinkling

½ cup plain dried bread crumbs

½ cup panko bread crumbs

2 teaspoons finely grated lemon zest

½ teaspoon cayenne pepper

½ teaspoon salt

¼ teaspoon freshly ground black pepper

Vegetable oil, for frying

RÉMOULADE

1 cup mayonnaise

¼ cup finely chopped cornichons or dill pickles

2 tablespoons finely chopped capers

1½ tablespoons minced shallot

1½ tablespoons tomato paste

1 tablespoon freshly squeezed lemon juice

1 tablespoon chopped fresh flat-leaf parsley

1 anchovy fillet, mashed

1 teaspoon dry mustard

1 teaspoon dried tarragon

1 teaspoon dried marjoram

Pinch of cayenne pepper

1. For the rémoulade, stir together the mayonnaise, cornichons, capers, shallot, tomato paste, lemon juice, parsley, anchovy, mustard, tarragon, marjoram, and cayenne in a small bowl. Cover with plastic wrap and refrigerate for at least 1 hour before serving.

2. Drain the oysters in a strainer, then place them in a bowl and add the buttermilk. Refrigerate for 30 minutes to 2 hours before continuing.

3. Cover 1 baking sheet with a thin layer of flour and line another baking sheet with a couple layers of brown paper or paper towels. Combine the flour, plain and panko bread crumbs, lemon zest, cayenne, salt, and pepper in a medium bowl and stir to mix.

4. Remove a few oysters at a time from the buttermilk and thoroughly coat them in the bread crumb mixture. Set the coated oysters on the floured baking sheet and continue with the remaining oysters. Let the oysters sit for about 15 minutes, then toss them once again in the bread crumb mixture.

5. Preheat the oven to 200°F. Pour about 2 inches of oil into a deep fryer or large, deep pot, such as a Dutch oven (it's important the oil comes no more than halfway up the sides of the pan for safety). Heat the oil over medium heat to 375°F.

6. Slip 4 or 5 of the coated oysters carefully into the hot oil and fry for 1 to 2 minutes, until nicely browned. Transfer the oysters to the paper-lined baking sheet, sprinkle lightly with salt, and keep warm in the oven while frying the remaining oysters.

7. Arrange the fried oysters on individual plates and spoon a generous dollop of rémoulade alongside.

Menu Ideas: These fried oysters are great for a cocktail party spread or to pass as your guests arrive. Or serve them as a seated first course before Mardi Gras Gumbo (page 100)—or any main course that has a little spice to it.

Do-Ahead Tips: The rémoulade can be made up to 4 days in advance and refrigerated. The coated oysters can be prepared up to 2 hours in advance and refrigerated; they are best when fried just before serving.

MINTY MEATBALLS

On trips to Spain I have sampled many different versions of the meatball in tapas bars—some in sauce, others on skewers to simply enjoy as is. For buffet service, I set a small dish of toothpicks alongside a platter of these meatballs, so guests can easily spear a meatball to enjoy as finger food.

I like the combination of ground pork and veal, a light flavor that allows the seasonings to shine through. Alter the combination to include ground beef and/or lamb if you like. Note that you may need to pre-order ground veal or lamb from your regular market, or make a trip to a specialty butcher. **MAKES 8 SERVINGS**

2 tablespoons plus 2 teaspoons vegetable oil

¼ cup minced yellow onion

1 tablespoon all-purpose flour

2 slices white sandwich bread, crusts removed

⅓ cup whole milk

1 pound lean ground pork

½ pound ground veal

1 egg, lightly beaten

2 cloves garlic, pressed or minced

2 teaspoons minced fresh mint, or 1 teaspoon dried mint

1 teaspoon minced fresh oregano, or ½ teaspoon dried oregano

¾ teaspoon salt

¼ teaspoon freshly ground black pepper

Mint sprigs, for garnish

1. Heat 2 teaspoons of the oil in a small skillet over medium-low heat. Add the onion and cook 2 to 3 minutes, until tender but not browned. Sprinkle the flour over and stir to mix. Let cool.

2. Tear the bread into pieces and place in a small bowl. Drizzle the milk over and let sit to fully moisten the bread.

3. Combine the ground pork and veal in a large bowl. Squeeze the milk from the bread and add the bread to the meat, along with the sautéed onion, egg, garlic, mint, oregano, salt, and pepper. Blend the ingredients well with your hands, then form into balls about 1 inch across (you should have about 40 meatballs). Cover with plastic wrap and refrigerate for at least 15 minutes before cooking.

4. Heat the remaining 2 tablespoons oil in a large skillet over medium heat. In 3 or 4 batches, cook the meatballs, , turning a few times, for 8 to 10 minutes, until evenly browned and cooked through. Transfer the meatballs to individual plates or a platter. Arrange mint sprigs around and serve.

Menu Ideas: These meatballs make a wonderful appetizer before most any meal, but will be ideal paired with Smoky Moroccan Meatballs (page 11) before Paella with Chicken and Shellfish (page 120) or the Chicken Tagine with Apricots and Almonds (page 116). You could also pair the meatballs with your favorite red pasta sauce (or the Spicy Tomato Topping on page 13, omitting the red pepper flakes), braised together a bit before serving over pasta.

Do-Ahead Tips: You can form the meatballs up to 1 day ahead and keep them, wrapped well, in the refrigerator. You can cook them up to 1 hour in advance and keep them warm in a low oven, covered with foil so they stay moist. The uncooked meatballs freeze well: Freeze them first on a baking sheet until solid, then transfer them to an airtight container to freeze for up to 1 month. Thaw slowly in the refrigerator before cooking.

PICKLED SHRIMP
WITH CAPERS

I like to leave the tail end of the shell on when peeling shrimp for this recipe, providing a little "handle" for guests to use when eating the pickled shrimp. For a more casual buffet service, arrange the drained shrimp on a decorative platter with fresh herb sprigs around for garnish. Capers—I prefer the tiny nonpareil type—are the pickled flower buds of a bush native to the Mediterranean. Caper berries, which I use to garnish this dish, are the fruit that is formed on the same bush, also pickled. MAKES 6 TO 8 SERVINGS

4 cups water

½ cup coarsely chopped celery leaves

¼ cup pickling spice

1 tablespoon salt

2½ pounds large shrimp, peeled and deveined

½ large sweet onion, thinly sliced

6 dried bay leaves

1 head butter lettuce, trimmed, rinsed, and dried

12 caperberries, halved

MARINADE

1½ cups vegetable oil

¾ cup white wine vinegar

¼ cup nonpareil capers, plus 2 tablespoons
of their brine

2½ teaspoons celery seeds

1 teaspoon salt

1. Combine the water, celery leaves, pickling spice, and salt in a large sauce-pan and bring to a boil over medium-high heat. Add the shrimp, decrease the heat to medium, and cook, stirring occasionally, for about 4 minutes, or just until the shrimp are evenly pink and cooked through. Drain the shrimp.

2. Choose a nonreactive bowl just large enough to hold the shrimp and onion with a little spare room. Place half of the still-warm shrimp (with the celery and spices) in the bowl, top with half the onion and half the bay leaves; repeat with a layer of the remaining shrimp, onion, and bay leaves.

3. For the marinade, whisk together the oil, vinegar, capers and brine, celery seeds, and salt in a small bowl until the salt is dissolved. Pour the marinade slowly over the shrimp. Cover the bowl with plastic wrap and refrigerate for at least 24 hours, gently stirring the ingredients once or twice. Drain the shrimp just before serving (reserve the marinade), shaking off any spices or celery that cling to them and discarding the bay leaves.

4. Arrange a couple leaves of the butter lettuce on each plate, cupped-side up. Spoon the marinated shrimp (with some of the onion and capers) into the lettuce cups and set a few of the caperberry halves alongside. Drizzle some of the marinade over and serve.

Menu Ideas: This dish is particularly good for picnic fare, as the pickled shrimp hold up well in transit. The marinated shrimp are great as part of a casual buffet as well, perhaps partnered with Chili with Fire-Roasted Peppers (page 94) and Mini Corn Muffins with Roasted Garlic and Fresh Herbs (page 136) for Super Bowl sustenance. If you have any leftovers, store them in the marinade, refrigerated, for up to a few days.

Do-Ahead Tips: The recipe can be fully prepared up to 5 days in advance and refrigerated.

FETA AND MINT PHYLLO PACKETS

Feta is often sold packed in briny water, in which case be sure to drain it well and pat dry with paper towels to keep the filling from being too damp. Different brands of feta can range from dry and crumbly to softer and almost creamy. If the feta you're using is rather dry, add another ounce of cream cheese to the filling. **MAKES 6 TO 8 SERVINGS**

8 ounces feta cheese, finely crumbled
    (about 2 cups)

4 ounces cream cheese, at room temperature

⅓ cup thinly sliced green onions

2 tablespoons minced fresh mint

½ teaspoon ground cumin

Freshly ground black pepper

8 ounces frozen phyllo dough, thawed

Olive oil, for brushing

Menu Ideas: These flaky pastries will be a perfect match for Choux Puffs with Salmon and Shrimp (page 36) and Grilled Pork Kebabs (page 21) to serve before dinner. The feta cheese has a very distinct flavor, so it's best not to serve this with dishes that feature other types of cheese. A dish of olives is always a good accent alongside. Follow with Veal Chops with Green Peppercorns and Rosemary (page 117) or Salmon with Nasturtium Butter (page 90).

Do-Ahead Tips: You can make the phyllo packets up to 2 hours ahead and refrigerate them on the baking sheet, covered with plastic wrap to avoid drying out. They are best served when still warm, shortly after baking.

1. Preheat the oven to 375°F. Line a baking sheet with a silicone baking mat or parchment paper.

2. Combine the feta, cream cheese, green onions, mint, and cumin in a small bowl and stir well to mix. Season to taste with pepper.

3. Lay out 1 sheet of phyllo dough on the work surface (keep the remaining sheets covered with a kitchen towel). Brush lightly with oil and lay another sheet on top as evenly as you can. Brush lightly with oil. Cut the phyllo sheets into strips 14 inches long and 4½ inches wide (into halves or quarters, depending on the size of your phyllo sheets).

4. Scoop 1 tablespoon of the feta filling onto a phyllo strip about 1½ inches from the bottom. Fold the bottom edge of dough upward to cover the filling, then fold the filling upward 2 more times. Fold in both long edges, to enclose the sides of the filling, then continue folding the phyllo upward to form a tidy packet.

5. Set the packet seam side down on the baking sheet, cover with a kitchen towel, and repeat with the remaining filling and phyllo dough. You should have about 20 packets in all. Lightly brush the pastry tops with oil. Bake for about 15 minutes, until puffed and brown. Serve warm or at room temperature.

GRILLED SCALLOPS
WITH RED PEPPER-HARISSA COULIS

This is an elegant way to start off a meal—fat, succulent scallops grilled and served with a silky sauce embellished with harissa, a North African chile sauce. Look for harissa in specialty food shops, or you can buy it online from Seattle-based Mustapha's Moroccan (see www.mustaphas.com). If you are unable to find harissa, you may use another chile sauce instead, such as the Asian sambal oelek; you may need to use less, as chile sauces vary greatly in their heat intensity.

I like to serve the scallops and coulis in large scallop shells, the bright red sauce a vivid complement to the pale shell and scallop. I usually serve three scallops per serving as a first course. But if this dish will be part of a larger multi-course menu, one scallop per person will suffice. You could also serve this as part of a buffet, spearing each scallop at the end of a bamboo skewer, the coulis alongside for dipping. If your scallops still have the small tough side muscle attached, cut it away before cooking. **MAKES 6 SERVINGS**

18 large sea scallops
¼ cup freshly squeezed lime juice
Freshly ground white pepper

RED PEPPER-HARISSA COULIS

2 red and 1 yellow or orange bell peppers,
    roasted, peeled, seeded, and chopped
    (see page 220)
2 tablespoons grated or minced yellow onion
2 tablespoons harissa
2 tablespoons water
2 tablespoons olive oil
1 tablespoon balsamic vinegar
1 clove garlic, pressed or minced
Salt

1. For the coulis, purée the roasted peppers in a food processor with the onion, harissa, water, olive oil, balsamic vinegar, and garlic until smooth, scraping down the side once or twice. Transfer the coulis to a small saucepan, season to taste with salt, and set aside until ready to serve, preferably at least 30 minutes to allow the flavors to meld.

2. Preheat an outdoor grill. When the grill is heated, lightly rub the grill grate with oil. Grill the scallops 30 to 60 seconds per side, until nicely browned on the surface but still rare. Set the scallops on a platter, drizzle the lime juice over, and season lightly with pepper.

3. Gently warm the coulis over medium-low heat. Spoon the coulis onto individual plates or large scallop shells. Set each scallop on top of the sauce.

Menu Ideas: This slightly spicy appetizer would be ideally paired with Cheese Crackers (page 39), Smoky Moroccan Meatballs (page 11), and/or the Feta and Mint Phyllo Packets (page 7) for a cocktail spread. As a seated first course, it pairs beautifully with Lamb Shanks Tagine with Preserved Lemon (page 126) or the Grilled Rack of Pork with Mango Salsa (page 92).

Do-Ahead Tips: The coulis can be made up to 2 days in advance and refrigerated; warm gently over low heat before serving. Note that the sauce will become spicier the longer it sits, so if making in advance you may want to use just 1 tablespoon harissa and adjust with more, to taste, just before serving. The scallops should be grilled just before serving.

OLIVE PECAN BITES

My friend Joe McDonnal taught me to make this great recipe. Joe owns The Ruins, a wonderful private dinner club in Seattle that is also one of the city's top catering companies. The blend of crisp pastry and salty-nutty filling makes them the ideal nibble with cocktails or wine before dinner. I've had more than a few friends confess to me that they're addicted to this aperitif snack.

One of the best things about this recipe is how convenient it can be for last-minute plans. With a couple of the logs in the freezer (I often quadruple the recipe), I can be ready to go with a snack in no time flat. **MAKES 16 TO 20 SERVINGS**

1½ cups all-purpose flour

1 teaspoon sweet Hungarian paprika

¾ teaspoon salt

½ cup unsalted butter, cut into pieces and chilled

½ cup sour cream

OLIVE PECAN FILLING

1 cup finely chopped toasted pecans
  (see page 220)

1 cup grated Cheddar cheese (medium or half
  sharp/half medium)

1 cup finely chopped green olives with pimientos

2 tablespoons mayonnaise

Menu Ideas: These bites will be great paired with other cocktail snacks such as Clam and Chive Dip with Pita Chips (page 17), Pickled Shrimp with Capers (page 6), and Choux Puffs with Salmon and Shrimp (page 36).

Do-Ahead Tips: You can assemble the filled logs of dough, wrap each well in a couple layers of plastic wrap, and freeze for up to 1 month. The pastry can be unwrapped and baked directly from the frozen state; add about 10 minutes to the baking time.

1. Combine the flour, paprika, and salt in a food processor and pulse to blend. Add the butter pieces and pulse until evenly blended to a sand-like consistency. Add the sour cream and pulse just until the mixture is pebbly. Turn the mixture out onto the work surface and form into a ball. Wrap the dough in plastic wrap and refrigerate for at least 30 minutes.

2. Preheat the oven to 400°F. Line a baking sheet with a silicone baking mat or parchment paper.

3. For the filling, stir together the pecans, cheese, olives, and mayonnaise in a medium bowl until well blended.

4. Roll the chilled dough on a lightly floured work surface to a rectangle about ⅛ inch thick, then trim it to a tidy rectangle 12 inches by 10 inches. Cut the dough into 4 lengthwise strips, each 3 inches wide and 10 inches long.

5. Spoon one quarter of the filling down the center of a pastry strip, using your fingers to form it into a compact cylinder about 1 inch wide. Roll the pastry around the filling, pinching well all along the seam to seal. (This is an important step to ensure the log doesn't burst when baked; take care to fully seal that edge.) Repeat to make 3 more logs.

6. Set the logs seam side down on the baking sheet. Bake for about 20 minutes, or until nicely browned. Let cool for a few minutes on the baking sheet, then transfer to a cutting board. Cut the logs into ½-inch slices (discard, or snack on, the end pieces), arrange on a serving platter, and serve warm.

SMOKY MOROCCAN MEATBALLS

My friends always rave about this recipe, which is a takeoff of an appetizer that I learned to make in Morocco on my first trip there in 1997. Sometimes I'll serve both the Minty Meatballs (page 5) and these, which have a more aromatic character from the cumin and smoked paprika. Rather than sautéing the meatballs, you could grill them. To do so, thread onto bamboo skewers that have been soaked in water, then grill until just cooked through, 5 to 7 minutes. **MAKES 8 SERVINGS**

1 pound lean ground pork

½ pound ground veal

⅓ cup finely chopped yellow onion

2 teaspoons ground cumin

2 teaspoons Spanish smoked paprika

2 teaspoons minced fresh flat-leaf parsley

1 teaspoon pressed or minced garlic

1 teaspoon olive oil

1 teaspoon salt

½ teaspoon freshly ground black pepper

6 tablespoons all-purpose flour

2 tablespoons vegetable oil

1. Combine the pork, veal, onion, cumin, paprika, parsley, garlic, olive oil, salt, and pepper in a large bowl and use your hands to thoroughly blend the ingredients. Form the mixture into balls about 1 inch across (you should have about 40 meatballs). Dust the meatballs in the flour, patting gently to remove the excess.

2. Heat the vegetable oil in a large skillet over medium heat. In 3 or 4 batches, cook the meatballs, turning them a few times, for 8 to 10 minutes, until evenly browned and cooked through. Transfer the meatballs to individual plates or a platter and serve.

Menu Ideas: Don't feel obligated to save these meatballs for a Moroccan-themed dinner. They'd be delicious before Paella with Chicken and Shellfish (page 120) or Grilled Honey and Mustard Ribs (page 108). Consider pairing the meatballs with Clam and Chive Dip with Pita Chips (page 17) and the Pickled Shrimp with Capers (page 6).

Do-Ahead Tips: The meatballs can be formed and cooked up to a day in advance. Gently reheat 8 to 10 minutes in a 325°F oven just before serving. You may also freeze the uncooked meatballs. First freeze them thoroughly on a baking sheet until solid, then transfer the frozen meatballs to a resealable plastic freezer bag to store for up to 1 month. Allow the meatballs to thaw overnight in the refrigerator before cooking.

CEVICHE WITH PAPAYA AND MINT

This bright, refreshing preparation of raw seafood is a great way to start a light summertime dinner. The fish needs to sit in its lime juice–based marinade, which gives a semblance of cooked texture and color, for at least 4 hours, so plan accordingly. The most important thing about this dish is the quality and freshness of the seafood since it's served raw; this is a good time to patronize the best seafood market in town. **MAKES 10 TO 12 SERVINGS**

1 medium yellow onion, thinly sliced

2 teaspoons finely grated lime zest

1 cup freshly squeezed lime juice

½ cup seasoned rice wine vinegar

4 cloves garlic, pressed or minced

1 pound bay scallops

1 pound halibut, skin and bones removed, cut into ½-inch dice

½ pound medium shrimp, peeled, deveined, and chopped

1 small fennel bulb, trimmed, cored, and thinly sliced (reserve green fronds)

1 red bell pepper, cored, seeded, and diced

1 small cucumber, peeled, seeded, and diced

1 small papaya, peeled, seeded, and diced

¼ cup chopped fresh cilantro

2 tablespoons minced fresh mint

2 tablespoons minced fresh chives

10 to 12 small tender lettuce leaves

1. Combine the onion, lime zest, lime juice, vinegar, and garlic in a large bowl and stir to mix. Add the scallops, halibut, and shrimp. Finely chop enough of the tender green fennel fronds to make 1 tablespoon and add to the bowl. Stir well to mix, then cover the bowl with plastic wrap and refrigerate to marinate for at least 4 hours, stirring each hour.

2. One half hour before serving, stir the fennel, bell pepper, cucumber, papaya, cilantro, mint, and chives into the ceviche. Let sit until ready to serve.

3. Lay the lettuce leaves on individual plates, spoon the ceviche onto the lettuce, and serve.

Menu Ideas: This ceviche makes a great starter for menus of Latin American character, particularly dishes that have a little spice to them. Consider serving this before Grilled Rack of Pork with Mango Salsa (page 92) or Chiles Rellenos with Potatoes and Cheese (page 114). It may double as a salad course if you like; just add more lettuce and drizzle a bit of extra-virgin olive oil over all just before serving. I've also served it as a passed hors d'oeuvre, serving the ceviche in small scallop shells with cocktail forks, so guests can nibble easily while walking around.

Do-Ahead Tips: The ceviche can be marinated up to 8 hours in advance; much longer than that and the seafood will become overly firm and tart from the lime juice.

FETTUCCINE WITH LEMON CREAM AND SPICY TOMATO TOPPING

Although this could easily be served as a main course, I typically serve the rich pasta as a small starter course. The spicy tomato and zesty lemon elements contrast perfectly with the richness of the cream sauce. When serving this as an entrée, I'll often add sautéed shrimp for a little more substance.

The tomato topping makes more than is needed here (it's really a finishing touch), but you'll be happy to have extra on hand to toss with sautéed green beans or to spoon over baked fish. **MAKES 8 TO 10 SERVINGS**

1 pound dry fettuccine

SPICY TOMATO TOPPING

⅓ cup olive oil

1 large yellow onion, thinly sliced

2 large shallots, chopped

6 cloves garlic, chopped

1 carrot, diced

1 can (28 ounces) diced plum tomatoes, drained, liquid reserved

¾ teaspoon dried red pepper flakes

Salt

LEMON CREAM SAUCE

1½ cups whipping cream

½ cup whole milk

½ cup unsalted butter, cut into pieces

¼ cup freshly squeezed lemon juice

2 teaspoons finely grated lemon zest

2 cups grated Parmesan cheese

1. For the topping, heat the olive oil in a large saucepan over medium heat. Add the onion, shallots, and garlic and sauté for 10 minutes, until the onion begins to soften. Add the carrot and continue cooking, stirring frequently, for 30 to 40 minutes, until the onion and carrots are tender and lightly browned; decrease the heat if needed to avoid burning. Add the tomatoes (reserving the liquid) and simmer 45 minutes longer, stirring occasionally. The sauce should be rather thick, but if it seems too dry, add ¼ cup or so of the tomato liquid. Stir in the red pepper flakes with salt to taste. Let cool, then purée in a food processor with 8 to 10 pulses, until moderately smooth but still a bit chunky, scraping down the side of the bowl once or twice.

2. For the lemon sauce, combine the cream, milk, and butter in a medium saucepan. Bring to a low boil over medium heat, stirring occasionally and taking care that the cream doesn't boil over. Decrease the heat to medium-low and simmer 10 minutes to reduce the sauce slightly. Remove the pan from the heat, stir in the lemon juice, and set aside.

3. Bring a large pot of salted water to a rolling boil. Add the fettuccine and cook for 10 to 12 minutes, until al dente. Drain the pasta well, then return to the empty pot. Add the lemon cream sauce, lemon zest, and half of the Parmesan. Toss to evenly coat the fettuccine.

4. Transfer the pasta to individual warmed pasta bowls, spoon ¼ cup of the spicy tomato topping on top, and pass the remaining Parmesan cheese separately.

Menu Ideas: This rich, filling dish goes well as a precursor to grilled meats and fish. Consider Salmon with Nasturtium Butter (page 90) and Old-Fashioned Green Beans with Bacon (page 142) to follow this flavorful first course.

Do-Ahead Tips: The tomato sauce can be made up to 2 days in advance and refrigerated, or frozen for up to a month. The lemon sauce should be made no more than 1 hour in advance. The pasta should be cooked and the dish assembled just before serving.

PROSCIUTTO PINWHEELS

I have made these crisp savory treats for many years and the platters always quickly return to the kitchen empty, a testament to their popularity. I tasted a similar snack in Italy and remember falling for the combination of flaky dough with rich, salty prosciutto and cheese.

Puff pastry is available in the freezer section of most grocery stores these days. Be sure to plan ahead and allow a day for it to thaw in the refrigerator before using. Most 1-pound packages will hold 2 folded sheets of pastry. When forming the cylinders, it's important to form the dough into a snug, tight roll to make cutting easier, and ensuring neat pinwheels. **MAKES 10 TO 12 SERVINGS**

1 pound frozen puff pastry, thawed

3 tablespoons Dijon mustard

1 tablespoon freshly squeezed lemon juice

1 teaspoon olive oil

8 ounces thinly sliced prosciutto

2 cups grated provolone cheese

¼ cup grated Parmesan cheese

¼ cup minced fresh basil

Menu Ideas: This is another ideal candidate for a tapas-type spread, perfect finger food for a buffet table, or for passing on platters at a cocktail party.

Do-Ahead Tips: You can prepare the pinwheels up to 6 hours in advance, to the point just before baking. Refrigerate them on the baking sheet, covered with plastic wrap (I prop it on top of other things in the refrigerator). Bake them just before serving.

1. Preheat the oven to 425°F. Line 2 baking sheets with silicone baking mats or parchment paper.

2. Lay 1 of the puff pastry sheets on a lightly floured work surface and roll it out to a 14-inch square (keep the remaining pastry wrapped, in the refrigerator). Stir together the mustard, lemon juice, and olive oil in a small bowl. Brush half of the mustard mixture over the pastry square and cover it with a layer of half the prosciutto, overlapping the slices slightly and leaving a ½-inch border of dough open along 1 edge. Sprinkle the prosciutto with half of the provolone and Parmesan cheeses and half of the basil.

3. Roll the pastry tightly up into a cylinder, beginning from the side opposite the bare border. Pinch the seam to seal the roll securely; if the seam doesn't seem well sealed, dab a little water onto the pastry. Repeat with the remaining pastry and filling ingredients to make another roll.

4. Use a good serrated knife and a gentle sawing motion to cut each of the cylinders into ½-inch-thick slices, discarding the end trimmings. Set the slices on the baking sheets at least 1½ inches apart. Bake the pinwheels for 16 to 18 minutes, or until puffed and lightly browned. If baking both sheets at once, switch pans about halfway through to ensure even cooking.

5. Let the pinwheels sit a few minutes on the baking sheets, then transfer to a wire rack to cool a bit. Serve warm or at room temperature. They're even tasty the next day, gently rewarmed if you like.

GRILLED MOZZARELLA
AND MUSHROOM SANDWICHES

Few comfort foods satisfy like grilled cheese sandwiches. I particularly like this variation, pairing the smooth tang of mozzarella cheese and the earthy richness of sautéed mushrooms, a combination that's hard to resist. I can guarantee that a tray of these will disappear as quickly as you make them.

Mozzarella comes in a number of forms. I prefer fresh mozzarella that's sold in tubs of brine. It has a softer, less stringy texture than the firmer, dryer mozzarella commonly used on pizzas—both types will work, just with different results. For the bread, choose a loaf with relatively square slices.

This is a great time to use a griddle pan that sits over two burners, which allows you to cook four sandwiches at once. Otherwise, use two large skillets at the same time. **MAKES 12 SERVINGS**

2 tablespoons unsalted butter, plus more softened butter for bread

1 tablespoon vegetable oil

¾ pound mushrooms, trimmed and thinly sliced

½ teaspoon salt

¼ teaspoon freshly ground black pepper

16 slices whole wheat sandwich bread, crusts removed

1 pound mozzarella cheese, thinly sliced

1 tablespoon minced fresh oregano or marjoram

1. Melt the butter with the vegetable oil in a large skillet over medium-high heat. Add the mushrooms, season with the salt and pepper, and sauté for 8 to 10 minutes, until they are tender and the liquid they give off has evaporated. Transfer to a bowl and set aside to cool.

2. Set 8 of the bread slices on the work surface and top with half of the mozzarella slices in layers as even as you can manage. Arrange the sautéed mushrooms evenly over the cheese and sprinkle with the oregano. Top with the remaining mozzarella and finish with the remaining bread slices. Spread a thin layer of softened butter on the top of each sandwich.

3. Preheat a griddle or 2 large heavy skillets over medium heat. Add the sandwiches buttered side down and cook for 2 minutes, or until nicely browned. While the sandwiches cook, butter the top slices of bread. Flip the sandwiches and cook for 2 minutes longer, until well browned and the cheese is melted.

4. Transfer the sandwiches to a cutting board and cut each into 3 strips. Transfer to individual plates or a platter to serve hot.

Menu Ideas: : This will be a delicious start to dinner that continues with Braised Brisket with Onions (page 109) and Braised Red Cabbage (page 138), and finishes with the ever-popular Sunken Chocolate Cupcakes (page 175). You could also serve the sandwiches whole, alongside bowls of Roasted Butternut Squash Soup (page 77) on a cold winter evening.

Do-Ahead Tips: You can sauté the mushrooms several hours ahead and refrigerate until needed. The sandwiches will be best cooked just before serving.

CLAM AND CHIVE DIP
WITH PITA CHIPS

Right up there as one of the top retro classics for entertaining, there's a certain timeless, comfort-food appeal to clam dip. Here, I've updated the classic with a big dose of chopped fresh chives, which adds bright flavor and color. I sometimes add chopped dill as well. This is one of the few times when canned clams, which couldn't be more convenient, are a better choice than fresh.

Although you can serve the dip simply with crackers or really good potato chips, I like to add easy-to-make pita toasts for a change of pace. Choose the pocket-type of pita bread, rather than the thicker, more bread-like pita. **MAKES 8 SERVINGS**

8 ounces cream cheese, at room temperature

½ cup crème fraîche or sour cream

¼ cup mayonnaise

2 cans (6½ ounces each) minced clams, drained, liquid reserved

¼ cup finely chopped fresh chives

2 tablespoons freshly squeezed lemon juice

1 tablespoon finely grated or minced yellow onion

1 teaspoon Worcestershire sauce

½ teaspoon garlic powder

4 pita bread rounds (white or whole wheat)

1. Stir together the cream cheese, crème fraîche, and mayonnaise with 2 tablespoons of clam juice until smooth. Stir in the chives, lemon juice, onion, Worcestershire sauce, and garlic powder. Fold in the clams. If the dip is too stiff, stir in a bit more of the clam juice. Cover and refrigerate for at least 1 hour before serving.

2. Preheat the oven to 350°F.

3. Cut each pita into 8 wedges and separate each wedge at the outer edge into 2 triangles. Arrange the triangles in an even layer on 2 baking sheets. Toast in the oven 12 to 15 minutes, until lightly browned and crisp. Switch the baking sheets once or twice so the pita toasts evenly. Set aside to cool.

4. To serve, transfer the clam dip to a serving bowl, set it on a platter surrounded by the pita chips, and serve.

Menu Ideas: This is my husband's favorite treat to have before main courses like Four-Star Fried Chicken (page 110) and Barbecued Flank Steak (page 91). I don't think we've sat through many Super Bowls without the dip (which disappears fast), lots of potato chips, and bowls of Chili with Fire-Roasted Peppers (page 94).

Do-Ahead Tips: The dip will be best if made at least 1 hour before serving; it can be made up to 2 days in advance and refrigerated. The pita toasts can also be prepared up to 2 days ahead, and stored in an airtight container. If the dip seems too thick after sitting, thin with a little clam juice or milk.

PAKISTANI VEGETABLE SAMOSAS

My wonderful Pakistani neighbor, Shelina, has shared many plates of her samosas, crisp savory stuffed pastries that are commonly served as an afternoon snack or at the beginning of the evening meal. I've sampled many different types of samosas on trips to India, typically filled with some combination of meat and/or spiced vegetables.

This recipe of Shelina's uses a secret ingredient: the cross-cultural egg roll wrapper (or lumpia wraps, from the Philippines) in place of the traditional samosa dough. Look for the square wrappers at Asian markets or in the grocery refrigerator case. It takes some time and patience to fill and wrap the samosas, but you'll find the time well spent when you see how much your friends love them.

The tamarind dipping sauce comes compliments of my friend Suvir Saran, the amazing Indian chef and owner of Devi in New York City. Suvir has also published two cookbooks that I use often to inspire me when I'm craving great Indian food. You could instead serve the samosas with tamarind chutney or other types of chutney, such as mango or mint. **MAKES 16 SERVINGS**

¼ cup olive oil

½ teaspoon whole black mustard seeds

1 red bell pepper, cored, seeded, and cut into ¼-inch dice

1 carrot, cut into ¼-inch dice

1 teaspoon pressed or minced garlic

½ cup fresh or thawed frozen peas

½ cup fresh or thawed frozen corn kernels

1½ teaspoons ground cumin

1½ teaspoons ground coriander

1 teaspoon mild curry powder

1 teaspoon salt

½ to 1 teaspoon dried red pepper flakes

½ teaspoon garam masala

3 medium white boiling potatoes (12 ounces), boiled, peeled, and cut into ¼-inch dice

¼ cup minced fresh cilantro

2 tablespoons minced fresh mint

¼ cup all-purpose flour

¼ cup cold water

1 package (1 pound) egg roll wrappers or lumpia wrappers

Vegetable oil, for frying

1. For the dipping sauce (page 20), heat the oil in a medium saucepan over medium heat. Add the cumin seeds, ginger, fennel seeds, garam masala, and cayenne. Cook, stirring, for 1 to 2 minutes, until aromatic and slightly toasty. Add the water, sugar, and tamarind concentrate. Bring to a boil over medium-high heat, then decrease the heat to medium and simmer, stirring often, for about 30 minutes, until the sauce is thick enough to coat the back of a spoon. Set aside until ready to serve.

2. Heat the olive oil in a medium skillet over medium heat. Add the mustard seeds and quickly cover with the lid. When the seeds stop popping after 1 to 2 minutes, add the bell pepper and carrot. Cook, stirring occasionally, for 2 minutes. Add the garlic and cook for about 1 minute, until aromatic but not too browned. Stir in the peas and corn and cook for 2 minutes longer, stirring frequently. Add the cumin, coriander, curry, salt, red pepper flakes, and garam masala, and stir for 1 minute, until well blended. Add the potatoes, cilantro, and mint. Cook, stirring gently to avoid mashing the potato cubes, for 2 to 3 minutes longer, until evenly blended. Set the samosa filling aside to cool.

3. Stir together the flour and water in a small bowl; this will be used to seal the samosas.

4. Cut each of the wrappers in thirds, making strips 6 to 8 inches long and 2 to 3 inches wide (different brands of wrappers vary in size). Set one strip in front of you vertically and fold the bottom half upward and to the right at a 90-degree angle, then under and back to the left, forming a triangular pouch with two flaps. Holding the packet in the palm of your hand, spoon a scant tablespoon of the filling into the pouch. Use a finger to spread some of the flour paste on the flap ends and fold them securely around the filling to fully enclose it. Repeat with the remaining filling (you may not need all of the egg roll wrappers; you should have about 4 dozen samosas total).

TAMARIND DIPPING SAUCE

1 tablespoon vegetable oil

1 teaspoon cumin seeds

1 teaspoon ground ginger

½ teaspoon fennel seeds

½ teaspoon garam masala

¼ to ½ teaspoon cayenne pepper

2 cups water

1¼ cups sugar

3 tablespoons tamarind concentrate

Menu Ideas: Don't feel limited to an Indian-themed meal for serving samosas. I enjoy them with Lemon and Sage Cornish Game Hens (page 122) or Braised Brisket with Onions (page 109). Be sure to plan for a crisp salad and green vegetable, since the fried samosas, with their potato filling, are a bit heavy.

Do-Ahead Tips: The uncooked samosas freeze well for up to 2 months; no need to thaw before frying, though they will require a little extra time. I find they should be frozen standing upright in an airtight container to help preserve their shape. The dipping sauce can be made up to 3 days in advance and refrigerated; allow to come to room temperature before serving.

5. Pour 3 to 4 inches of oil in a deep fryer or in a large, deep pot, such as a Dutch oven (it's important the oil comes no more than halfway up the sides of the pan for safety). Heat the oil over medium heat to 375°F. Carefully slip 4 or 5 of the samosas into the hot oil and fry for about 3 minutes, until well browned. Drain on paper towels while frying the remaining samosas, allowing the oil to reheat between batches as needed.

6. Serve the samosas warm or at room temperature, with tamarind sauce alongside for dipping.

GRILLED PORK KEBABS

I've sampled similar kebabs to these in tapas bars across the Andalusia region of Spain, with slight variations in seasoning, sometimes with a sauce and sometimes without. The key idea is that with just a few small cubes of pork at one end of each skewer, they are easily enjoyed as a one-bite snack.

Though outdoor grilling always adds an incomparable dose of flavor, you can certainly cook these kebabs under the broiler if you prefer. I've used the same marinated pork for main-course kebabs, cutting the meat into larger cubes and threading pieces of onion and green bell pepper between them. Twelve-inch skewers will be best for main-dish kebabs, which would serve six. MAKES 10 TO 12 SERVINGS

3 tablespoons finely chopped fresh flat-leaf
    parsley

1 tablespoon finely grated lemon zest

3 tablespoons freshly squeezed lemon juice

2 tablespoons dry sherry

2 tablespoons olive oil

2 teaspoons ground cumin

2 teaspoons ground fennel seeds

2 teaspoons Spanish smoked paprika or sweet
    Hungarian paprika

4 cloves garlic, crushed

2 dried red chiles, crushed, or 1 teaspoon dried
    red pepper flakes

½ teaspoon freshly grated or ground nutmeg

½ teaspoon salt

2 pounds pork tenderloin, cut into ¾-inch cubes

1. Combine the parsley, lemon zest, lemon juice, sherry, olive oil, cumin, fennel, paprika, garlic, dried chiles, nutmeg, and salt in a large bowl and whisk to thoroughly blend. Add the pork cubes and stir to evenly coat. Cover the bowl with plastic wrap and refrigerate for at least 12 hours, or overnight. (Alternately, you may transfer the pork and marinade to a resealable plastic bag for marinating.)

2. Preheat an outdoor grill. If using bamboo skewers, soak about 32 six-inch skewers in cold water for 30 minutes.

3. Thread 2 or 3 pork cubes onto the end of each skewer. When the grill is heated, lightly rub the grill grate with oil. Grill the kebabs for 8 to 10 minutes, until the pork is nicely browned and just a hint of pink remains in the center. Set the skewers aside on a platter, cover with foil, and let sit for 10 minutes before serving.

Menu Ideas: As part of an appetizer spread, these kebabs could be served with Mushrooms à la Grecque (page 22), Choux Puffs with Salmon and Shrimp (page 36), and a simple tray with a few varieties of cheeses and roasted nuts. Served as a main course, consider pairing them with Lemon Israeli Couscous (page 161) and finishing with Blueberry Tart (page 184).

Do-Ahead Tips: The pork can be marinated for up to 2 days. The skewers can be assembled up to 4 hours before grilling. You can keep the grilled pork warm in a low oven before serving, but they are best if grilled just before serving.

MUSHROOMS À LA GRECQUE

The French term "à la Grecque" refers to vegetables that are marinated—often with lemon juice and spices, as I do here—to serve cold as an appetizer. The mushrooms for this recipe should be small, with tight caps that don't have exposed dark gills underneath. These will be most tender and are ideal for marinating whole. If you can only find mushrooms that are larger than bite-sized, halve or quarter them before marinating. Keep in mind, though, that the mushrooms will shrink a bit when cooked. This recipe is easy to double or triple for a bigger crowd. **MAKES 6 TO 8 SERVINGS**

1 pound small button mushrooms

1¾ cups water

½ cup olive oil

¼ cup freshly squeezed lemon juice

2 tablespoons white vinegar

1 teaspoon salt

1 dried bay leaf

½ teaspoon dry mustard

Pinch of sugar

2 stalks celery with leaves, coarsely chopped

6 sprigs fresh flat-leaf parsley

3 sprigs fresh thyme

10 whole black peppercorns

2 cloves garlic, quartered

½ teaspoon fennel seeds

½ teaspoon coriander seeds

1 tablespoon minced fresh flat-leaf parsley

1 teaspoon finely grated lemon zest

1. Trim the stems of the mushrooms level with the bottoms of the caps.

2. Combine the water, olive oil, lemon juice, vinegar, salt, bay leaf, mustard, and sugar in a large saucepan. Cut an 8-inch square of cheesecloth and place the celery, parsley sprigs, thyme sprigs, peppercorns, garlic, fennel seeds, and coriander seeds in the center. Draw the edges up and tie securely with kitchen string. Add the spice packet to the saucepan.

3. Bring the marinade mixture to a boil over high heat, then decrease the heat to medium and simmer, covered, for 5 minutes. Add the mushrooms and simmer, uncovered, for 10 minutes. Remove the pan from the heat and let cool. Cover the pan and refrigerate overnight.

4. To serve, drain the mushrooms, discarding the marinade and spice bundle. Transfer the mushrooms to a serving bowl. Add the parsley and lemon zest, toss to mix evenly, and serve.

Menu Ideas: This is an ideal addition to a tapas-oriented array of appetizers, which might also include Minty Meatballs (page 5), Prosciutto Pinwheels (page 15), and Baked Clams with Bacon and Rosemary (page 29). The mushrooms will also be delicious served with cheese and olives as a simple antipasti plate before an Italian meal, or packed along on your next picnic.

Do-Ahead Tips: The mushrooms hold well for up to a week, fully covered by the marinade, the bowl covered with plastic wrap, and refrigerated. Let come to room temperature before serving.

SAVORY PUFF PASTRY BITES

The Spanish have perfected the art of the pre-dinner snack. When the dinner hour doesn't come until 10 P.M. or later, as is common in Spain, friends gather first at a tapas bar to sample some small bites with a glass of wine, tiding them over until dinner. These simple tapas begin with prepared puff pastry, which you cut into any bite-sized shape and top with a wide range of colorful, flavorful toppings before baking. The greater variety you choose, the more mosaic-like the presentation on a large, simple platter. Make sure you allow at least one of each variety per guest. Rather than hand-cutting shapes, you could use small pastry cutters to form the dough into festive shapes.

One of my favorite cheeses to use for these bites is manchego, a sheep's milk cheese, though you could use good Parmesan or other nutty, firm cheese in its place. **MAKES 16 TO 20 SERVINGS**

1 pound frozen puff pastry, thawed

TOPPINGS

Pimiento-stuffed green olives, drained (whole, or halved lengthwise if large)

Marcona almonds, or other toasted almonds, with sea salt

Sun-dried tomatoes (oil-packed) with small fresh basil leaves or slivered basil

Chorizo, thinly sliced, with grated manchego cheese

Anchovy paste, with small pieces of sliced manchego cheese

Menu Ideas: These small puffs are ideal for an afternoon card party, served with a dish of nuts, or as a before-dinner snack paired with a glass of Champagne. It's an easy recipe that is really very versatile.

Do-Ahead Tips: These simple bites can be made up to 4 hours ahead and held at room temperature. And they'll store well in an airtight container for up to 12 hours. Or, arrange the unbaked bites on the baking sheets and refrigerate for up to 6 hours, covered with plastic wrap; bake just before serving.

1. Preheat the oven to 400°F. Line 2 baking sheets with silicone baking mats or parchment paper.

2. Unfold the thawed pastry sheets on a lightly floured work surface and roll out a bit, to about a 10½-inch square. Cut the pastry into a variety of bite-sized shapes: 1½-inch circles, squares, and diamonds, and rectangles about 1½ inches long and ½ inch wide.

3. Top the pastry pieces with toppings of your choice, pressing them down into the pastry to help them adhere during baking.

4. Arrange the pastry on the prepared baking sheets and bake for 10 to 12 minutes, until well puffed and nicely browned. Shift the pans halfway through to ensure even cooking. Transfer the pastry puffs to a platter or plates and serve warm or at room temperature.

CHEESE-STUFFED ZUCCHINI BLOSSOMS

We have a sizeable garden that produces dozens of different vegetables, fruits, and herbs from late spring into the fall. When the first zucchini and other squash blossoms begin appearing in early summer, this wonderful, delicate hors d'oeuvre always leaps to mind. If you don't have zucchini blossoms in your own garden, they are often available at farmers' markets and well-stocked produce sections. Choose blossoms that are of similar size, with tender bright blooms that are not torn or bruised. You may sometimes find them with the baby zucchini still attached, which is a bonus! All I do to clean them is to shake the blossoms, to remove any stray debris or the occasional ladybug.

The basic batter used here is the same as that used for classic Japanese tempura. It has a thin consistency that offers light, crisp results with most any fresh vegetable or shrimp. **MAKES 6 SERVINGS**

18 large zucchini blossoms

1 package (5 ounces) Boursin cheese (pepper or garlic and herb flavor)

4 ounces herb- or pepper-seasoned goat cheese

½ cup mascarpone

1 tablespoon minced fresh herbs (basil, thyme, and/or tarragon)

1 clove garlic, pressed or minced

Vegetable oil, for frying

Salt

TEMPURA BATTER

1 cup all-purpose flour

1 egg yolk

1¼ cups ice water

Menu Ideas: As an elegant seated first course, I usually allow 3 blossoms per person. The blossoms can also be served as finger food, with napkins to catch any drips of the rich cheese filling.

Do-Ahead Tips: The zucchini blossoms can be stuffed up to 2 hours in advance and refrigerated, draped with damp paper towels to keep them from drying out. The blossoms should be battered and fried just before serving.

1. Shake and/or gently brush the blossoms if needed; I often find they're perfectly tidy to use as is.

2. Combine the Boursin and goat cheeses in a medium bowl and use a fork to mash and soften them. Add the mascarpone, herbs, and garlic and stir until evenly blended and smooth.

3. Carefully open one of the zucchini blossoms and use a small spoon to fill the blossom with about 1½ tablespoons of the cheese mixture. Twist the tips of the blossom to fully enclose the filling. Continue with the remaining blossoms and filling.

4. Pour about 2 inches of oil in a deep fryer or in a large, deep pot, such as a Dutch oven (it's important the oil comes no more than halfway up the sides of the pan for safety). Heat the oil over medium heat to 375°F.

5. While the oil is heating, make the batter. Place the flour in a medium bowl and make a well in the center. Beat the egg yolk with a fork in a small bowl, then stir in the ice water. Add this to the flour and quickly stir with the fork to blend. Avoid overmixing; the batter may be a bit lumpy.

6. When the oil is preheated, dip a few of the blossoms in the batter, allowing the excess to drip off, and carefully slide into the oil. Fry for 1 to 2 minutes, until browned and crisp. Use a large slotted spoon or tongs to gently transfer the fried blossoms to paper towels to drain, sprinkling them with salt. Continue with the remaining blossoms, allowing the oil to reheat between batches as needed.

7. Serve the stuffed zucchini blossoms while warm, on individual plates as a seated first course or on a large platter to pass as an appetizer.

FRESH SUMMER TOMATO
AND CRAB PASTA

There's a universal anticipation that builds for summer's first sweet, juicy vine-ripe tomatoes in our local farmers' markets, or, if you're as lucky as we are, from our own garden. Use any combination of tomatoes here, including cherry tomatoes, grape tomatoes, or heirlooms of different colors and varieties. If you're only able to find standard large beefsteak tomatoes, peel them (see page 223) before using.

Italians usually don't add cheese to seafood dishes, so this pasta remains light, allowing the flavor of the juicy tomatoes and sweet crab to shine through. I wouldn't recommend canned crab in this dish, so if freshly cooked crab is not available, use bay shrimp instead. I prefer the delicate flavor of the pasta without red pepper flakes, although my husband Carl enjoys the hint of heat they provide.
MAKES 8 SERVINGS

3 cups diced fresh tomatoes (about 3 medium)

¾ cup olive oil

3 tablespoons minced shallot

2 cloves garlic, pressed or minced

12 ounces dry fettuccine

¾ to 1 pound fresh crabmeat

1¼ cups chopped green onions

1 teaspoon minced fresh thyme

Salt and freshly ground black pepper

2 tablespoons freshly squeezed lemon juice

¼ teaspoon dried red pepper flakes (optional)

Menu Ideas: This slightly substantial first course would be perfect before a lighter entrée such as Halibut with Nut Crust and Apple Vinaigrette (page 106) or Lemon and Sage Cornish Game Hens (page 122).

Do-Ahead Tips: You can make the shallot/garlic oil and combine the crab with the green onions and thyme up to 2 hours in advance and refrigerate. Cook the pasta, warm the crab in the oil, and finish the dish just before serving.

1. Drain the tomatoes in a medium sieve over a bowl for 30 minutes, stirring occasionally. (Excess water from the tomatoes can dilute the flavor of the dish.)

2. Heat the olive oil in a medium skillet or small saucepan over medium heat. Add the shallot and garlic and cook gently for 3 to 5 minutes, until the oil is aromatic but the shallot and garlic not browned. Set aside.

3. Bring a large pot of salted water to a rolling boil. Add the fettuccine and cook for 10 to 12 minutes, until al dente.

4. While the pasta is cooking, rewarm the oil mixture over medium heat. Add the crab, green onions, and thyme and cook gently for about 5 minutes, until the crab is heated through. Season to taste with salt and pepper.

5. Drain the pasta well and return to the empty pot. Add the drained tomatoes, stir to mix, then add the crab mixture, lemon juice, and red pepper flakes and toss well. Serve in warmed pasta plates or shallow bowls.

GORGONZOLA PITA BITES

Pears and blue cheese is a delicious combination, often paired up in salads and on after-dinner cheese plates. Here I match the sweet-and-salty duo in a simple appetizer, small bites that are packed with flavor. Look for the thicker Greek-style pitas, which are a sturdier option, though the pocket-type pita may be used as well. Instead of peeling away "curls" of pear with the vegetable peeler as described below, you could core and quarter the pear, cutting each quarter into thin slices. **MAKES 8 TO 10 SERVINGS**

3 pita bread rounds

5 ounces (about 1½ cups) crumbled Gorgonzola cheese

1 tablespoon soy sauce

1 large ripe pear

½ lemon

1. Preheat the oven to 400°F.

2. Halve each pita crosswise, then cut each half into 6 wedges. Lay the wedges on a baking sheet and toast in the oven for 8 to 10 minutes, until lightly browned but not crisp-dry.

3. Stir together the cheese and soy sauce in a medium bowl.

4. Peel the pear and rub the cut side of the lemon over the surface to avoid browning. Use a vegetable peeler to peel away thin strips of pear, working from the stem end down, frequently rubbing lemon over the pear as you go.

5. Spread about 1 teaspoon of the cheese on the broad end of each pita triangle and top with 1 or 2 strips of the pear, twisted into a curl or folded. Arrange the pita bites on a platter and serve.

Menu Ideas: These tasty appetizers are a great alternative to bread served with a green salad before dinner. And they're also delicious alongside Roasted Butternut Squash Soup (page 77), the tangy cheese and sweet pear an ideal complement to the roasted squash. For a cocktail party, consider serving the bites with Pickled Shrimp with Capers (page 6) and Grilled Pork Kebabs (page 21).

Do-Ahead Tips: The pita wedges can be toasted up to a day in advance and stored in an airtight container. The cheese topping can be added up to 3 hours before serving. Because the pear will brown after prolonged sitting, it should be prepared just before serving.

CRUDITÉS
WITH SPICY RED PEPPER DIP AND ROQUEFORT DIP

Both of these dips may be used in a variety of ways. The red pepper dip is a great option for dunking Smoky Moroccan Meatballs (page 11), and can also be tossed with freshly steamed green beans or cauliflower for a zesty finish. The Roquefort dip, thinned with a little milk, makes an ideal salad dressing. This is a good time to splurge on imported Roquefort cheese or other top-quality crumbly blue cheese (creamier Cambozola will not work well here). **MAKES 12 SERVINGS**

2½ pounds mixed vegetables (carrots, celery, turnips, cauliflower, cucumber, green and/or red bell peppers, green beans)

SPICY RED PEPPER DIP

1 tablespoon olive oil

2 cloves garlic, pressed or minced

1 red bell pepper, roasted, peeled, seeded, and chopped (see page 222)

8 ounces mascarpone cheese

2 teaspoons harissa

½ teaspoon finely grated lemon zest

Salt

ROQUEFORT DIP

4 ounces Roquefort cheese

2 ounces cream cheese, at room temperature

¼ cup crème fraîche or sour cream

¼ cup mayonnaise

3 tablespoons olive oil

3 tablespoons freshly squeezed lemon juice

2 tablespoons minced yellow onion

1 clove garlic, pressed or minced

½ teaspoon minced fresh tarragon

Salt and freshly ground black pepper

1. For the red pepper dip, heat the olive oil in a small skillet over medium-low heat, add the garlic, and cook for about 1 minute, until tender but not browned. Set aside to cool. Combine the oil mixture, roasted pepper, mascarpone, harissa, and lemon zest in a food processor. Process to a smooth paste, scraping down the side once or twice. Transfer the dip to a serving bowl. Season to taste with salt, cover, and refrigerate for at least 1 hour before serving.

2. For the Roquefort dip, combine the Roquefort, cream cheese, crème fraîche, mayonnaise, olive oil, lemon juice, onion, garlic, and tarragon in a food processor and pulse until smooth, scraping down the side once or twice. Transfer the dip to a serving bowl, season to taste with salt and pepper, cover, and refrigerate for at least 1 hour before serving.

3. Trim and prepare the vegetables as needed: Cut carrots, celery, and turnips into sticks; break cauliflower into small florets; cut cucumber in slices on the bias; core, seed, and slice bell peppers; and blanch green beans for 1 to 2 minutes.

4. Set the dips on a large platter, or transfer them to smaller individual dishes and set on individual plates. Arrange the vegetables around the dips and serve.

Menu Ideas: The crudités with both dips is a versatile appetizer to serve at a cocktail party, picnic, or casual dinner buffet. For a sit-down first course, you could serve just one dip in small individual bowls set on plates with an array of the vegetables alongside. The spicy red pepper dip is well suited as a prelude to Lamb Shanks Tagine with Preserved Lemon (page 126), and the Roquefort dip is ideal before Braised Brisket with Onions (page 109).

Do-Ahead Tips: Both dips can be made up to 3 days in advance and refrigerated. The vegetables can be prepared up to 4 hours in advance. Wrap them loosely in dampened paper towel and refrigerate in a plastic bag (not sealed) to keep them crisp until ready to serve.

BAKED CLAMS
WITH BACON AND ROSEMARY

This is a recipe that takes me back to my early 20s, when work led me to New York City and I tasted clams Casino for the first time in Little Italy. I add fresh rosemary to my version of that classic dish, with the traditional bacon blended into the cooked clam mixture rather than simply topping the whole clam. As a sit-down first course, I'd recommend serving six clams per person on a small plate. For cocktail party–style service, I'll serve just two clams on a smaller plate, with a two-pronged cocktail pick. **MAKES 10 TO 12 SERVINGS**

3 strips thick-cut bacon, cut into ¼-inch pieces

4 tablespoons unsalted butter

4 cloves garlic, pressed or minced

½ cup dry vermouth

½ cup finely chopped yellow onion

3 pounds live Manila or other hard-shell clams
    1½ to 2 inches across, rinsed

⅓ cup plain dried bread crumbs

¼ cup chopped green onions

¼ cup chopped fresh flat-leaf parsley

1 tablespoon olive oil

½ teaspoon finely grated lemon zest

1 tablespoon freshly squeezed lemon juice

2 teaspoons minced fresh rosemary

½ teaspoon salt

½ teaspoon freshly ground black pepper

¼ cup grated Parmesan cheese

Menu Ideas: The aromatic clams will be great served before Osso Buco (page 113) or Barbecued Flank Steak (page 91). Chocolate would be a wonderful finish, perhaps Sunken Chocolate Cupcakes (page 175).

Do-Ahead Tips: You can prepare and stuff the clams up to 4 hours in advance and refrigerate them on the baking sheet. Bake just before serving.

1. Preheat the oven to 400°F. Line a baking sheet with aluminum foil.

2. Cook the bacon in a small skillet over medium heat, stirring occasionally, 3 to 4 minutes, until crisp. Drain on paper towels and set aside. Melt the butter in a small skillet or saucepan over medium-low heat, stir in the garlic, and set aside.

3. Combine the vermouth and onion in a large pot and cook over medium heat 1 to 2 minutes, until the onion is tender. Add the clams, cover, and steam, gently shaking the pot occasionally, for 8 to 10 minutes, until the clams open. Every couple of minutes, use a large slotted spoon to scoop the open clams into a bowl. Discard any clams that haven't opened after 10 minutes; reserve the cooking liquid in the pot.

4. When the clams are cool enough to handle, remove the meat from the shells, reserving the shells. Separate the shell halves and keep half of each, rinsing and drying the shells.

5. Combine the bacon, garlic butter, 1 tablespoon of the clam cooking liquid, the bread crumbs, green onions, parsley, oil, lemon zest, lemon juice, rosemary, salt, and pepper in a food processor and pulse 4 or 5 times to blend well; don't overprocess to a smooth paste. Scrape down the sides, add the clam meat, and pulse 3 or 4 more times to chop the clams. Transfer the mixture to a bowl and stir to be sure ingredients are well blended.

6. Mound about 1 teaspoon of the clam mixture into each of the reserved clam shells (the exact amount needed will vary with the size of the shells) and set them on the baking sheet. Top each clam with a pinch of the cheese and bake for 10 to 12 minutes, until heated through and the cheese is lightly browned. Transfer the clams to individual plates or a platter to serve.

KIBBE
(MIDDLE EASTERN MEAT AND BULGUR BALLS)

There are dozens of types of kibbe found throughout the Middle East. This version comes from one of our best friends, Jim Hanna, whose Syrian mother would visit from Portland, bringing along kibbe to share with us all. Jim's wife, Ga, and I have also cooked this recipe together many times, based on the family recipe, with a few minor updates made over the years.

In many recipes, this one included, I like to grate onion rather than simply chopping it. Grating breaks the onion into fine slivers, while also releasing the onion's juices, which adds flavor and moisture to the dish. For a large volume of grated onion, use your food processor's grating attachment; smaller amounts I'll just grate on a classic box grater. **MAKES 12 SERVINGS**

2½ cups bulgur

2 teaspoons salt

1 medium yellow onion, grated

¼ teaspoon freshly ground black pepper

⅛ teaspoon ground allspice

⅛ teaspoon ground cinnamon

¼ cup olive oil

2 pounds ground lamb

STUFFING

2 tablespoons unsalted butter

¼ cup pine nuts

½ pound ground lamb

1½ cups minced yellow onions

1½ teaspoons minced fresh basil

½ teaspoon salt

⅛ teaspoon ground cinnamon

⅛ teaspoon ground allspice

1. Preheat the oven to 375°F. Lightly oil 2 large rimmed baking sheets.

2. For the stuffing, melt the butter in a medium skillet over medium heat. Add the pine nuts and brown gently for 2 to 3 minutes, stirring often. Add the ½ pound of lamb and cook for 10 minutes, breaking the meat into small pieces as it cooks. Add the minced onions, basil, salt, cinnamon, and allspice and continue cooking for 5 minutes, or until the onions are tender. Set aside to cool.

3. While the stuffing is cooling, place the bulgur in a large bowl and add cold water to cover by an inch or so. Let sit for 10 minutes, then drain well in a sieve and sprinkle with 1 teaspoon of the salt. (This keeps the bulgur from getting mushy.)

CUCUMBER YOGURT DIPPING SAUCE

1 clove garlic, coarsely chopped

1 tablespoon finely chopped fresh mint

1 teaspoon salt

2 cups Greek yogurt or other plain yogurt
    (preferably not nonfat)

1 cucumber, peeled, seeded, and finely diced

¼ cup grated yellow onion

Menu Ideas: This delicious, rather exotic appetizer is on the substantial side, so I'd follow it with a lighter entrée such as Salmon with Wild Mushroom Sauce (page 128) or Seattle Cioppino (page 105).

Do-Ahead Tips: The kibbe can be frozen in the raw or cooked state. Either way, they can be baked frozen, without thawing first, just until warmed if precooked, about 35 minutes if raw. The yogurt sauce can be made up to 2 days in advance and refrigerated.

4. Combine the grated onion, remaining 1 teaspoon salt, pepper, allspice, and cinnamon in a large bowl and stir well to mix. Add the bulgur and olive oil and stir to mix, then add the 2 pounds of lamb and work with your hands to fully blend the ingredients, kneading with your palms to form a cohesive mixture.

5. Scoop about 2 tablespoons of the bulgur mixture into your hand and form a ball. Use a finger to form a large indentation in the ball. Spoon about 1 teaspoon of the stuffing into the indentation and pinch it closed. Roll the ball in your palms to form it into a football shape about 2½ inches long. Repeat with the remaining bulgur and stuffing mixtures; you should have about 3 dozen kibbe.

6. Arrange the kibbe on the baking sheets, not touching. Bake for 18 to 20 minutes, until just cooked through. Turn the kibbe a few times and switch the baking sheets halfway through to ensure even cooking.

7. While the kibbe are baking, make the dipping sauce. Mash together the garlic, mint, and salt in a mortar and pestle, then transfer to a medium bowl. (Alternatively, press or mince the garlic and stir with the mint and salt in a medium bowl, pressing with the back of the spoon to crush the ingredients together.) Stir in the yogurt, cucumber, and grated onion.

8. Transfer the warm kibbe to individual plates, with a small bowl of the cucumber yogurt sauce alongside. Or arrange the kibbe on a large serving platter, with the sauce alongside for dipping.

LETTUCE WRAPS
WITH CHICKEN AND HERBS

Many Asian countries have their own version of this lettuce-wrapped appetizer (which reminds me of an Asian-style taco). The recipe, similar to one that I've sampled in Vietnam, is versatile: Try adding other ingredients, such as cilantro leaves, pickled ginger, and kaffir lime leaves, to vary the flavors. I really enjoy the character of Thai basil, which grows like mad in my garden, in these rolls. The main thing is to make sure your lettuce is very cold and crisp. For a little more color and crunch, add shredded carrots and/or chopped roasted peanuts to the filling.

Peanut sauce is a popular condiment in Southeast Asia. For a shortcut, try a commercially made sauce rather than making your own. (The peanut sauce would also be wonderful with Grilled Pork Kebabs, page 21.) The ginger-lime sauce is a snap to make. You may certainly serve the wraps with just one sauce or the other. **MAKES 6 TO 8 SERVINGS**

1¼ pounds ground chicken or turkey

¼ cup freshly squeezed lime juice

3 cloves garlic, pressed or minced

1 jalapeño chile, cored, seeded, and finely minced

2 tablespoons soy sauce

1 tablespoon unseasoned rice wine vinegar

1 tablespoon garlic chili paste

1 teaspoon granulated sugar

2 tablespoons sesame oil

1 head butter lettuce or iceberg lettuce, trimmed, rinsed, and dried

½ cup lightly packed fresh mint leaves

½ cup lightly packed fresh basil leaves

3 tablespoons chopped green onions

GINGER-LIME DIPPING SAUCE

1½ tablespoons hot water

1 tablespoon granulated sugar

¼ cup freshly squeezed lime juice

¼ cup Asian fish sauce, such as *nam pla*

2 tablespoons minced or grated ginger

1 clove garlic, pressed or minced

1. For the ginger-lime sauce, combine the water and sugar in a small bowl and let sit, stirring occasionally, until the sugar is dissolved and the mixture cool. Whisk in the lime juice, fish sauce, ginger, and garlic. Transfer to a small bowl and set aside.

2. For the peanut sauce, heat the vegetable oil and chili oil in a small saucepan over medium heat. Add the garlic and cook, stirring, for about 1 minute, until tender and aromatic but not browned. Add the peanut butter and stir until softened, then stir in the water, soy sauce, hoisin sauce, lime juice, brown sugar, and ginger. Bring just to a low simmer, then decrease the heat to medium-low and cook for 1 to 2 minutes, until the sauce thickens slightly. Transfer to a small bowl and set aside.

3. Combine the chicken, lime juice, garlic, jalapeño, soy sauce, vinegar, chili paste, and sugar in a medium bowl and stir well to blend. Heat the sesame oil in a large heavy skillet over medium heat. Add the chicken mixture and cook, stirring to break the meat into small pieces, for about 5 minutes, until the chicken is cooked through.

4. To serve, arrange the lettuce leaves around the edge of a large platter. Pile the mint leaves and basil leaves alongside the lettuce. Spoon the cooked chicken into a bowl, sprinkle with the green onions, and set it in the center of the platter, with the dipping sauces alongside. Alternatively, you may arrange the components on individual plates. Tell your guests to hold a lettuce leaf, cupped upward, in the palm of one hand and spoon some of the chicken mixture into the leaf. Add a couple mint and basil leaves, roll up, and enjoy, dipping into either of the sauces.

PEANUT DIPPING SAUCE

1 tablespoon vegetable oil

¼ teaspoon chili oil

2 cloves garlic, pressed or minced

¼ cup creamy peanut butter

¾ cup water

2 tablespoons soy sauce

2 tablespoons hoisin sauce

2 tablespoons freshly squeezed lime juice

1 teaspoon dark or light brown sugar

1 teaspoon minced or grated ginger

Menu Ideas: These crisp, fresh wraps can take the place of a salad course, either served on individual plates or family-style. Follow with a slightly rich main course, such as Salmon with Nasturtium Butter (page 90). Very Citrus Cheesecake (page 178) would make a wonderful finale.

Do-Ahead Tips: The dipping sauces can be made up to 3 days in advance, covered with plastic wrap, and refrigerated. The chicken mixture can be cooked up to 1 day in advance and warmed gently over low heat just before serving.

MEMORABLE RECIPES

MUSSELS À L'ESCARGOT

After having found myself too often maneuvering around my escargot dishes on the kitchen shelf, seldom using them, I decided to find some other uses for the simple porcelain dishes with their six snail-sized indentations. This is a garlicky-delicious alternative to the common steamed mussels. If you don't have escargot dishes, use other small dishes such as crème brûlée dishes or ramekins. Or, for a finger-food option, return the mussels to their shells and set on a rimmed baking sheet to bake.

You'll need 48 mussels in all; the in-shell weight will vary with the size of the mussels, but 1½ to 1¾ pounds should do the trick. Whenever buying mussels or clams in the shell, it's a good idea to buy a handful more than needed, in case you have to discard any with broken or gaping shells, or if any do not open when steamed. **MAKES 8 SERVINGS**

½ cup unsalted butter, cut into pieces

6 cloves garlic, pressed or minced

3 tablespoons minced shallot or yellow onion

½ cup minced fresh flat-leaf parsley

3 tablespoons olive oil

¼ teaspoon salt

¼ teaspoon freshly ground black pepper

¼ cup dry white wine or dry vermouth

1¾ pounds live mussels, scrubbed and debearded

2 to 3 tablespoons seasoned dried bread crumbs

1. Preheat the oven to 450°F.

2. To make the garlic butter, combine the butter, garlic, and 1 tablespoon of the shallot in a small saucepan and cook over medium-low heat, stirring occasionally, for 5 to 7 minutes, until the garlic and shallot are tender and aromatic but not browned. Set aside to cool. Stir in the parsley, olive oil, salt, and pepper. Let sit for 15 minutes before continuing to allow the flavors to meld.

3. Combine the wine and remaining 2 tablespoons shallot in a large saucepan and warm over medium heat for 3 minutes. Add the mussels, cover, and cook, shaking the pan gently a few times, for 6 to 8 minutes, until the mussels open. Transfer the mussels to a large bowl to cool; discard any mussels that do not open.

4. Spoon about 1 teaspoon of the garlic butter into each indentation of 8 escargot dishes, or spoon 2 tablespoons into each of 8 larger individual dishes. Remove the mussels from their shells and set a mussel in each indentation, or 6 in each larger dish. Top each mussel with about ⅛ teaspoon of the bread crumbs, or more to your taste.

5. Arrange the dishes on a baking sheet and bake for 8 to 10 minutes, until the juices are bubbly and the top is lightly browned. Transfer the dishes to serving plates and serve.

Menu Ideas: Because of its richness, you may want to follow this dish with a less rich entrée such as Lemon and Sage Cornish Game Hens (page 122) or Grilled Rack of Pork with Mango Salsa (page 92). Be sure to serve warm crusty bread alongside, for sopping up the amazing cooking juices.

Do-Ahead Tips: The garlic butter can be made up to 1 day ahead and refrigerated. The mussels can be steamed and the dishes assembled up to 2 hours in advance and refrigerated. The mussels will be best if baked just before serving.

CHOUX PUFFS
WITH SALMON AND SHRIMP

The French choux (pronounced *shoo*) pastry—also known as cream puff pastry—is made in a different fashion than most other pastries. A simple paste of water, butter, and flour is made stovetop, then eggs are beaten in. The magic happens during baking when the dough puffs up to create light, hollow domes, ready to be stuffed with countless possible fillings. You'll find a dessert version on page 190.

Note that this recipe makes more puffs than are needed for the fillings; extras freeze well and you'll be thrilled to have them on hand for a last-minute appetizer when friends pop by unexpectedly. Either let the puffs sit on the counter for about 30 minutes to thaw, or warm the frozen puffs in a 325°F oven for 5 minutes (direct from the freezer, no thawing needed). You may also skip the choux puffs and simply serve the fillings in endive leaves or spooned onto thick slices of cucumber for a super shortcut option that's still impressive.

MAKES 8 TO 12 SERVINGS

CHOUX PASTRY

½ cup whole milk

½ cup water

7 tablespoons unsalted butter, cut into pieces

1 teaspoon salt

1½ cups all-purpose flour

5 or 6 eggs, at room temperature

EGG WASH

1 egg

1 teaspoon water

SALMON FILLING

2 tablespoons cream cheese, at room temperature

2 tablespoons finely minced yellow onion

1 tablespoon prepared horseradish

½ teaspoon finely grated lemon zest

1 tablespoon freshly squeezed lemon juice

1 teaspoon minced fresh flat-leaf parsley

1 teaspoon chopped fresh dill

1 cup (about 6 ounces) flaked cooked or smoked salmon, pin bones and skin removed

Salt and freshly ground black pepper

1. Preheat the oven to 400°F. Line 2 baking sheets with silicone baking mats or parchment paper.

2. For the pastry, combine the milk, water, butter, and salt in a medium saucepan and warm over medium heat until the butter is melted. Add the flour all at once and stir continuously for about 1 minute, until the flour is thoroughly incorporated and the dough begins to pull together into a ball.

3. Remove the pan from the heat and beat in the eggs 1 at a time, stirring well with a wooden spoon to fully incorporate each egg before adding the next. The first couple of eggs are the hardest to mix; as the dough softens, it gets easier. After you have incorporated 5 eggs, the dough should be smooth and satiny. If the dough detaches from the spoon in a few seconds' time when you lift it up, it is perfect and you do not need the extra egg. Otherwise beat in a sixth egg.

4. Transfer the dough to a large pastry bag fitted with a ½-inch plain tip. Pipe the dough onto the baking sheets in 1½-inch mounds, about 2 inches apart.

5. For the egg wash, beat the egg with a fork in a small bowl until frothy, then beat in the water. Use a soft pastry brush to brush the top of each mound lightly with egg wash, gently patting down any tails of dough sticking up.

6. Bake the puffs for 18 to 20 minutes, until the pastry is nicely puffed and deep brown. It's best to bake 1 sheet at a time, so pop the first in the oven while piping the second (which will be fine sitting to wait its turn). Allow the puffs to cool on the baking sheet, then transfer to a wire rack to cool completely before filling.

SHRIMP FILLING

1 cup (about 6 ounces) cooked shrimp, finely
    chopped

¼ cup minced celery

¼ cup Greek yogurt or mayonnaise

3 tablespoons minced green onions

2 teaspoons minced fresh dill

1 teaspoon freshly squeezed lemon juice

7. For the salmon filling, blend together the cream cheese, onion, horserad-ish, lemon zest, lemon juice, parsley, and dill in a medium bowl. Add the salmon and stir until thoroughly blended. Season to taste with salt and pepper.

8. For the shrimp filling, if the shrimp seem wet, pat them dry with paper towels. Combine the shrimp, celery, yogurt, green onions, dill, and lemon juice in a medium bowl and stir to thoroughly blend. Season to taste with salt.

9. Shortly before serving, use a serrated knife to cut off the top third of each puff. Spoon the shrimp filling into about 18 of the puffs and the salmon fill-ing into another 18 or so puffs (don't overfill). Top each puff with a lid, arrange on a serving platter, and serve.

Menu Ideas: The puffs are an ideal finger-food accompaniment to a glass of wine or cocktail, whether as part of a full cocktail party spread or solo before a sit-down dinner. Consider following them with Asparagus Salad with Champagne Vinaigrette (page 65), then Osso Buco with Sage Gremolata (page 113).

Do-Ahead Tips: The fully cooled puffs can be stored for up to 3 days in the refrigerator in an airtight bag, or up to 1 month in the freezer. Both fillings can be made up to 1 day in advance and refrigerated, covered. The puffs should be filled shortly before serving.

SAVORY HERBED CHOUX

The recipe above for choux pastry is an all-purpose one, ideal for a wide variety of fillings. But for an added dose of flavor in the puffs them-selves, you might want to try this version. It's flavorful enough that the puffs may be served plain, whole and without any filling, in which case you may want to bake them in smaller, bite-sized mounds. To make onion juice, simply grate about one-quarter of a yellow onion and strain, pressing on the onion to extract a maximum of juice MAKES ABOUT 50 CHOUX

¾ cup whole milk

3 tablespoons onion juice

1 tablespoon water

7 tablespoons unsalted butter,
    cut into pieces

1 teaspoon salt

1½ cups all-purpose flour

5 or 6 large eggs, at room temperature

1 teaspoon minced fresh dill

1 teaspoon minced fresh chives

Follow the instructions above, using the blend of milk, onion juice, and water in place of the milk/water combination. Stir the dill and chives into the dough just before adding it to the piping bag. Pipe, brush with egg wash, and bake as directed.

SOUTHERN POPCORN SHRIMP

This ever-popular bar menu snack is often made with crawfish tails instead of shrimp, particularly in the South. I like to use large shrimp instead, and cut them into bite-sized pieces. I soak the shrimp in buttermilk before frying to keep them extra juicy and tender. Use the maximum of cayenne pepper if you like spice; with just 1 teaspoon there will be moderate heat.

Although they're delicious as is, popped in your mouth like popcorn, I sometimes serve them with homemade Tartar Sauce (page 104). And maybe a dash or two of Tabasco sauce for extra zing. For a less casual first course, leave the shrimp whole, with the tails on for visual appeal and doubling as a handle. **MAKES 6 TO 8 SERVINGS**

1½ **pounds large shrimp, peeled, deveined, and cut into ½-inch pieces**

2 **cups buttermilk**

1½ **cups all-purpose flour**

½ **cup panko bread crumbs**

1 **tablespoon chili powder**

1 **tablespoon garlic powder**

1 **to 2 teaspoons cayenne pepper**

1 **teaspoon sweet Hungarian paprika**

1 **teaspoon onion powder**

1 **teaspoon salt**

½ **teaspoon freshly ground black pepper**

2 **cups vegetable oil**

Menu Ideas: Complement the richness of the fried shrimp with a refreshing platter of Crudités with Spicy Red Pepper Dip and Roquefort Dip (page 28) or Mushrooms à la Grecque (page 22).

Do-Ahead Tips: The shrimp can be soaked up to 1 hour in advance and flour coated up to 15 minutes in advance. They will be tastiest if fried just before serving; the shrimp don't reheat or store well once cooked.

1. Combine the shrimp and buttermilk in a medium bowl, stir, and let sit for 15 minutes (refrigerate if soaking longer).

2. Stir together the flour, bread crumbs, chili powder, garlic powder, cayenne, paprika, onion powder, salt, and pepper in a shallow dish, such as a pie pan.

3. Heat the oil in a large, heavy skillet over medium-high heat (it's important the oil comes no more than halfway up the sides of the pan for safety; use a little less oil if needed). Line a platter or baking sheet with brown paper or layers of paper towels.

4. Drain the shrimp well and toss in the flour-spice mixture to evenly coat. Let the shrimp sit in the flour for 1 to 2 minutes (allowing the coating to set), then toss them one more time. Shake to remove excess flour and transfer to a plate.

5. In 2 or 3 batches, fry the shrimp for 1 to 2 minutes, until lightly browned and crisp. Use a slotted spoon to transfer to the paper-lined baking sheet to drain briefly. Sprinkle the shrimp with a bit more salt if you like and serve hot.

CHEESE CRACKERS

These little savory crackers—really more like cookies—are great passed with the salad course or set out on a table with olives and nuts while your guests enjoy a drink before dinner. I also like to make batches to offer as a tasty hostess gift, wrapped up in cellophane on a cute plate.
MAKES 12 TO 16 SERVINGS

1 cup unsalted butter, at room temperature

8 ounces sharp Cheddar cheese, grated

¼ teaspoon salt

Pinch of cayenne pepper

2 cups all-purpose flour

About 2 cups pecan halves

Menu Ideas: The flavor in this crisp snack is a perfect way to start a dinner showcasing Mardi Gras Gumbo (page 100). The savory cookies are also a perfect addition to a cocktail party spread that pair wonderfully with tasty bites such as Mushrooms à la Grecque (page 22) and Choux Puffs with Salmon and Shrimp (page 36).

Do-Ahead Tips: The crackers can be made up to 2 days before serving and stored in an airtight container. They can also be frozen for up to 1 month.

1. Preheat the oven to 375°F. Line a baking sheet with a silicone baking mat or parchment paper.

2. Combine the butter, cheese, salt, and cayenne in a large bowl and stir until thoroughly blended. Stir in the flour and knead gently but quickly with your hands until the mixture is firm and smooth.

3. Roll the dough into balls, using about 2 teaspoons for each. Set the balls on the baking sheet about 1½ inches apart. Bake for 10 minutes. Carefully press a pecan half onto each cracker. Bake for 18 to 20 minutes longer, until the crackers and pecans are lightly browned. Let cool a few minutes on the pan, then transfer to a wire rack to cool.

SALADS

Salad is a course for which there are virtually no rules. It is most generically considered a mix of lettuce and raw vegetables with a dressing—the classic "starter salad." But from there the variants are truly endless. Countless vegetables and fruits come into play, as do grains, pastas, nuts, seafood, and meats. This is an arena in which there is always room for creativity. And salads are versatile within the meal: They can be served as a first course, alongside the main course, as the main course, or—in the case of light, fresh greens and herbs—after the main course, before dessert.

Though not all salads include greens, I can't resist this opportunity to talk briefly about lettuces. I think they often get overlooked as the background, rather than the star, of most salads. Choose lettuce greens that are crisp and fresh looking; I prefer not to use bagged lettuces, they just don't have the same crispness and fresh flavor. Wash the lettuce in cold water as soon as you get home, dry the leaves well, and wrap in paper towels or a kitchen towel to refrigerate until ready to serve. For a simple green salad, choose greens that complement one another, such as mild red leaf lettuce with peppery arugula, or crisp romaine with feathery frisée.

Dressing plays a big role in the character of a salad, whether it's a simple splash of vinegar and oil or a more robust dressing with spices and mustards that elevates the flavor profile distinctly. Greens should be dressed just before serving, to avoid wilting. Too much dressing will weigh down the greens and overwhelm their flavor and texture. Toss just enough dressing to evenly coat the greens but not pool at the bottom of the bowl. Salads can be wonderfully complementary to each other. I think it's fun and a bit of a surprise to serve two or three salads that offer varying flavors and textures that go well together. For lunch, a buffet party, or a light supper, I may make a few salads that add up to a wonderful meal in themselves.

ENDIVE AND RADICCHIO SALAD

Radicchio is often bitter, so I like to soak the leaves in ice water for 15 to 20 minutes, which mellows the bitterness, then spin them dry. For the vinaigrette dressing, regular Dijon mustard is a classic component but I sometimes like to use a flavored mustard for a little twist, such as varieties with herbes de Provence or green peppercorns.

Use a really good, artisanal bread for the croutons, one that has a distinctive crust and chewy-firm center. Fluffy, airy bread doesn't make the best croutons. Instead of baking, I sometimes fry the croutons in a large skillet in olive oil with a crushed garlic clove, though you need to take care to watch that the garlic doesn't burn. **MAKES 6 TO 8 SERVINGS**

3 cups baguette cubes (about ½-inch cubes)

2 to 3 tablespoons extra-virgin olive oil

3 large heads Belgian endive, trimmed and cut into 1-inch pieces

1 head radicchio, rinsed, dried, cored, and torn into bite-sized pieces

1 small cucumber, peeled, seeded, and thinly sliced

6 green onions, thinly sliced

⅔ cup freshly grated Parmesan cheese

SHERRY VINAIGRETTE

2 tablespoons sherry vinegar

1 tablespoon balsamic vinegar

1 tablespoon Dijon mustard

1 clove garlic, pressed or minced

⅓ cup extra-virgin olive oil

2 tablespoons vegetable oil

Salt and freshly ground black pepper

1. Preheat the oven to 350°F.

2. Arrange the baguette cubes in an even layer on a baking sheet and bake, tossing a few times to ensure even toasting, for 10 to 12 minutes, until golden. Drizzle the toasted croutons with the olive oil, toss to evenly coat, and set aside.

3. For the vinaigrette, combine the sherry and balsamic vinegars, mustard, and garlic and whisk to blend. Whisk in the olive and vegetable oils, season to taste with salt and pepper, and set aside.

4. In a large bowl, combine the endive, radicchio, cucumber, green onions, croutons, and half the cheese. Whisk the vinaigrette to reblend and drizzle two-thirds over the salad. Toss to evenly mix and arrange the salads on individual plates. Sprinkle the remaining cheese over and pass the remaining dressing separately for guests to add more to their taste.

Menu Ideas: I feel this salad is best enjoyed with fall and winter foods. The richness of hearty dishes like Braised Brisket with Onions (page 109) or Wine-Braised Corned Beef with Brown Sugar Glaze (page 124) is a great complement to the slight bitter taste of the endive and radicchio.

Do-Ahead Tips: The croutons can be made up to 2 days in advance and stored in an airtight container. The vinaigrette can be made up to 1 day in advance and refrigerated. The salad ingredients can be prepared up to 4 hours in advance and refrigerated, covered with damp paper towels to keep crisp. The salad should be assembled and tossed just before serving.

BASIC VINAIGRETTE

Everyone should know how to make basic vinaigrette; my favorite is this simple recipe. I'll sometimes add a tablespoon or two of minced fresh herbs (tarragon, chervil, basil, flat-leaf parsley, and/or celery leaves) to the oil, allowing them to infuse for an hour or two before making the dressing. On occasion, I'll also use freshly squeezed lemon juice in place of the vinegar. This is enough dressing for about 8 cups of lettuce greens. **MAKES ABOUT ⅓ CUP**

¼ cup peanut oil or top-quality extra-virgin olive oil

1 tablespoon red or white wine vinegar

¼ teaspoon dry mustard

Pinch of salt and freshly ground black pepper

Whisk together the oil, vinegar, mustard, and salt.

To dress a salad, place greens in a bowl. Add about half of the vinaigrette along with a grinding of pepper. Toss well to mix, adding another tablespoon or two of the dressing to suite your taste. Any leftover vinaigrette will keep, refrigerated, for a week or more.

SPINACH AND HEARTS OF PALM SALAD

Though this salad is delicious without the fried oysters, which can be found on page 4, I find I'm always frying up a batch to top the colorful spinach salad embellished with hearts of palm and fresh tomato. **MAKES 6 SERVINGS**

1½ cups chopped, seeded tomatoes

1 can (14 ounces) hearts of palm, drained

8 green onions, sliced

¾ cup Champagne Vinaigrette (page 63)

6 cups lightly packed spinach leaves, rinsed, dried, and tough stems removed

24 Fried Oysters (without rémoulade, page 4; optional)

1. Drain the tomatoes in a medium sieve over a bowl for 30 minutes, stirring occasionally to help release excess liquid. Place the hearts of palm in a heat-proof bowl and cover with boiling water. Let sit for 3 to 4 minutes, then drain well and let cool. Discard any tough outer layers from the hearts of palm and cut them into ¼-inch slices. Toss together the tomatoes, hearts of palm, and green onions with half of the vinaigrette.

2. Arrange the spinach on individual salad plates. Spoon the tomato mixture into the center of each salad and arrange the oysters around the tomato mixture. Drizzle the remaining vinaigrette over the oysters and spinach.

Menu Ideas: I love to serve this boldly flavored salad before Mardi Gras Gumbo (page 100). You can also let it stand alone as a main-course salad for your oyster-loving friends.

Do-Ahead Tips: The vinaigrette can be made up to 1 day in advance and refrigerated. The tomato and hearts of palm mixture can be combined and dressed up to 2 hours in advance. The oysters should be fried and the salads assembled just before serving.

RADISH AND FENNEL SALAD

I love to use fennel—which is packed with flavor and crunch—in many ways. Here the flavor of the fresh fennel is echoed in the fennel seeds in the dressing. When the fennel plant in my garden has gone to seed, I'll capture some of those fresh seeds and use them here, which contributes an outstanding boost in flavor.

This is an ideal time to use a V-slicer; both the firm radishes and dense fennel will slice like a dream. Note that the lemon juice and salt isn't added to the salad until the last minute; this helps preserve the crisp character of the vegetables. **MAKES 6 SERVINGS**

1 medium fennel bulb, trimmed, cored, and thinly sliced (reserve green fronds)

2 cups thinly sliced radishes (about 1 bunch)

6 green onions, white and light green portions, minced

6 tablespoons extra-virgin olive oil

2 tablespoons white wine vinegar

1 teaspoon minced shallot

1 teaspoon fennel seeds, toasted and ground or crushed (see page 222)

2 teaspoons freshly squeezed lemon juice

Salt and freshly ground black pepper

4 ounces baby spinach or mixed baby greens

1. Combine the fennel and radishes in a large bowl.

2. Mince enough of the fennel fronds to make 2 tablespoons and place in a medium bowl. Add the green onions, olive oil, vinegar, shallot, and fennel seeds and whisk to blend. Pour over the fennel and radishes, tossing to evenly coat the vegetables. Set aside for 1 hour, refrigerated.

3. Just before serving, add the lemon juice with salt and pepper to taste. Toss to blend, then toss in the baby spinach and serve.

Menu Ideas: This salad is a perfect start to most any meal. Consider serving it before your favorite grilled steak and Roasted Smashed Potatoes with Garlic and Herbs (page 159), or The Best Roasted Chicken (page 112) with Old-Fashioned Green Beans with Bacon (page 142).

Do-Ahead Tips: The dressing can be made up to 1 day in advance and refrigerated. The fennel and radishes can be tossed with the dressing up to 4 hours in advance and refrigerated. Add the lemon juice and season just before serving.

GINGER ASIAN SLAW

Napa cabbage is perfect for this crisp salad but it does not hold up as well as regular green cabbage, so plan to serve the slaw within an hour of dressing it. I like to make the dressing a couple of hours in advance, at least, so that the ginger, jalapeño, lime, and other flavorful ingredients have a chance to meld and develop before serving. For a main-course salad, add slivers of cooked chicken breast, either mixed in or perched across the top of the plated salad.

When I measure shredded or sliced vegetables in a recipe such as this, I'll moderately pack the ingredient into the cup. For the 4-cup measure of the Napa cabbage, you could use a quart measure. Yes, it's typically used for measuring liquids, but it works well for this type of ingredient.   MAKES 6 TO 8 SERVINGS

4 cups finely shredded Napa cabbage

1 cup finely shredded red cabbage

1 cup coarsely grated carrot

1 red bell pepper, cored, seeded, and thinly sliced

½ cup finely chopped green onions

¼ cup minced fresh mint

¼ cup minced fresh cilantro

Salt and freshly ground black pepper

3 tablespoons chopped roasted peanuts (optional)

2 teaspoons toasted sesame seeds (see page 222)

GINGER DRESSING

1 teaspoon finely grated lime zest

3 tablespoons freshly squeezed lime juice

2 tablespoons minced shallot

2 tablespoons sesame oil

2 tablespoons unseasoned rice wine vinegar

1½ tablespoons minced or grated ginger

1 tablespoon minced jalapeño chile

1 tablespoon soy sauce

2 teaspoons honey

1 teaspoon pressed or minced garlic

⅓ cup peanut or vegetable oil

1. For the dressing, whisk together the lime zest, lime juice, shallot, sesame oil, vinegar, ginger, jalapeño, soy sauce, honey, and garlic in a small bowl. Drizzle in the oil, whisking constantly. Refrigerate the dressing, covered with plastic wrap, for at least 2 hours before serving.

2. When ready to dress the slaw, combine the Napa and red cabbages, carrot, bell pepper, green onions, mint, and cilantro in a large bowl. Drizzle the dressing over, toss well, and let sit for 10 minutes. Taste the salad for seasoning, adding salt and pepper to taste. Arrange the slaw on individual plates and sprinkle with the peanuts and sesame seeds.

Menu Ideas: This slaw—vibrant in both color and flavor—is great with simple grilled or roasted meats, or served at a summer picnic with cold Four-Star Fried Chicken (page 110).

Do-Ahead Tips: The dressing can be made up to 24 hours in advance. The vegetables can be prepped and blended up to 6 hours in advance and refrigerated in the large bowl with a damp paper towel draped on top. The vegetables and dressing should be tossed together shortly before serving.

SALADE NIÇOISE WITH GRILLED AHI TUNA

I grill fresh tuna, usually with a delicious sesame crust (page 95), for this twist on the classic Niçoise salad. Traditionally a high-quality canned tuna is featured, which you can certainly use if you prefer. I also make three different dressings to toss with the different salad elements, so the individual character of each stands out a bit more. MAKES 6 SERVINGS

2 pounds small Yukon Gold potatoes, scrubbed and halved

½ cup Crème Fraîche–Tarragon Dressing (page 59)

1 pound green beans, trimmed and halved crosswise

6 green onions, finely chopped

1 tablespoon olive oil

1 to 1½ pounds ahi tuna fillets, 1 inch thick

1 head Boston or Bibb lettuce, rinsed, dried, and torn into bite-sized pieces

¼ cup minced fresh herbs (tarragon, chives, thyme, and/or flat-leaf parsley)

4 medium tomatoes, cut into 1-inch wedges

6 hard-cooked eggs (see page 221), peeled and quartered

¾ cup Niçoise olives or other cured black olives

TARRAGON VINAIGRETTE

2 tablespoons tarragon vinegar

1 tablespoon freshly squeezed lemon juice

½ teaspoon Dijon or tarragon mustard

7 tablespoons extra-virgin olive oil

1 tablespoon minced fresh herbs (tarragon, basil, chives, and/or flat-leaf parsley)

Salt and freshly ground black pepper

RICH VINAIGRETTE

¼ cup Champagne vinegar

½ teaspoon Dijon mustard

1 clove garlic, pressed or minced

1 egg yolk

½ cup extra-virgin olive oil

1. For the tarragon vinaigrette, whisk together the vinegar, lemon juice, and mustard in a small bowl. Whisk in the olive oil and herbs with salt and pepper to taste. Set aside. For the rich vinaigrette, whisk together the vinegar, mustard, garlic, and egg yolk in a small bowl. Whisk in the olive oil to make a smooth dressing. Season to taste with salt and pepper. Set aside.

2. Steam the potatoes until tender when pierced with the tip of a knife, about 20 minutes. When cool enough to handle (but not fully cooled), peel the potatoes and cut into 1-inch dice. In a large bowl, toss the potatoes with the Crème Fraîche–Tarragon dressing and set aside.

3. Bring a large pan of salted water to a boil. Add the green beans and cook until just tender but still bright green, 2 to 3 minutes. Drain and run under cold water to stop the cooking. Drain well and pat dry with paper towels. Place the beans in a medium bowl and add the green onions. Set aside.

4. Heat a grill pan or large cast-iron skillet over medium-high heat (allow enough time for the skillet to fully heat). Add the oil, then add the tuna steaks and cook for about 1 minute per side, until lightly browned and medium. Transfer the tuna pieces to a cutting board, cover loosely with foil, and let sit while assembling the salads.

5. Arrange the lettuce on individual plates or in the center of a large platter, sprinkle the herbs over, and drizzle with half of the rich vinaigrette. Toss the green beans with the tarragon vinaigrette. Arrange the green beans, potatoes, tomatoes, eggs, and olives around the edge of the salad(s). Drizzle the remaining rich vinaigrette over the tomatoes.

6. Cut the tuna steaks on the bias into slices about ½ inch thick. Arrange the tuna in the center of the salad(s), slightly overlapping.

Menu Ideas: Serve with crusty French bread and follow with a selection of French cheeses.

Do-Ahead Tips: All of the salad elements can be prepared up to 4 hours in advance and refrigerated. Let them sit at room temperature for about 30 minutes before plating. Dress the green beans just before serving, to avoid discoloration.

FRISÉE SALAD
WITH TOASTED HAZELNUTS

Frisée, a lettuce with spiked, flavorful leaves, is among those gourmet greens that have begun to show up more and more in well-stocked produce sections. On big heads that have darker outer greens, you'll want to discard the larger, tough leaves and use only the pale green to nearly white tender leaves at the center. If you prefer to serve this salad nut-free, the hazelnuts may be omitted and the hazelnut oil replaced with more of the olive oil. **MAKES 8 TO 10 SERVINGS**

2 heads romaine lettuce

2 heads frisée, trimmed, rinsed, and dried

6 green onions, thinly sliced

1 large cucumber, peeled, seeded, and thinly sliced

1 medium fennel bulb, trimmed, cored, and thinly sliced

½ cup chopped toasted hazelnuts (see page 222)

½ cup coarsely grated Parmigiano-Reggiano cheese

HAZELNUT DRESSING

3 tablespoons hazelnut oil

2 tablespoons extra-virgin olive oil

½ teaspoon finely grated lemon zest

2 tablespoons freshly squeezed lemon juice

1 clove garlic, pressed or minced

½ teaspoon roasted garlic mustard or Dijon mustard

½ teaspoon sugar

Salt and freshly ground black pepper

1. For the dressing, whisk together the hazelnut oil, olive oil, lemon zest, lemon juice, garlic, mustard, and sugar in a small bowl. Season to taste with salt and pepper; set aside.

2. Remove the few outer layers of leaves from the romaine heads and discard or save for another use. Rinse the remaining leaves and dry well. Tear the romaine into pieces, discarding the larger tough ribs. Tear the frisée into pieces.

3. Combine the romaine, frisée, green onions, cucumber, and fennel in a large bowl. Drizzle the dressing over and toss well.

4. Arrange the salad on individual plates, scatter the hazelnuts and cheese over, and serve.

Menu Ideas: This crisp salad is great any time of year, with flavors and textures that complement a range of dishes, including The Best Roasted Chicken (page 112) and Salmon with Wild Mushroom Sauce (page 128).

Do-Ahead Tips: The dressing can be made up to 1 day in advance and refrigerated. The salad elements can all be prepared up to 4 hours in advance and refrigerated. Cover the greens and vegetables with damp paper towels to keep them crisp and store the nuts and cheese in airtight containers. The salad should be dressed and assembled just before serving.

WHITE BEAN AND TUNA SALAD
WITH ROASTED PEPPERS

I created this salad 20 years ago when we began taking picnics along with us for spring skiing. It packs well and can be scooped up with pieces of pita bread, keeping cleanup at a minimum. **MAKES 6 TO 8 SERVINGS**

8 cups cold water

2 cups dry small white beans (such as Great Northern)

2 dried bay leaves

1 tablespoon salt

2 cans (6 ounces each) albacore tuna in water, drained

2 red bell peppers, roasted, peeled, seeded, and chopped (see page 222)

6 green onions, chopped

3 stalks celery, thinly sliced

1 tablespoon chopped fresh dill

GARLIC AND MUSTARD VINAIGRETTE

½ cup vegetable oil

¼ cup extra-virgin olive oil

¼ cup red wine vinegar

2 tablespoons freshly squeezed lemon juice

2 cloves garlic, pressed or minced

2 teaspoons Dijon mustard

1 teaspoon dry mustard

Salt and freshly ground black pepper

1. Bring the water to a boil in a large saucepan over medium-high heat and add the beans. Boil for 2 minutes. Remove the pan from the heat and let stand for 1 hour. Return the pan to the heat and add the bay leaves and salt. Bring to a low boil over medium-high heat. Decrease the heat to medium and simmer for about 45 minutes, until the beans are tender but not mushy. (The water should not boil vigorously; decrease to medium-low if needed.) Drain the beans, discard the bay leaves, and let cool to room temperature.

2. For the dressing, whisk together the vegetable oil, olive oil, vinegar, lemon juice, garlic, Dijon mustard, and dry mustard. Season to taste with salt and pepper. Set aside for 10 minutes to allow the flavors to blend.

3. Break the tuna into bite-sized pieces and stir into the beans along with the roasted peppers, green onions, celery, dill, and dressing. Let sit for 30 minutes before serving (refrigerate if made further in advance). Taste the salad for seasoning, adding more salt or pepper if needed.

Menu Ideas: This salad makes a wonderful addition to a buffet, served alongside sliced meats, grilled fish, or roasted chicken. Serve with dishes that don't have heavy sauces or complex flavors. As a main course, serve with sliced, vine-ripe tomatoes and steamed asparagus— a perfect meal for a warm day.

Do-Ahead Tips: The dressed salad will be at its best made 1 day in advance so the flavors have a chance to meld. Allow to come to room temperature before serving.

BIBB LETTUCE AND GRAPEFRUIT SALAD

Bibb lettuce tends to have more delicate leaves than other lettuces. I don't use a salad spinner when cleaning Bibb lettuce because the soft leaves of Bibb lettuce can bruise; instead, rinse it in cold water then wrap the leaves in a large thick kitchen towel to dry. I often serve a couple of water crackers or thin slices of baguette alongside this salad, to complement the Brie cheese that accents the plates. You could embellish the salad with other ingredients that complement the grapefruit, such as diced avocado or shrimp. MAKES 8 SERVINGS

2 large pink grapefruit, peeled and sectioned (see page 221)

6 green onions, chopped

½ cucumber, peeled, seeded, and diced

1 head Bibb lettuce, leaves separated, rinsed, and dried

8 ounces Brie cheese, cut into 8 slices

GRAPEFRUIT DRESSING

3 tablespoons extra-virgin olive oil

3 tablespoons grapefruit juice (from sectioning the grapefruit)

1 tablespoon white balsamic vinegar or white wine vinegar

1 teaspoon minced shallot

1 teaspoon minced fresh tarragon

½ teaspoon sugar

Salt and freshly ground black pepper

1. For the dressing, combine the olive oil, grapefruit juice, vinegar, shallot, tarragon, and sugar in a small bowl and whisk well to blend. Season to taste with salt and pepper.

2. Combine the grapefruit sections, green onions, and cucumber in a medium bowl. Drizzle the dressing over and toss gently to mix.

3. To serve, arrange the lettuce leaves, partly overlapping, on individual plates. Top the lettuce with the grapefruit mixture and set a piece of Brie alongside each salad.

Menu Ideas: This is an easy, refreshing, and versatile salad. It can complement a meal with robust or spicy flavors, such as Chili with Fire-Roasted Peppers (page 94) or Clam and Mussel Cataplana with Chorizo (page 98). It also makes a great start to a dinner with softer flavors, such as Salmon with Nasturtium Butter (page 90).

Do-Ahead Tips: The dressing can be made up to 1 day in advance and refrigerated. You can section the grapefruit early in the day, place the sections in their juice, and refrigerate until ready to serve. The salads should be assembled just before serving.

ROASTED CORN SALAD

When I was growing up, our family garden produced quite a lot of what ended up on our dinner table. Few crops each year elicited as much anticipation as the corn; we couldn't wait for those first ears to be plucked from the stalks to have with dinner. We were also surrounded by roadside stands selling fresh corn to supplement our own harvest throughout the summer.

This corn salad has a Moroccan twist with the addition of cumin and coriander. During a visit to Morocco a few years ago, I had a similar salad on a few different occasions, served at wonderful leisurely lunches under the cool shade of trees. If you've got the grill going for other parts of dinner, you can grill the corn rather than broiling. It'll take less time; be sure to turn the ears frequently to avoid burning.

MAKES 10 TO 12 SERVINGS

8 ears sweet corn, husks and silk removed

2 tablespoons olive oil

1 yellow and 1 red bell pepper, roasted, peeled,
　　seeded, and diced (see page 222)

1 cup finely diced red or sweet onion

8 ounces arugula, rinsed, dried, and trimmed

CUMIN DRESSING

6 tablespoons extra-virgin olive oil

3 tablespoons freshly squeezed lemon juice

2 tablespoons cider vinegar

1 teaspoon ground cumin, toasted (see page 222)

½ teaspoon ground coriander, toasted
　　(see page 222)

⅛ teaspoon cayenne pepper

Salt

Menu Ideas: This is an ideal late summer recipe, when corn is at its best and sweetest, perfect for a picnic or al fresco dining. I like to pair it with Four-Star Fried Chicken (page 110) or Grilled Honey and Mustard Ribs (page 108). It also makes a great side dish to Chiles Rellenos with Potatoes and Cheese (page 114).

Do-Ahead Tips: The corn can be roasted and combined with the onion and roasted peppers up to 1 day in advance. The dressing also can be made up to 1 day ahead and refrigerated. The salad should be assembled with the arugula shortly before serving.

1. Preheat the broiler. Set the oven rack about 5 inches below the heating element.

2. Brush the ears of corn with the olive oil and set them on a broiler pan or rimmed baking sheet. Broil the corn, turning a few times, for 5 to 10 minutes, until evenly tender and lightly browned on all sides. Set aside to cool. Cut the kernels from the ears. Place the corn in a large bowl with the roasted peppers and onion and toss to mix.

3. For the dressing, combine the olive oil, lemon juice, vinegar, cumin, coriander, and cayenne. Whisk to blend and season to taste with salt.

4. Pour the dressing over the corn mixture and toss to blend. Let sit at room temperature for 30 minutes, or refrigerate up to 2 hours in advance. Taste the salad for seasoning, adding more salt to taste.

5. Just before serving, arrange the arugula leaves on a serving platter or individual plates and spoon the corn salad over.

CONFETTI PASTA SALAD
WITH TANGY YOGURT DRESSING

In early May when the weather begins to show signs of summer in the Northwest, everyone begins to talk about outside dining and picnics. These casual meals often include a wide array of salads, and pasta salads are a perennial favorite. I think one of the downfalls of pasta salad is when it is overly heavy with dressing (often made with lots of mayonnaise). With yogurt in this dressing, the salad is lighter and the flavors come through better. I love Greek-style yogurt, which is thicker and tangier than the more common yogurts we see in grocery stores.

MAKES 8 SERVINGS

8 ounces fusilli or rotini pasta

1 red and 1 yellow bell pepper, roasted, peeled, seeded, and diced (see page 222)

3 stalks celery, diced

6 green onions, minced

¾ cup diced sweet onion

¾ cup sliced Kalamata olives

½ cup diced sweet pickles

TANGY YOGURT DRESSING

½ cup plain yogurt (not nonfat), preferably Greek

2 tablespoons mayonnaise

1 tablespoon Dijon mustard

¼ cup extra-virgin olive oil

3 tablespoons minced fresh basil

3 tablespoons minced fresh flat-leaf parsley

1 teaspoon finely grated lemon zest

2 tablespoons freshly squeezed lemon juice

2 tablespoons sweet pickle juice

Salt and freshly ground black pepper

1. Bring a large pot of salted water to a rolling boil. Add the pasta and cook for about 10 minutes, until al dente. Drain the pasta well, place in a large bowl, and let cool slightly. Add the roasted peppers, celery, green onions, sweet onion, olives, and pickles and stir to mix.

2. For the dressing, whisk together the yogurt, mayonnaise, and mustard in a medium bowl until well blended. Whisk in the olive oil, basil, parsley, lemon zest, lemon juice, and pickle juice. Season to taste with salt and pepper.

3. Pour the dressing over the pasta mixture and stir to thoroughly incorporate. Cover the bowl with plastic wrap and refrigerate for at least 1 hour before serving. Taste the salad again for seasoning before serving, adding more salt or pepper if needed.

Menu Ideas: Pasta salads go best with simple meat or fish preparations, or even just a good grilled burger or any kind of sandwich. This salad holds up well to travel, great for potlucks and family gatherings.

Do-Ahead Tips: This salad can be made up to 2 days in advance and refrigerated, and will have the best flavor if made at least 1 day in advance. Let the salad sit at room temperature for about 30 minutes before serving.

CURRIED SEAFOOD SALAD

I've sampled different versions of this salad for many years here in the Northwest, since it's such a simple choice for a great lunch. Use fresh crab and shrimp if possible, rather than frozen or canned. I use sweet, delicious Dungeness crab and small pink Oregon shrimp, but other types may be used instead.

Fresh water chestnuts are a true luxury, available in Asian grocery stores. If you're able to get your hands on some, peel the water chestnuts and blanch them for a minute or two in boiling water. Drain and let cool before dicing to add to the salad. MAKES 6 TO 8 SERVINGS

1¾ cups frozen petite peas

1 can (8 ounces) water chestnuts, drained and rinsed

4 ounces crabmeat, picked over to remove bits of shell or cartilage

8 ounces cooked shrimp

2 cups thinly sliced celery

1¼ cups fresh bean sprouts

6 green onions, finely chopped

CURRY DRESSING

⅓ cup mayonnaise

⅓ cup crème fraîche or sour cream

2 tablespoons freshly squeezed lemon juice

1 tablespoon mild curry powder

1 teaspoon soy sauce

¼ teaspoon garlic powder

Salt and freshly ground black pepper

1. Bring a small pan of salted water to a boil, add the frozen peas, and simmer for 2 minutes. Drain well and set aside to cool. Place the water chestnuts in a small bowl, pour boiling water over to cover, and let sit for 5 minutes. Drain well and dice.

2. For the dressing, in a small bowl, whisk together the mayonnaise, crème fraîche, lemon juice, curry powder, soy sauce, and garlic powder. Season to taste with salt and pepper.

3. In a bowl, combine the cooled peas, chestnuts, crabmeat, shrimp, celery, bean sprouts, and green onions. Drizzle the dressing over the salad and toss to mix. Cover with plastic wrap and refrigerate for at least 2 hours to allow the flavors to meld.

Menu Ideas: This is a great lunch salad, with cups of Chilled Cucumber-Buttermilk Soup (page 78) served beforehand. I also often take this salad to potlucks, a wonderful contribution your friends will love. You can also serve it as a distinctive appetizer at a dinner party, spooning the salad onto pineapple slices, or into scallop shells with a mint garnish.

Do-Ahead Tips: It's best to make this salad not more than 4 hours in advance, so it doesn't become watery. You can prepare the dressing and other ingredients up to 1 day in advance and refrigerate them separately, tossing the salad just a couple hours before serving.

CELERY ROOT AND APPLE SALAD
WITH DIJON DRESSING

While we often tend to think that "salad" always includes some type of lettuce, in France they've perfected the art of the salad, going well beyond salad greens. Celery root is one such French favorite, often served with the type of tangy, mustardy dressing that I use here. I've added grated crisp apple to the mix, a perfect contrast to the earthy-nutty celery root.

Crisp, sweet Fuji apples are my favorite choice for this recipe, but Gala or Cameo would work well too. Be sure to hold off on peeling and grating the apple until just before serving, to avoid browning. Knobby celery root has a coarse skin that takes extra care in peeling. I trim both ends from the root first, cut it into quarters, and then use a small paring knife to cut away the skin rather than relying on a vegetable peeler.

MAKES 6 TO 8 SERVINGS

1 tablespoon freshly squeezed lemon juice

1½ teaspoons salt

1 (1½-pound) medium celery root, peeled

2 Fuji apples

3 tablespoons minced fresh flat-leaf parsley

DIJON DRESSING

2 tablespoons Dijon mustard

2 tablespoons boiling water

⅓ cup extra-virgin olive oil

2 tablespoons apple cider vinegar

Freshly ground black pepper

Menu Ideas: This tart, crunchy salad makes a great picnic offering to serve with cold Four-Star Fried Chicken (page 110) and Mini Corn Muffins with Roasted Garlic and Fresh Herbs (page 136). Or, for a sit-down dinner, serve the salad alongside The Best Roasted Chicken (page 112) or Grilled Honey and Mustard Ribs (page 108).

Do-Ahead Tips: The celery root should be combined with the dressing and refrigerated at least 4 hours (or up to 1 day) before serving. The apple should be grated and added to the salad just before serving.

1. Stir together the lemon juice and salt in a small dish and let sit until the salt is dissolved. Coarsely grate the celery root and immediately drizzle the salted lemon juice over, tossing to mix well. Let sit at room temperature for 30 minutes. Rinse the celery root under cold water, squeeze in your hands to remove most of the water, and dry well with paper towels.

2. For the dressing, put the mustard in a medium bowl. Slowly add the boiling water, whisking gently. Add the oil in a slow stream, whisking constantly, to form a thick, creamy dressing. Whisk in the vinegar with pepper to taste.

3. Place the celery root in a large bowl and fold in the dressing until evenly blended. Refrigerate, covered, for at least 4 hours, or overnight.

4. Shortly before serving, peel, core, and coarsely grate the apples. Stir them into the salad, arrange on individual plates, and top with a sprinkling of parsley.

BEET AND FENNEL SALAD
WITH WALNUT DRESSING

Our family enjoys beets many ways and this is a favorite dish I prepare year-round. I know many people feel they don't like beets because they were served canned, often pickled, beets as children. If that includes you, this recipe will change your mind about beets.

Be sure to choose beets that are smaller and still have their leafy green tops attached. These have far sweeter, more delicate flavor and texture than the larger beets that are pre-trimmed. The greens can be saved to braise for a side dish to your main course. You may use another type of nut if you like, such as pecans or hazelnuts, instead of the walnuts; substitute a similar nut oil in place of the walnut oil in the dressing.

MAKES 8 SERVINGS

2½ pounds medium beets (preferably half red beets and half yellow beets), trimmed and scrubbed

4 tablespoons olive oil

2 cups lightly packed baby spinach leaves, rinsed, dried, and tough stems removed

1 cup thinly sliced sweet or yellow onion

1 small fennel bulb, trimmed, cored, and very thinly sliced

1 cup coarsely chopped, toasted walnuts (see page 222)

3 to 4 ounces crumbled blue cheese or goat cheese

WALNUT DRESSING

2 tablespoons white wine vinegar

½ teaspoon Dijon mustard

¼ cup walnut oil

1 tablespoon minced fresh flat-leaf parsley

1 tablespoon prepared pesto or minced fresh basil

¼ teaspoon sugar

Salt and freshly ground black pepper

1. Preheat the oven to 400°F.

2. Place the beets in a baking dish just large enough to hold them (if cooking 2 colors, bake them in separate dishes). Rub the beets with 2 tablespoons of the olive oil. Cover with aluminum foil and roast for about 1¼ hours, until the beets are tender when pierced with the tip of a knife. Set aside to cool.

3. While the beets are roasting, make the dressing. Whisk together the vinegar and mustard in a small bowl, then whisk in the oil in a slow stream. Whisk in the parsley, pesto, and sugar with salt and pepper to taste. Set aside.

4. Use your fingers to slip the skin from the beets, then thinly slice them (I use a mandoline to get even, thin slices). Toss the spinach with the remaining 2 tablespoons olive oil and arrange in even beds on individual plates. Scatter the onion over, followed by the fennel. Arrange the beet slices on top, slightly overlapping, then sprinkle the beets with the walnuts and cheese. Drizzle the dressing over and serve.

Menu Ideas: While this salad is delicious served solo before most any meal, I like to serve small portions as part of a trio—including Celery Root and Apple Salad with Dijon Dressing (page 57) and either Radish and Fennel Salad (page 46) or simply sliced cucumbers drizzled with a vinaigrette. It makes for a vibrant start to a meal featuring Grilled Rack of Pork with Mango Salsa (page 92) or Lemon and Sage Cornish Game Hens (page 122), with spoonfuls of fluffy Roasted Pepper and Corn Spoon Bread (page 155) alongside.

Do-Ahead Tips: The beets can be roasted up to 1 day ahead and refrigerated. Peel and slice them just before serving. The dressing can be made 1 day ahead as well. The other salad ingredients can be prepped up to a couple hours in advance, then draped with damp paper towels to keep fresh. The salad should be assembled just before serving.

GRAND COBB SALAD

Cobb salad is often served on individual plates, with all the ingredients arranged on, or tossed into, the greens. Instead, I like to serve Cobb salad on a large platter, with the components mounded around a pile of greens. Not only does this make for quite a "wow" factor in its presentation, but guests can customize their own serving, helping themselves to greens and then adding small or large spoonfuls of the accents to suit their preferences. It's also nice to serve the dressing from a bowl on the side, so guests may add only as much as they'd like. Toss the cubed avocado with a bit of lemon juice to avoid browning, or preferably cut it just before using. MAKES 6 SERVINGS

6 thick strips bacon, cut into ½-inch pieces

1 head romaine lettuce, rinsed, dried, and cut into ribbons

½ head iceberg lettuce, rinsed, dried, and cut into ribbons

½ cup chopped green onions

2 ripe avocadoes, pitted, peeled, and cut into ½-inch cubes

4 cups diced cooked chicken breast (see below)

1 cup crumbled blue cheese

2 beefsteak tomatoes, diced

6 hard-cooked eggs (see page 221), peeled and chopped or grated

DRESSING

2 tablespoons water

2 tablespoons red wine vinegar

1 clove garlic, pressed or minced

1 teaspoon freshly squeezed lemon juice

½ teaspoon dry mustard

¼ teaspoon Worcestershire sauce

¼ teaspoon sugar

¼ cup olive oil

¼ cup vegetable oil

Salt and freshly ground black pepper

1. For the dressing, whisk together the water, vinegar, garlic, lemon juice, dry mustard, Worcestershire sauce, and sugar in a medium bowl. Whisk in the olive oil, adding it in a thin stream, then whisk in the vegetable oil in a thin stream until the dressing is emulsified. Season to taste with salt and pepper.

2. Fry the bacon in a large skillet over medium heat for 5 to 7 minutes, until browned and crisp. Use a slotted spoon to transfer to paper towels to drain.

3. In a large bowl, toss together the romaine and iceberg lettuces. Arrange the greens as a bed on a large serving platter and scatter the green onions over. Arrange mounds of the bacon, avocado, chicken, blue cheese, tomatoes, and eggs around the outer edge of the salad greens. Drizzle the dressing over the greens, or serve alongside for guests to add themselves.

SIMPLE COOKED CHICKEN BREASTS: For the cooked chicken needed for this salad recipe (or for any recipe that requires cooked chicken meat, such as chicken salad for sandwiches), you have a couple of options. You could poach them in gently simmering water with aromatics such as sliced onion, celery, and carrot; crushed garlic; and a few peppercorns; 10 to 12 minutes should be enough to cook them through. Or you can bake the breasts—with a drizzle of olive oil and seasoned with a sprinkle of salt and pepper—at 375°F for about 25 minutes, until no longer pink in the center.

Three skinless boneless chicken breasts, about 1½ pounds total, will give you roughly the 4 cups needed for this recipe.

Menu Ideas: This elaborate salad serves as its own centerpiece for a luncheon, with crisp baguette slices alongside. Or, for a casual supper, serve with Tomato and Roasted Red Pepper Soup with Chile Cream (page 87) and a basket of bread. Top things off with a Berry Galette (page 164).

Do-Ahead Tips: Most of the salad components, including the dressing, can be prepared up to 6 hours in advance and refrigerated, though the avocadoes should be prepared just before serving. The salad should be assembled and dressed just before serving.

FRENCH POTATO AND GREEN BEAN SALAD
WITH TARRAGON

Tarragon embellishes this salad with a distinctly French touch. The types of potatoes usually found in France are similar to our Yukon Golds or small red potatoes, rather than russets, which I don't recommend here. Be sure to add the dressing to the potatoes while they are still warm; they'll absorb more flavor.   **MAKES 8 TO 10 SERVINGS**

2½ pounds small Yukon Gold potatoes, scrubbed and halved

1 pound green beans, trimmed and cut into ¾-inch pieces

1 cup finely chopped celery

¾ cup finely chopped sweet onion

6 green onions, minced

CRÈME FRAÎCHE–TARRAGON DRESSING

½ cup mayonnaise (light is okay)

½ cup crème fraîche or light sour cream

3 tablespoons finely chopped fresh tarragon

3 tablespoons freshly squeezed lemon juice

3 tablespoons extra-virgin olive oil

2 teaspoons Dijon mustard

1 teaspoon salt

½ teaspoon freshly ground black pepper

Menu Ideas: This tangy salad is particularly wonderful paired with Grilled Honey and Mustard Ribs (page 108) or The Best Roasted Chicken (page 112) served cold, with Asparagus with Garlic (page 134) alongside.

Do-Ahead Tips: The dressing can be made up to 2 days in advance and refrigerated. The salad is at its best made at least 30 minutes before serving, so flavors can meld; a day in advance is even better. Serve the salad at room temperature; too cold, and the flavors will be dulled. If the salad has been refrigerated, let it sit at room temperature for 15 to 20 minutes before serving.

1. For the dressing, whisk together the mayonnaise, crème fraîche, tarragon, lemon juice, olive oil, mustard, salt, and pepper in a medium bowl. Set aside.

2. Bring a medium saucepan of salted water to a boil, add the green beans, and simmer 2 to 3 minutes, until just tender but still bright green. Drain and rinse under cold water to cool quickly. Drain well on paper towels.

3. Steam the potatoes until tender when pierced with the tip of a knife, 15 to 17 minutes. When cool enough to handle (but not fully cooled), peel the potatoes and cut into 1-inch dice.

4. In a large bowl, combine the potatoes (while they're still warm) with the dressing, green beans, celery, sweet onion, and green onions. Toss gently to mix.

5. Cover the salad with plastic wrap and refrigerate until ready to serve, at least 30 minutes. Taste the salad again before serving, adding more salt or pepper to taste. If the salad seems a bit dry, stir in a little more olive oil before serving.

WINTER POMEGRANATE
AND ENDIVE SALAD

As a child, I always loved the joy of eating a pomegranate and picking each kernel from the skin. Now I use the fresh seeds in many salads, sauces, and fish and meat dishes. They partner well here with crisp endive and other vegetables, tossed with a tangy pomegranate vinaigrette. If you're using English cucumbers, skip peeling and seeding them. The creamy lemon topping is an optional flourish for this wintry salad.
MAKES 8 SERVINGS

1½ pounds Belgian endive

2 cucumbers, peeled, seeded, halved lengthwise, and thinly sliced

1 cup shaved fennel bulb (about ½ small bulb)

½ cup finely diced celery

1 bunch green onions, chopped

½ cup pomegranate seeds

POMEGRANATE VINAIGRETTE

3 tablespoons pomegranate juice

2 tablespoons white balsamic vinegar

2 tablespoons minced shallot

1 tablespoon pomegranate molasses or fig balsamic vinegar

1 tablespoon chopped fresh chives

½ teaspoon dry mustard

¼ cup extra-virgin olive oil

2 tablespoons vegetable oil

Salt and freshly ground black pepper

LEMON CREAM TOPPING (OPTIONAL)

2 tablespoons crème fraîche

2 tablespoons whipping cream

2 tablespoons freshly squeezed lemon juice

Pinch of sugar (optional)

1. For the vinaigrette, whisk together the pomegranate juice, vinegar, shallot, pomegranate molasses, chives, and dry mustard in a medium bowl. Whisking constantly, slowly drizzle in the olive oil followed by the vegetable oil. Season to taste with salt and pepper; set aside.

2. For the cream topping, whip together the crème fraîche, cream, lemon juice, and sugar in a small bowl until just fluffy, not stiff. Season to taste with salt and pepper; set aside.

3. Discard any bruised outer leaves from the endive heads. Peel away 3 to 4 whole leaves from each head and set them aside. Chop the rest of each endive head, working from the tip toward the stem, discarding the last tough inch or so of the stem.

4. Combine the chopped endive, cucumbers, fennel, celery, and green onions in a large bowl. Drizzle the vinaigrette over and toss to mix evenly. Arrange the whole endive leaves, 3 to 4 per plate, spoke-like around the outer edge of each plate. Spoon the salad into the center of the plate, sprinkle the pomegranate seeds over each salad, and drizzle with the lemon cream.

SEEDING A POMEGRANATE: The trick to seeding a whole pomegranate is to cut the whole fruit into 4 pieces. Hold each quarter of the fruit in a bowl of cool water and flick out the seeds under water, so the staining juices don't stray. Strain the seeds and pick out any small white membrane pieces.

Menu Ideas: This salad works well with most main courses. It will be a particularly nice contrast to Chiles Rellenos with Potatoes and Cheese (page 114) served with Spicy Spanish Rice (page 139). Finish with the decadent Black and White Cocoa Bars (page 173).

Do-Ahead Tips: The vinaigrette and lemon cream can be made up to 1 day in advance and refrigerated. You can prepare the vegetables for the salad up to a few hours in advance; cover with a damp paper towel to keep them moist and crisp. The salad should be assembled just before serving.

WATERMELON AND RED ONION SALAD

This salad may seem a rather odd combination, sweet watermelon with peppery onion, but the results are surprisingly delicious. Our friend Claudia Nelson gave me the recipe—she likes to add sliced avocado just before serving. Half of a small seedless watermelon, weighing about 4½ pounds when halved, should give you the 8 cups of trimmed, cubed watermelon needed. **MAKES 6 TO 8 SERVINGS**

1 medium red onion, thinly sliced

3 tablespoons red wine vinegar

8 cups cubed seedless watermelon

2 tablespoons chopped fresh cilantro (optional)

ORANGE DRESSING

⅓ cup freshly squeezed orange juice

6 tablespoons extra-virgin olive oil

1 teaspoon freshly squeezed lime juice

Salt and freshly ground black pepper

1. Combine the red onion and vinegar in a medium bowl and marinate at room temperature for 15 to 30 minutes, stirring occasionally. Drain the onions, reserving the vinegar for the dressing.

2. For the dressing, whisk together 2 tablespoons of the reserved vinegar, the orange juice, olive oil, and lime juice. Season to taste with salt and pepper.

3. Just before serving, combine the marinated onion and watermelon in a large bowl. Drizzle the dressing over, add the cilantro, toss to mix well, and serve.

Menu Ideas: This salad is perfect when served with another summertime treat, such as grilled Herb-Rubbed Lamb Chops with Raita (page 125) or Grilled Honey and Mustard Ribs (page 108). For a delightful finish, consider Rhubarb and Strawberry Crisp (page 170) or Peanut Butter Cream Pie (page 180).

Do-Ahead Tips: The onions can be marinated with the vinegar at room temperature up to 4 hours in advance. The watermelon can be cubed and the dressing made 4 hours in advance as well, refrigerated separately (drain liquid that collects from the watermelon before using). The salad should be assembled and dressed just before serving.

COLESLAW
WITH LEMON-CAPER DRESSING

It's an all-American classic, this salad—perfect for a summertime picnic, ideal with your next backyard barbecue, and a welcome addition to any home-style dinner. My version is particularly colorful and flavorful, with bell peppers, green onions, and basil added to the traditional trio of green cabbage, purple cabbage, and carrots.

I'm a big fan of mustards and have many different types in my refrigerator at any time. For this recipe, I use lemon mustard, which has a lovely bright citrus flavor. You can use regular Dijon mustard and add ½ teaspoon grated lemon zest to the dressing.
MAKES 8 SERVINGS

4 cups finely shredded green cabbage

1½ cups finely shredded purple cabbage

2 large carrots, coarsely grated

½ cup sliced green onions

½ cup finely chopped red bell pepper

½ cup finely chopped yellow bell pepper

⅓ cup chopped fresh basil

LEMON-CAPER DRESSING

½ cup crème fraîche or sour cream

½ cup mayonnaise

¼ cup extra-virgin olive oil

1 tablespoon capers

2 teaspoons lemon mustard

1 teaspoon Tabasco sauce

Salt and freshly ground black pepper

1. In a large bowl, combine the green and purple cabbages, carrots, green onions, bell peppers, and basil. Toss to mix.

2. For the dressing, stir together the crème fraîche, mayonnaise, olive oil, capers, mustard, and Tabasco in a medium bowl. Season to taste with salt and pepper.

3. Pour the dressing over the vegetables and toss to evenly coat. Set the coleslaw aside for at least 15 minutes before serving, or refrigerate, covered, until ready to serve.

Menu Ideas: This salad works for any summer buffet, and travels well for get-togethers with friends or school potlucks. The coleslaw is delicious with Salmon with Nasturtium Butter (page 90) or Grilled Honey and Mustard Ribs (page 108); serve with Tiny Potatoes with Hot Bacon Dressing alongside (page 132). Finish your meal with a hot fudge sundae, using the chocolate sauce from Individual Chocolate Fondues (page 192) and top-quality vanilla ice cream.

Do-Ahead Tips: The coleslaw can be fully assembled a day in advance, covered with plastic wrap, and refrigerated, although the vegetables lose some of their crispness over time. For best results, prepare the vegetables (minus the basil) and store them undressed in a large bowl. Lay a couple pieces of damp paper towels directly on the vegetables, cover the bowl with plastic, and refrigerate. The dressing can be made a day ahead and refrigerated. Toss the two together, with the basil, 15 minutes before serving.

ASPARAGUS SALAD
WITH CHAMPAGNE VINAIGRETTE

I prefer thick asparagus spears rather than thinner ones, they have the best flavor and texture in my opinion and are the most versatile. I always cut off 1 or 2 inches from the tough, often woody, bottom of the spear, then peel away the skin from the lower couple inches. If you're using thin spears, peeling is unnecessary. Soaking the spears in cold water for at least 1 hour before cooking rehydrates the stalks, keeping them plump and juicy when cooked. **MAKES 6 SERVINGS**

1½ cups diced, seeded tomatoes

1 pound asparagus, trimmed

¾ cup finely diced sweet onion

2 tablespoons minced fresh tarragon

CHAMPAGNE VINAIGRETTE

3 tablespoons Champagne vinegar

2 tablespoons freshly squeezed lemon juice

2 tablespoons minced shallot

1 tablespoon balsamic vinegar

1 tablespoon Dijon mustard

1 clove garlic, pressed or minced

½ teaspoon sugar

5 tablespoons extra-virgin olive oil

Salt and freshly ground black pepper

1. Drain the tomatoes in a medium sieve over a bowl for 30 minutes, stirring occasionally to help release excess liquid.

2. Bring a deep skillet or large saucepan of lightly salted water to a boil; fill a large bowl with ice water. Add the asparagus to the boiling water and blanch for 1 to 2 minutes. With a slotted spoon, transfer to the ice water and let cool, then drain well on a kitchen towel or paper towels.

3. For the vinaigrette, whisk together the Champagne vinegar, lemon juice, shallot, balsamic vinegar, mustard, garlic, and sugar in a small bowl. Whisk in the olive oil and season to taste with salt and pepper.

4. Stir together the drained tomatoes, onion, and tarragon in a large bowl. Just before serving, add the blanched asparagus, pour the vinaigrette over, and toss gently to mix.

Menu Ideas: There are very few meals this salad doesn't pair well with. Since the dressing is light, the sweet flavor of the vegetable comes through, so it's ideal alongside the simplest grilled fish or pan-fried steak. If your menu has more pronounced flavors, you could use a more flavorful vinegar, such as more balsamic vinegar or sherry vinegar, in place of the Champagne vinegar.

Do-Ahead Tips: You can blanch the asparagus up to 3 days in advance and refrigerate, rolled in a kitchen towel and slipped into a plastic bag (unsealed). The vinaigrette can be made up to 1 day in advance and the tomato/onion/tarragon mixture tossed up to 1 hour in advance. Add the asparagus and toss just before serving. (The asparagus will discolor if dressed in advance.)

PARMESAN CONES
WITH BABY GREENS AND HERB SALAD

This salad will delight guests, with crisp baked Parmesan cornucopias spilling out delicate salad greens. Seek out the most tender young salad greens and fresh-from-the-garden herbs for best flavor and texture. This is the time to pull out your best extra-virgin olive oil; with the delicate, tender greens and bright herbs, the flavor of the olive oil will really come through. You can easily double the recipe for a larger table of guests.

Forming the cones takes a little practice. That's why I suggest baking two rounds of the cheese at a time, so you can take your time to form them. I use a pizzelle roller to form the cones, a tool meant for shaping cookies. But you can make a cone out of thin cardboard or use another similar tool from your kitchen. Or leave the Parmesan rounds flat and serve them perched on top of the salad. MAKES 4 SERVINGS

¾ cup freshly grated Parmesan cheese

4 cups (about 4 ounces) loosely packed baby greens

8 large radishes, julienned or coarsely grated

¼ cup finely minced tender fresh herbs (chives, tarragon, flat-leaf parsley, basil, and/or thyme)

PESTO VINAIGRETTE

3 tablespoons Champagne vinegar

2 teaspoons prepared pesto

½ teaspoon sugar

Salt and freshly ground black pepper

⅓ cup extra-virgin olive oil

Menu Ideas: This is a great way to start a fancy dinner party, with Halibut with Nut Crust and Apple Vinaigrette (page 106), and Zucchini Fritters with Fresh Herbs (page 157) to follow. Consider Puff Pastry Tart with Plums (page 188) for dessert.

Do-Ahead Tips: The Parmesan cones can be made up to 2 days in advance and stored in an airtight container, layered between pieces of waxed paper. You should plan to make them at least a couple hours in advance, as they take some careful attention.

1. Preheat the oven to 400°F. Line 2 baking sheets with silicone baking mats or parchment paper.

2. Sprinkle the Parmesan cheese on the baking sheets into rounds about 5 inches across, 2 rounds per sheet. Bake, 1 sheet at a time, for about 5 minutes, until the cheese is melted and just lightly brown. Remove the sheet from the oven.

3. Use a spatula (preferably nonstick) to carefully lift one of the warm cheese rounds from the baking sheet and drape it over the pizzelle roller so that one edge of the round meets the point, wrapping the sides around to form a cone. Hold it for a few moments until set. Cool on a wire rack and repeat with the second cheese round. If needed, pop the baking sheet back in the oven for 30 to 60 seconds to rewarm so the round is easily pliable. Bake the second sheet and repeat the process to form 4 cones total. Set aside until ready to serve (in an airtight container if more than 2 hours in advance).

4. For the vinaigrette, whisk together the vinegar, pesto, and sugar with salt and pepper to taste. Drizzle in the olive oil, whisking to emulsify the dressing.

5. Combine the greens, radishes, and herbs in a large bowl and toss to mix. Pour over the dressing and toss to evenly coat.

6. Gently stuff some of the salad into the Parmesan cones. Arrange the remaining greens on each plate, top with the cones, and serve while the Parmesan is crisp.

SOUPS

Soup is one of the most universally appealing foods. From simple broth with a few accents to complex blends of seafood, meat, grains, and vegetables, soup serves as a versatile meal component that plays a role in virtually every cuisine worldwide. Equally at home at lunch or dinner, soup can play a starring role as the main course or supporting role at the start of a meal. And wherever it goes, soup is often equated with comfort food as well. It's warming, aromatic, satisfying, and grounding.

With each of the four seasons, distinct soup options come to mind. Wintertime, we lean toward soups that are more filling to warm us from the inside out on those cold dreary days. Spring welcomes us with fresh vegetables for soups, such as garden peas, tender young beets, and other fresh tastes of the season. As temperatures warm in summer, our soup selections tend to cool, with refreshing gazpachos, and other chilled soups from which to choose. Come autumn, we return to more rustic flavors with rich chowders and other soups featuring ingredients that echo the harvest season like squash, wild mushrooms, and grains.

A couple of practical notes: Most hearty soups and stews freeze well, so when you make a pot of soup consider making extra so you'll have some to freeze for a later date. Also, when menu planning, I recommend serving very few appetizers before a meal that starts with soup, since they are often rather filling.

ASIAN SPINACH SOUP WITH SHRIMP

Soup is a common element in meals across Asia, often with the aromatic elements that I've included here: ginger, lime, coconut milk, and lemongrass. Asian cooks would more likely use water spinach, which has narrower leaves and hollow stems, but its distant cousin, our common spinach, works well too. For a heartier soup you can add a couple of tablespoons of cooked white rice or diced silky tofu to each bowl just before serving.

Smashing the lemongrass tenderizes the tough stalk and brings out its aromatic character. To do so, I lay the broad side of a cleaver over the lemongrass and smash it hard with my fist. You can also smash it with the bottom of a small heavy skillet. MAKES 8 SERVINGS

1 tablespoon peanut or canola oil

2 stalks lemongrass, trimmed and smashed

2 (½-inch) pieces ginger, peeled and smashed

3 cloves garlic, pressed or minced

1 serrano chile, cored, seeded, and minced

10 cups vegetable broth

3 cups packed spinach leaves, rinsed, dried, tough
    stems removed, and coarsely chopped

1½ pounds large shrimp, peeled and deveined

¾ cup reduced-fat coconut milk

⅓ cup freshly squeezed lime juice

2 to 3 tablespoons soy sauce

3 tablespoons minced fresh chives

1. Heat the oil in a large saucepan over medium heat. Add the lemongrass, ginger, garlic, and chile and cook for 1 to 2 minutes, until aromatic and tender but not browned.

2. Add the vegetable broth and bring to a low boil. Simmer for 10 minutes (the broth should not boil vigorously, decrease the heat to medium-low if needed). Add the spinach and shrimp and simmer 5 minutes, until the shrimp are evenly pink and just cooked through. Remove the pan from the heat and use a slotted spoon or tongs to lift out and discard the lemongrass and ginger. Stir in the coconut milk and lime juice with soy sauce to taste. Ladle the soup into warmed bowls and sprinkle with the chives.

Menu Ideas: You'll have a wonderful, light Asian-inspired meal pairing this soup with Lettuce Wraps with Chicken and Herbs (page 32), Grilled Pork Kebabs (page 21), and plain steamed white rice.

Do-Ahead Tips: The soup can be made up to 6 hours in advance, but set aside the shrimp and spinach to add when reheating the soup just before serving. In fact, the soup will have more developed flavor if it is made at least 2 hours in advance.

CORN CHOWDER WITH ROASTED PEPPERS

This recipe produces a light chowder that is a wonderful way to highlight summer's fresh sweet corn. You can use frozen corn off-season, but the flavor will be quite different, lacking the gentle sweetness of fresh seasonal corn. If you prefer a spicy version, add ¼ cup or so of chopped canned green chiles and/or use pepper bacon in place of the regular bacon. And if that touch of chowder richness is what you love, use cream or half-and-half instead of the milk I call for. MAKES 6 TO 8 SERVINGS

3 thick strips bacon, cut into ½-inch pieces

2 medium russet potatoes, peeled and diced

1 large yellow onion, diced

2 stalks celery, diced

2 cloves garlic, pressed or minced

1 cup water

3 cups chicken stock (page 83) or top-quality chicken broth

1 tablespoon tomato paste

1 teaspoon salt

1 teaspoon minced fresh thyme or ¼ teaspoon dried thyme

1 dried bay leaf

3 cups fresh corn kernels (cut from 5 to 6 ears)

1 yellow and 1 red bell pepper, roasted, cored, seeded, and diced (see page 222)

1½ cups whole milk

2 tablespoons minced fresh flat-leaf parsley

Menu Ideas: A large bowl of this chowder can be a light meal, simply with crusty bread alongside. For a more substantial dinner, I'll serve this before Four-Star Fried Chicken (page 110) and Coleslaw with Lemon-Caper Dressing (page 64). A slice of Orange Cake (page 182) is a great finish.

Do-Ahead Tips: The bell peppers can be roasted up to 2 days in advance and refrigerated. The soup can be made 1 day in advance; take care when reheating that it does not boil, which may cause curdling.

1. Fry the bacon in a large saucepan over medium heat for 5 to 7 minutes, until browned and crisp. Use a slotted spoon to transfer the bacon to paper towels to drain, reserving the bacon fat in the pan.

2. Add the potatoes, onion, and celery to the pan and cook for 3 to 4 minutes, until beginning to soften. Add the garlic and cook 1 minute longer. Stir in the water and simmer 3 to 4 minutes. Add the chicken stock, tomato paste, salt, thyme, and bay leaf. Continue to simmer until the potatoes are tender, 10 to 12 minutes. Discard the bay leaf.

3. Add the bacon, corn, roasted bell peppers, milk, and parsley to the chowder and simmer gently for 5 to 7 minutes, just until heated through; do not allow the chowder to boil. Taste for seasoning, adding more salt to taste.

FRESH CORN KERNELS: To cut kernels from a shucked ear of corn, set the ear upright on a cutting board or in a large roasting pan, which will help contain the kernels that tend to fly all over. Cut downward on the cob to remove most of the tender kernels with a minimum of the tough base from the core. Depending on the recipe, I may then go back around the ear, scraping the back of the knife down the cob, removing the remaining bits of tender, milky flesh. This is an ideal, flavorful addition to a recipe such as this chowder or a corn pudding, but some recipes, such as a corn salad or salsa, are better with just the firm whole kernels.

There are also a couple of handy kitchen tools that make easy work of stripping kernels from the ears. I really like the slitter, which splits each kernel before it is cut away from the ear, releasing a maximum of its rich, sweet flavor.

SPICY MANHATTAN CLAM CHOWDER

This flavorful chowder starts with fresh clams, which I prefer to cook by sautéing rather than steaming. In a pinch, you could use three 6½-ounce cans of minced clams with their juice or 1 pound of frozen clam meat (available in some well-stocked grocery stores) in place of the fresh clams. Russet, or Idaho baking, potatoes are not the best choice here: Waxy thin-skinned types, like Yukon Golds, hold up better. Other golden potatoes can be used, or small white or red potatoes. MAKES 6 TO 8 SERVINGS

5 strips thick-cut pepper bacon, diced

1 large yellow onion, finely chopped

4 cups water

3 carrots, diced

3 stalks celery, diced

1 can (28 ounces) diced tomatoes (with basil, preferably)

1 bottle (8 ounces) clam juice

1 green bell pepper, cored, seeded, and diced

½ red bell pepper, cored, seeded, and diced

3 cloves garlic, pressed or minced

1 teaspoon chopped fresh thyme

1 dried bay leaf

2 tablespoons olive oil

2½ pounds Manila or other hard-shell clams, rinsed

1 pound small Yukon Gold potatoes, peeled and diced

¼ cup chopped fresh flat-leaf parsley

¼ teaspoon cayenne pepper, or more to taste

Salt

1. Fry the bacon in a large saucepan over medium heat for 5 to 7 minutes, until browned and crisp. Use a slotted spoon to transfer the bacon to paper towels to drain, reserving the bacon fat in the pot.

2. Add the onion to the pot and cook, stirring occasionally, for 3 to 5 minutes, until tender and translucent. Stir in the water, carrots, celery, tomatoes (with their juice), clam juice, bell peppers, garlic, thyme, and bay leaf. Simmer for about 30 minutes, until the carrots are tender. The liquid should just bubble gently, not boil; decrease the heat to medium-low if needed.

3. While the chowder base is cooking, heat the olive oil in a large, deep skillet over medium-high heat. Add the clams and cook, stirring gently and scooping the clams into a bowl with a slotted spoon as they pop open. Discard any clams that haven't opened after 7 or 8 minutes. Pour the liquid from the skillet into the bowl with the clams and set aside until the clams are cool enough to handle. Remove the meat from the shells and let sit in the juices until needed.

4. Add the potatoes to the soup and simmer for about 15 minutes, until tender. Stir in the bacon, clams with their liquid, parsley, and cayenne. Simmer gently an additional 5 minutes. Discard the bay leaf. Season the chowder to taste with salt (which may not be needed because clam juice can be rather salty) and more cayenne, if needed.

Menu Ideas: This chowder makes a delicious main course for lunch or a light supper, with Asparagus with Garlic (page 134) or Beet and Fennel Salad with Walnut Dressing (page 59) alongside. Have some crunchy bread and good butter on hand as well.

Do-Ahead Tips: The clam chowder can be made up to 3 days in advance and refrigerated. You can freeze it as well, but I wouldn't recommend doing so for longer than 2 weeks; I find the soup begins to lose flavor after that time.

BEET SOUP WITH DILL AND CHIVES

Roasted beets are a favorite vegetable in my house and we use them many ways, especially in salads (page 41) and in soups such as this one. I shop for beets with the greens still on for the best flavor. This soup can be served warm or cold; we tend to prefer it warm, when the flavors are more pronounced. MAKES 8 TO 10 SERVINGS

6 medium red beets (about 1½ pounds), trimmed and scrubbed

1 tablespoon olive oil

2 medium russet potatoes, peeled and cut into ½-inch dice

6 cups chicken stock (page 83) or top-quality chicken broth

2 large carrots, diced

1 medium yellow onion, diced

Salt and freshly ground black pepper

½ to ¾ cup sour cream or crème fraîche

¼ cup minced fresh chives

¼ cup minced fresh dill

Menu Ideas: A cup of this lovely soup would be an ideal starter before a simple supper of grilled steak. Or consider serving bowls of the soup as a light main course with Garlic-and-Herb Baked Artichokes (page 150) Cheese-Stuffed Tomatoes with Linguine (page 141) alongside. A simple dessert, such as the Chocolate Espresso Pots de Crème (page 167), would finish the meal splendidly.

Do-Ahead Tips: The beets can be roasted a day or two in advance, peeled, and refrigerated, wrapped in plastic. The soup can be made 1 day ahead and gently reheated before serving. The herb garnish can also be chopped in advance, preferably not more than a few hours. Top with lightly dampened paper towels and refrigerate until needed.

1. Preheat the oven to 350°F.

2. Rub the beets with the olive oil and place in a baking dish just large enough to hold them. Cover the dish with aluminum foil and roast for about 1¼ hours, or until tender when pierced with the tip of a knife. Set aside to cool.

3. While the beets are roasting, place the potatoes in a medium pan of salted water. Bring the water just to a boil, then decrease the heat to medium and simmer for about 5 minutes, until the potatoes are about half cooked. Drain well and set aside.

4. In a large pan, combine 5 cups of the stock, the carrots, and onion and bring just to a boil over medium-high heat. Decrease the heat to medium-low and simmer until the vegetables are tender, about 5 minutes. Scoop the vegetables with a slotted spoon into a bowl and set aside, reserving the stock in the pan.

5. When the roasted beets are cool enough to handle, use your fingers to slip off the skins. Dice the beets. Purée half of the diced beets with about ½ cup of the remaining stock in a blender or food processor. Add the beet purée to the stock. Purée the carrots and onions with the remaining ½ cup of broth and then add to the soup. Add the remaining beets and the potatoes and season to taste with salt and pepper. Simmer over medium-low heat for about 15 minutes, until the soup is well heated, the potatoes are tender, and the flavors have blended. Taste for seasoning, adding more salt or pepper if needed.

6. To serve, ladle the soup into warmed bowls, top with dollops of sour cream, and sprinkle with the chives and dill.

CHICKEN SOUP
WITH MEATBALLS

I often make chicken vegetable soup or, during the holidays, the old standby, turkey noodle soup. But I gained a new inspiration for the soup during a trip to Italy when I tasted a wonderful chicken soup with small meatballs and a fresh grating of Parmesan cheese on top. You can add other vegetables to the soup: Quick-cooking vegetables, such as spinach or zucchini, should be added with the meatballs near the end. Denser diced turnips or rutabaga should be added earlier, with the onion, carrot, and celery. The flavorful, light meatballs are also delicious added to a red pasta sauce and served over spaghetti. MAKES 6 TO 8 SERVINGS

5 tablespoons olive oil

1 cup finely diced yellow onion

1 cup finely diced carrot

1 cup finely diced celery

8 cups chicken stock (page 83) or top-quality chicken broth

1 cup chopped green beans (fresh or thawed frozen)

Salt and freshly ground black pepper

Coarsely grated Parmesan cheese, for serving

TURKEY MEATBALLS

¾ pound ground raw turkey or chicken

½ cup plain dried bread crumbs

¼ cup finely grated Parmesan cheese

3 tablespoons minced fresh flat-leaf parsley

1 tablespoon minced fresh oregano or 1 teaspoon dried oregano

1 tablespoon minced fresh thyme or 1 teaspoon dried thyme

2 cloves garlic, pressed or minced

¾ teaspoon salt

½ teaspoon freshly ground black pepper

½ teaspoon sweet Hungarian paprika

Pinch of freshly grated or ground nutmeg

½ cup all-purpose flour

1. For the meatballs, combine the turkey, bread crumbs, Parmesan, parsley, oregano, thyme, garlic, salt, pepper, paprika, and nutmeg in a large bowl. Use your hands or a large wooden spoon to thoroughly blend the ingredients. Form the mixture into balls about 1-inch across (you should have about 36 meatballs). Place the flour in a rimmed baking sheet or other shallow pan. Add the meatballs and roll them around to evenly coat with flour. Let sit for 5 minutes, then roll around a bit more to ensure they're well coated.

2. Heat 3 tablespoons of the olive oil in a large skillet, preferably nonstick, over medium heat. Working in batches, toss the meatballs in your hands or in a small sieve to remove the excess flour. Brown them well on all sides, 5 to 7 minutes; be sure not to crowd the pan or they won't brown well. Transfer the meatballs to paper towels and set aside.

3. Heat the remaining 2 tablespoons olive oil in a large saucepan over medium heat. Add the onion, carrot, and celery and cook, stirring occasionally, for 5 to 7 minutes, until tender and aromatic. Add the stock and simmer for 15 minutes. Add the meatballs and green beans and simmer for 10 minutes longer. Taste the soup for seasoning, adding salt and pepper to taste. Ladle the soup into individual bowls, sprinkle with Parmesan, and serve.

Menu Ideas: The soup stands alone as a meal in itself with Grilled Mozzarella and Mushroom Sandwiches (page 16) or other grilled cheese sandwiches alongside. You can make the soup itself more substantial with the addition of cooked rice, but you only need a small amount or the broth will become too thick.

Do-Ahead Tips: The meatballs can be made 1 month ahead and frozen raw, first on a tray until solid, then transferred to a heavy resealable bag. To defrost, scatter on a tray so the meatballs aren't touching. Do not fry the meatballs until you are ready to add to the soup. The soup with vegetables freezes well but I take out any meatballs before freezing and freeze them separately. They tend to get mushy when frozen in the soup.

CURRIED RED LENTIL SOUP

A staple of Indian cuisine, red lentils are smaller, more delicate lentils than the more common brown lentils. They add great texture and color to this soup that is bursting with flavor. You can easily make this a vegetarian recipe by replacing the chicken stock with vegetable broth. If the mango chutney you're using has large chunks of fruit, chop it up before adding to the soup. MAKES 6 TO 8 SERVINGS

1 tablespoon vegetable oil

1 large yellow onion, chopped

1 jalapeño chile, cored, seeded, and minced

2 tablespoons minced or grated ginger

2 cloves garlic, pressed or minced

1½ tablespoons curry powder

1½ teaspoons ground cinnamon

1 teaspoon ground cumin

2 dried bay leaves

1½ cups red lentils

8 cups chicken stock (page 83) or top-quality chicken broth

2 tablespoons freshly squeezed lemon juice

Salt and freshly ground black pepper

3 tablespoons chopped fresh cilantro or flat-leaf parsley, plus more for garnish

3 tablespoons mango chutney

⅓ cup plain yogurt

1. Heat the oil in a medium, heavy stockpot over medium heat. Add the onion and cook, stirring, for 3 to 5 minutes, until tender and aromatic. Add the jalapeño, ginger, garlic, curry powder, cinnamon, cumin, and bay leaves and cook, stirring constantly, for about 1 minute longer, until aromatic.

2. Stir in the lentils to blend well with the vegetable mixture, then add the chicken stock. Bring just to a boil over medium-high heat. Decrease the heat to low and simmer, partially covered, for 35 to 45 minutes, until the lentils are tender. Discard the bay leaves and stir in the lemon juice with salt and pepper to taste.

3. Just before serving, stir in the cilantro and chutney. Ladle the soup into individual bowls, add dollops of the yogurt, and sprinkle with additional cilantro.

Menu Ideas: This flavorful soup would be a great start to a meal featuring The Best Roasted Chicken (page 112) or Herb-Rubbed Lamb Chops with Raita (page 125), with Cauliflower and Tomato Gratin (page 154) and steamed broccoli alongside. I also love the soup for lunch with a salad or sandwich alongside.

Do-Ahead Tips: The soup can be prepared up to 2 days in advance and refrigerated. Gently reheat before serving. This soup will also freeze well, but I wouldn't recommend doing so for more than a few weeks.

MEMORABLE RECIPES

ROASTED BUTTERNUT SQUASH SOUP

Butternut squash is consistently available and it's a sure bet here. But during those couple of months in fall when wonderful sugar pumpkins are available, I will use them in place of the butternut squash. Roasting the squash before adding to the soup brings out its wonderful sweet flavor; the results are very much worth that extra step. If you like a slightly more savory flavor, add some minced sage shortly before serving. Or if a touch of sweetness suits your palate, try stirring in a drizzle of maple syrup. MAKES 8 SERVINGS

1 (3-pound) butternut squash

3 tablespoons plus 1 teaspoon olive oil

1½ teaspoons salt

2 tablespoons unsalted butter

1 large Fuji or Golden Delicious apple, cored, peeled, and chopped

½ cup finely chopped yellow onion

5 cups chicken stock (page 83) or top-quality chicken broth

1 cup canned pumpkin purée (unseasoned)

2 tablespoons finely grated orange zest

½ cup freshly squeezed orange juice

2 tablespoons light or dark brown sugar

½ teaspoon freshly ground or grated nutmeg

¼ teaspoon ground mace

1 cup whole milk or half-and-half

½ cup raw pumpkin seeds

Coarse sea salt

Menu Ideas: Serve this before Halibut with Nut Crust and Apple Vinaigrette (page 106) served with Lemon Israeli Couscous (page 161) and steamed asparagus. For dessert, try the Applesauce Cake with Cinnamon–Cream Cheese Frosting (page 168). As a main course, the soup pairs well with Grilled Mozzarella and Mushroom Sandwiches (page 16).

Do-Ahead Tips: The soup will keep in the refrigerator for up to 3 days. When reheating, add chicken stock or water as needed. The squash can be roasted up to a day ahead and refrigerated.

1. Preheat the oven to 350°F.

2. Cut the squash in half, then cut each half in quarters. Scoop out and discard the seeds and pulp. Rub the squash pieces with 2 tablespoons of the olive oil and set on a roasting pan, cut side up. Sprinkle with ½ teaspoon of the salt. Roast, turning the pieces several times, for about 1 hour, until the squash is easily pierced with a fork. Allow the squash to cool, then scoop the tender flesh from the skins. Set aside.

3. Heat the butter with 1 tablespoon of the remaining olive oil in a large saucepan over medium heat. Add the apple and cook for 3 to 4 minutes, until partly tender but not browned. Add the onion and cook for 3 to 4 minutes longer, until the onion is tender.

4. Stir in 2 cups of the chicken stock and simmer until the apple is fully tender, about 5 minutes. Stir in the pumpkin, orange zest, orange juice, brown sugar, nutmeg, mace, and remaining 1 teaspoon salt. Add the remaining 3 cups stock and simmer for 15 minutes.

5. Dice enough of the roasted squash to make 1½ cups and set aside. Coarsely chop the remaining squash and add to the soup. Cook over medium-low heat for 15 minutes. Add the milk and simmer 5 minutes longer. Allow to cool slightly. Working in batches, purée the soup in a blender or food processor until very smooth, returning the soup to the pot. Gently reheat the soup over medium-low heat.

6. Just before serving, heat the remaining 1 teaspoon olive oil in a small skillet over medium heat. Add the pumpkin seeds and toast, stirring often, for 1 to 2 minutes, until crisp and lightly browned (be careful, the seeds may pop out of the pan). Spoon the seeds onto a small plate to avoid burning.

7. Heat the reserved diced squash in a microwave for 30 seconds or warm in a small saucepan with 1 cup of the soup over medium-low heat. Spoon the diced squash into warmed soup bowls and ladle the hot soup over. Top each bowl with toasted pumpkin seeds and a few grains of sea salt.

CHILLED CUCUMBER-BUTTERMILK SOUP

Buttermilk is an ingredient that tends to turn off some people, but in this soup it's a perfect partner to cool cucumber, adding a richness of flavor and texture in a surprisingly low-fat form. English cucumbers have a thinner skin and don't need seeding, but I prefer the flavor of regular cucumbers, which do require peeling and seeding. MAKES 8 SERVINGS

5 cucumbers, peeled and seeded

2 tablespoons salt

½ cup lightly packed fresh flat-leaf parsley leaves

6 green onions, coarsely chopped

3 tablespoons chopped fresh chives

½ cup chopped fresh dill

4 cups buttermilk

1 cup sour cream (light or regular)

¼ cup freshly squeezed lemon juice

Freshly ground white pepper

½ cup thinly sliced radishes

1. Finely dice enough cucumber to make ½ cup and set aside for the garnish. Cut the rest of the cucumber into 1-inch pieces, place in a colander, and sprinkle with the salt. Let sit in the sink for 30 minutes (this draws off excess liquid), then rinse under cold water and pat dry with paper towels.

2. Working in a few batches, purée the cucumbers in a blender with the parsley, green onions, chives, and 3 tablespoons of the dill until smooth, adding about ½ cup buttermilk with each batch. Transfer the mixture to a large bowl and stir in the remaining buttermilk with the sour cream and lemon juice. Season to taste with salt and pepper. Cover and refrigerate for at least 1 hour before serving.

3. To serve, ladle the soup into individual bowls and garnish each bowl with the finely diced cucumber, the remaining dill, and sliced radishes.

Menu Ideas: This soup lends itself to summer, warm-weather meals, particularly pretty if served in glass cups or bowls. Follow the soup with Fresh Dungeness Crab with Two Sauces (page 104), Sautéed Tiny Tomatoes with Chile Flakes (page 144), and corn on the cob. The Berry Galette (page 164) is always a great finish.

Do-Ahead Tips: The soup should be chilled for at least an hour, but is best served within a few hours of making. Use a whisk to blend before serving, as the soup may have separated a bit.

OYSTER SOUP

We have the best oysters here in the Northwest and locals use them in a wide variety of recipes, with fried oysters and barbecue-grilled oysters among the favorites. I was not a big fan of oysters in soup, however, until one of Seattle's best-known chefs, Tom Douglas (owner of Dahlia Lounge, Etta's Seafood, and other popular restaurants), made some for my birthday dinner. I've been a fan ever since, and even came up with my own recipe based on Tom's inspiration: a flavorful, creamy steaming hot broth that you slip oysters into just a few minutes before serving.

For this easy soup, you can use either oysters freshly shucked from the shells or jarred oysters (two 10-ounce jars of "extra small" oysters will do the trick). MAKES 6 TO 8 SERVINGS

6 tablespoons unsalted butter

1 large shallot, minced

¼ cup finely diced yellow onion

1 medium Yukon Gold potato, peeled and diced

2 stalks celery, minced

¼ cup finely chopped fresh flat-leaf parsley

1 cup water

¼ cup dry white wine

2 cups whipping cream or half-and-half

1 cup clam juice

2 teaspoons freshly squeezed lemon juice

Salt and freshly ground white pepper

26 to 30 small raw shucked oysters, with their liquor

1 tablespoon minced fresh chives

1. Melt the butter in a large saucepan over medium heat. Add the shallot and onion and cook, stirring, for 2 to 3 minutes, until tender and aromatic. Stir in the potato, celery, and parsley and cook for 3 to 4 minutes longer. Stir in the water and white wine and simmer for 10 to 12 minutes, until the potato is tender.

2. Stir in the cream and clam juice and cook gently for 1 to 2 minutes to blend the flavors; be sure the mixture doesn't boil. Stir in the lemon juice with salt and pepper to taste (keeping in mind that the oysters will add salty flavor).

3. Add the oysters and their liquor to the pot and cook for 3 to 4 minutes longer, until the oysters are just firm. Ladle the soup into individual shallow bowls, distributing the oysters evenly. Sprinkle with chives and serve at once.

Menu Ideas: This lovely, velvety soup will be a great first course before The Best Roasted Chicken (page 112) and Tiny Potatoes with Hot Bacon Dressing (page 132). Finish off your meal with Ginger Cake with Lemon Cream (page 176).

Do-Ahead Tips: While many soups can be made in advance, this is one that will be at its best made just before serving. To ease the last-minute preparations for a dinner party you can, however, prepare the soup to the point just before the oysters are added up to 3 hours in advance. Reheat the soup gently and add the oysters just before serving.

OAXACAN TORTILLA SOUP
WITH ROASTED POBLANOS

Asadero cheese, used to garnish this soup, is a semi-soft cow's milk cheese from the Mexican state of Oaxaca; it has a mild flavor and nice melting texture, which is ideal for this recipe. Look for asadero cheese in Mexican or Latin American groceries or specialty cheese shops; Cheddar or Jack cheese can be substituted.

To make this a main-course soup, I add thin strips of grilled chicken breast just before the garnishes. You might want to pass a bottle of Tabasco sauce around the table so guests can add more heat to their taste. MAKES 6 TO 8 SERVINGS

1 medium yellow onion, chopped

6 corn tortillas

5 tablespoons corn or vegetable oil

6 cloves garlic, pressed or minced

2 poblano chiles, roasted, peeled, seeded, and diced (see page 222)

1 jalapeño chile, cored, seeded, and diced

2 tablespoons chopped fresh cilantro

1 tablespoon ground cumin, toasted (see page 222)

1 teaspoon freshly ground black pepper, toasted (see page 222)

2 dried bay leaves

8 cups chicken stock (page 83) or top-quality chicken broth

1 can (14½ ounces) diced tomatoes

1½ teaspoons chili powder

1½ teaspoons salt

GARNISHES

1 avocado, peeled, pitted, and diced

1 cup grated asadero cheese

¾ cup chopped, seeded plum tomatoes

¼ cup chopped fresh cilantro

½ cup sour cream

Lime wedges

1. Purée the chopped onion in a food processor until smooth. Cut 3 of the tortillas into ¼-inch dice.

2. Heat 3 tablespoons of the oil in a large saucepan over medium heat. Stir in the garlic and cook for a few seconds. Add the diced tortillas, stir to evenly coat, and cook for about 5 minutes, or until they begin to crisp (be sure the garlic doesn't get too brown, decrease the heat if necessary). Stir in the onion purée, poblanos, jalapeño, cilantro, cumin, pepper, and bay leaves. Cook, stirring, until the chiles and spices are aromatic, 3 to 4 minutes.

3. Add the chicken stock and diced tomatoes (with their liquid) and bring to a boil over medium-high heat. Decrease the heat to medium-low and simmer for 30 minutes. Stir in the chili powder and salt and simmer for 10 minutes longer. Discard the bay leaves.

4. Cut the remaining 3 tortillas into ¼-inch strips. Heat the remaining 2 tablespoons oil in a large skillet over medium heat. Add the tortilla strips and cook, stirring often, for about 5 minutes, until lightly toasted and aromatic. Drain on paper towels.

5. To serve, ladle the soup into individual warmed bowls. Garnish with the crisp tortilla strips, avocado, cheese, chopped tomatoes, cilantro, and dollops of sour cream. Add wedges of lime alongside for squeezing.

Menu Ideas: This make a great start, of course, for a menu with other Mexican influences such as Chiles Rellenos with Potatoes and Cheese (page 114); also try it before simple Herb-Rubbed Lamb Chops (page 125, minus the raita).

Do-Ahead Tips: The soup can be made up to 2 days in advance and refrigerated. Gently reheat before serving. Prepare the garnishes just before serving.

FIVE-ONION SOUP

Onion soup is a frequent favorite with its delicious blend of sweet and savory flavors. With so many types of onions available, I like to mix things up and make soup using different varieties for even more complex flavor. This recipe was inspired, too, by wanting to make onion soup one day when I didn't have my usual bag of yellow onions on hand.

An optional addition to the soup's garnishes is a sprinkle of lightly fried "frizzled" onions, described below. MAKES 6 SERVINGS

¼ cup olive oil

¼ cup unsalted butter

5 leeks (about 2 pounds total), white and pale green parts only, split, cleaned, and sliced

2 sweet onions, diced

1 white onion, diced

3 large shallots, diced

4 cloves garlic, pressed or minced

1 teaspoon salt

½ teaspoon freshly ground white pepper

1 large russet potato, peeled and diced

5 cups chicken stock (page 83) or top-quality chicken broth

1¼ cups half-and-half

3 tablespoons minced green onions

1 tablespoon crushed or coarsely ground pink peppercorns

Menu Ideas: For a light supper or lunch entrée, this soup can serve as the main course, with a crisp green salad alongside. As the start of the meal, I'd recommend following the soup with Grilled Rack of Pork with Mango Salsa (page 92) and Zucchini Fritters with Fresh Herbs (page 157).

Do-Ahead Tips: The soup can be made up to 1 day in advance and refrigerated, covered. Reheat gently just before serving. It will freeze fine for 1 month or so.

1. Heat the olive oil and butter in a Dutch oven or large saucepan over medium heat. Add the leeks, sweet onions, white onion, shallots, and garlic and cook, stirring often, for about 25 minutes, until the onions are tender. The onions will give off water as they cook, which will slowly evaporate. Stir in the salt and pepper.

2. Add the potato and chicken stock to the onions. Bring to a low boil over medium-high heat, then decrease the heat to medium-low and simmer for 25 to 30 minutes, until the potatoes are very tender and beginning to fall apart. Let cool to room temperature.

3. Stir in the half-and-half. Working in batches, purée the soup in a blender or food processor until very smooth, returning the soup to the pot. Gently reheat over medium-low heat. Add a little more stock or half-and-half if it seems too thick. Ladle the soup into warmed soup bowls and top with a sprinkle of green onion and pink peppercorns.

FRIZZLED ONIONS: Heat about 1 inch of vegetable oil in a large pot or deep sauté pan over medium-high heat. Toss 1 small onion, very thinly sliced, with ½ cup all-purpose flour, coating them well and shaking to remove excess flour. Add 1 handful of the coated onions to the hot oil and fry until crisp and lightly browned, 30 to 60 seconds. Scoop the onions onto paper towels, sprinkle with salt, and continue with the remaining onions. Store in an airtight container for up to 2 days.

HOMEMADE CHICKEN STOCK

Making stock from scratch can seem like a daunting task, particularly when it's just one part of a recipe. But the way I approach it is to make the stock in advance—up to a month or two, frozen in an airtight container—so when it comes time to make soup, the stock needs only to be thawed. Better yet, double the recipe and store the stock in different portion sizes—1 quart, 1 cup, even in ice cube trays for smaller doses. You'll be thrilled to have it on hand for quick addition to any number of recipes.

Ask your butcher if he can supply you with chicken backs and/or necks, which contribute great depth of flavor to the stock. Otherwise, use less-expensive pieces, such as legs and thighs, with most of the skin removed. If you have a whole chicken or turkey carcass from a recent meal, you can use that as well, embellished with raw chicken pieces for added flavor. MAKES ABOUT 12 CUPS

4 to 5 pounds mixed chicken pieces (backs, necks, legs, and/or thighs), most of the skin removed

1 large yellow onion, quartered

3 carrots, coarsely chopped

2 stalks celery, coarsely chopped

3 cloves garlic, crushed

1 dried bay leaf

1 sprig fresh thyme or ½ teaspoon dried thyme

1 teaspoon salt

12 cups cold water, more if needed

1. Combine the chicken pieces, onion, carrots, celery, garlic, bay leaf, thyme, and salt in a large stockpot. Add the cold water, which should cover the ingredients by 1 to 2 inches; add more water if needed.

2. Bring just to a boil over medium-high heat, using a slotted spoon to skim off the frothy foam that rises to the surface as the water heats. As soon as the water boils, decrease the heat to medium-low and simmer for 2 hours. The water should not bubble actively, nor be too placid; adjust the heat if needed.

3. Let the stock cool to near room temperature, then spoon off most of the fat from the surface. Strain the stock, reserving any leg or thigh meat for another use if you like.

ZIPPY GAZPACHO

Gazpacho is one of the wonderful signature dishes of Spain. I've been exploring the country by way of its cuisine—fueled by a few wonderful trips in recent years—which has included trying many different versions of gazpacho. This is a more traditional tomato- and vegetable-based example.

I often use a mix of both regular and spicy V8 juice for a little extra zip in the chilled soup. I prefer to add the reserved chopped vegetables to each bowl as a colorful garnish, but you could instead stir them into the puréed soup before chilling. If you're using English cucumbers, there is no need to peel and seed them. For regular cucumbers, halve them lengthwise and run the tip of a small spoon down the center of each half to remove the seeds. Peel the cucumbers after seeding, rather than before as the skin will help you hold the cucumber more securely. Cold poached shrimp or crisp croutons would be a great final addition to the soup. MAKES 8 SERVINGS

1 green bell pepper, cored, seeded, and finely diced

1 red bell pepper, cored, seeded, and finely diced

1 yellow or orange bell pepper, cored, seeded, and finely diced

1 cup finely chopped yellow onion

1 cucumber, seeded, peeled, and finely diced

1 beefsteak tomato, seeded and finely diced

½ cup chopped fresh flat-leaf parsley

1½ tablespoons pressed or minced garlic

3 cups tomato juice

2½ cups V8 vegetable juice

¼ cup plain dried bread crumbs

2 tablespoons extra-virgin olive oil

2 tablespoons red wine vinegar

1 tablespoon minced jalapeño chile

1 tablespoon Worcestershire sauce

1 teaspoon Tabasco sauce

1 teaspoon salt

½ teaspoon freshly ground black pepper

1. In a large bowl, combine the bell peppers, onion, cucumber, tomato, parsley, and garlic and stir well to evenly blend. Scoop out about half of the mixture and set aside. To the rest, add the tomato juice and V8. In a small bowl, stir together the bread crumbs, olive oil, vinegar, jalapeño, Worcestershire, Tabasco, salt, and pepper.

2. Working in batches, blend the tomato juice/vegetable mixture in a blender, adding some of the bread crumb mixture with each batch to be sure that it is thoroughly incorporated. Transfer all of the soup to a large bowl and blend well. Refrigerate the soup and the reserved vegetables for at least 2 hours before serving.

3. To serve, ladle the chilled soup into individual shallow bowls and spoon the reserved vegetables into the center of each. Pass the Tabasco bottle separately, in case your guests would like a bit more spicy flavor.

Menu Ideas: You can serve this soup in shot glasses as one of an array of appetizers at a summertime party. Or for a buffet dinner, serve cups of the gazpacho with platters of Grilled Pork Kebabs (page 21) and a big bowl of Roasted Corn Salad (page 53) for guests to help themselves. This would also be an ideal seated first course before Paella with Chicken and Shellfish (page 120).

Do-Ahead Tips: The soup can be made up to 2 days in advance; note it is best if allowed to sit for at least 2 hours so flavors can meld. Be sure to stir well before serving.

SHORT RIB–BARLEY STEW

I have always enjoyed barley soup and my husband loves short ribs, so I blended those two favorites in this richly flavored stew. With the long, gentle cooking, your kitchen will smell wonderful. You can thin the stew with more stock for a more soup-like consistency if you prefer. The few hours this dish requires are very much worth it. MAKES 8 TO 10 SERVINGS

4 pounds beef short ribs

Salt and freshly ground black pepper

¼ cup all-purpose flour

3 tablespoons vegetable oil

1 cup dry red wine

4 cups top-quality beef broth

2 cups water

1 large yellow onion, chopped

3 carrots, diced

3 stalks celery, diced

2 parsnips, diced

2 cloves garlic, chopped

¾ cup pearl barley

3 tablespoons finely chopped fresh flat-leaf parsley, plus coarsely chopped parsley for garnish

1 tablespoon chopped fresh thyme or ¾ teaspoon dried thyme

1 can (14½ ounces) diced tomatoes

Menu Ideas: This stew is hearty enough to stand alone as a main course, served with a crisp salad and a loaf of warm crunchy bread. A piece of Ginger Cake with Lemon Cream (page 176) would be the perfect finish.

Do-Ahead Tips: This stew can be made up to 3 days in advance and refrigerated. The barley will puff and thicken the stew over time, so you may want to add some broth or water when reheating to thin it a bit. The stew also freezes well for a month or so.

1. Preheat the oven to 350°F.

2. Season the short ribs with salt and pepper, then coat them in the flour, patting to remove the excess. Heat the oil in a Dutch oven or other large pot over medium heat. Working in batches, brown the ribs well on all sides, about 5 minutes per batch. Set the ribs aside on a plate.

3. Add the wine to the pot, bring to a boil over medium-high heat, and boil for 3 to 5 minutes, until reduced by about half. Stir frequently to scrape up cooked bits from the bottom of the pan. Return the ribs (with any juices) to the pot with 2 cups of the broth, the water, and onion. Cover the pot and braise in the oven for 1 hour.

4. Add the carrots, celery, parsnips, and garlic to the pot and simmer over medium heat for 5 minutes. Add the barley, parsley, thyme, and remaining 2 cups broth. Simmer, covered, for 1 hour over medium-low heat (the liquid should not boil actively; decrease the heat to low if needed). Stir in the tomatoes with their liquid and a good pinch of salt. Simmer, partly covered, for 1 hour longer, until the meat is very tender.

5. Use a slotted spoon to lift the ribs from the stew. When cool enough to handle, separate the meat from the bone, gristle, and fat. Shred the meat and return it to the stew.

6. Taste the stew for seasoning, adding more salt or pepper to taste. Reheat gently over medium-low heat. Ladle the stew into shallow soup bowls and sprinkle with parsley.

TOMATO AND ROASTED RED PEPPER SOUP
WITH CHILE CREAM

While this soup can be made any time of year, it will be at its very best in late summer when tomatoes are bursting with flavor. The soup can be either a first course or a main course of a light meal. For a lighter version, use half-and-half or whole milk instead of the cream. I often add a few minced chives and a small squeeze of lime juice just before serving. MAKES 6 TO 8 SERVINGS

2 large sprigs fresh flat-leaf parsley

3 sprigs fresh thyme

1 dried bay leaf

2 tablespoons olive oil

1 medium sweet onion, chopped

8 medium tomatoes (about 2 pounds total), peeled, seeded, and chopped (see page 223)

4 cups chicken stock (page 83) or top-quality chicken broth

3 cloves garlic, roasted (see page 221)

1 large yellow and 2 large red bell peppers, roasted, peeled, and chopped (see page 222)

1 cup whipping cream

5 tablespoons freshly squeezed lemon juice

CHILE CREAM

1 cup lightly packed spinach leaves, rinsed, dried, and tough stems removed

⅓ cup crème fraîche or sour cream

1 Anaheim chile, cored, seeded, and finely chopped

1 clove garlic, pressed or minced

1 tablespoon freshly squeezed lime juice

Salt and freshly ground black pepper

1. For the chile cream, bring a small pan of lightly salted water to a boil. Add the spinach leaves and cook for 15 to 30 seconds, until just wilted. Drain well and rinse under cold water to cool. Dry well on paper towels. Combine the spinach, crème fraîche, chile, garlic, and lime juice in a food processor and pulse until smooth. Season to taste with salt and pepper. Refrigerate until needed.

2. Tie together the parsley sprigs, thyme sprigs, and bay leaf in a piece of cheesecloth, secured with kitchen string.

3. Heat the olive oil in a large saucepan over medium heat. Add the onion and cook, stirring occasionally, until tender and aromatic, 3 to 5 minutes. Stir in the tomatoes, stock, and roasted garlic with a good pinch each of salt and pepper. Add the herb bundle to the pan and bring to a low boil over medium-high heat. Decrease the heat to medium and simmer for 10 minutes. Add the roasted peppers and cream and simmer 25 minutes longer (the soup should not boil; decrease the heat to medium-low if needed).

4. Discard the herb packet and allow the soup to cool slightly. Working in batches, purée the soup in a blender or food processor until very smooth, returning the soup to the pot. Stir in the lemon juice and gently reheat the soup over medium-low heat. Taste the soup for seasoning, adding more salt or pepper to taste.

5. Ladle the soup into warmed soup bowls and top with dollops of the chile cream.

Menu Ideas: This soup is a perfect starter for a dinner followed by My Grandmother's Cabbage Rolls (page 96) or Grilled Honey and Mustard Ribs (page 108). For lunch, I'd make some good garlic bread to serve alongside, then finish things off with a slice of decadent Very Citrus Cheesecake (page 178).

Do-Ahead Tips: The chile cream can be made up to 2 days in advance. The soup can be made up to 1 day in advance and refrigerated. Warm the soup gently over medium-low heat and add the lemon juice just before serving.

MAIN DISHES

This is the chapter you'll typically turn to first to find the anchor of your meal. It's only natural that we figure out the focal "star" at the center of the menu and then build the rest of the dishes around it. I like to start by thinking about those seasonal ingredients and impulses. I'll browse grocery sections and farmers' market stalls to see what looks the freshest and most grabs my attention. Cooking techniques also tend to follow the seasons. We turn to braised dishes such as brisket, corned beef, and tagines in the winter and lighter grilled fare in summer. Let your mood and your instincts be the guide.

As with other chapters, you'll find here a broad range of recipes that represent the array of influences I've had in the kitchen. From the rustic, flavorful cabbage rolls my grandmother used to make to the exotic aroma and flavor of a lamb tagine accented with preserved lemons and myriad spices, there is an entrée within the following pages to suit any style of dinner party.

Once the main course has been chosen, you start building. A saucy entrée will call out for an easy starch to help soak up the sauce. Or a simpler entrée of grilled fish or roasted meat will invite colorful, interesting side dishes to contrast. A time-consuming dish or one that requires last-minute attention (such as Chiles Rellenos with Potatoes and Cheese) should encourage you to pick easier, make-ahead items to serve before or alongside.

Some of these entrées are so visually impressive that they can literally be served as the centerpiece of the table. When you bring out your paella pan filled with aromatic rice, meats, and seafood, or the cataplana pan with shellfish, the energy at the table will become even more dynamic.

SALMON WITH NASTURTIUM BUTTER

One of many products from our prolific garden—which grows everything from garlic and Spanish flat beans to sweet corn and a variety of pumpkins—is seemingly endless vines of nasturtiums. The nasturtium blossoms that flourish in summer come in a wide range of colors from soft yellow and orange to deep red and striped patterns, and have a wonderful peppery flavor. They are a great partner for salmon in this pure-summer recipe.

Extra nasturtium butter is delicious tossed with steamed green beans, or simply served as a flavorful alternative to plain butter for spreading on bread. Be sure the flowers you use have not been sprayed; I don't rinse my blossoms, simply shake them a bit to dislodge any bugs or debris. MAKES 6 SERVINGS

2 tablespoons olive oil

6 (7- to 8-ounce) salmon fillet pieces,
 skin and pin bones removed

Salt and freshly ground white pepper

Whole nasturtium blossoms, for garnish

NASTURTIUM BUTTER

½ cup unsalted butter, at room temperature

¼ cup loosely packed, finely slivered nasturtium
 blossoms

1 tablespoon minced fresh chives

½ teaspoon salt

Menu Ideas: An ideal partner for this vibrant, slightly rich dish would be Artichoke Risotto with Spring Peas and Mint (page 146) or Asparagus with Garlic (page 134).

Do-Ahead Tips: The nasturtium butter can be made up to 1 week in advance and refrigerated, or frozen for up to 3 weeks. The salmon should be cooked just before serving.

1. For the nasturtium butter, stir together the butter, slivered nasturtium blossoms, chives, and salt in a small bowl until well blended. Cut a piece of foil or parchment paper about 8 inches long. Spoon the butter mixture down the center length of the foil and wrap the butter in a cylinder shape, twisting the ends to make a firm roll. Refrigerate until ready to serve, at least 2 hours.

2. Heat the olive oil in a large skillet over medium heat. Season the salmon with salt and pepper. Add the salmon to the skillet skin side down and cook, turning once, for 4 to 10 minutes, until lightly browned and nearly opaque through the thickest part; the time will vary with the thickness of the fillets.

3. Transfer the salmon pieces to warmed plates. Unwrap the nasturtium butter and cut 6 slices about ½ inch thick. Top each salmon piece with a slice of the butter, garnish with a whole blossom, and serve.

BARBECUED FLANK STEAK

Flank steak was a bargain when I was younger and just beginning to entertain. Though more expensive now, it is still a relatively good deal among steak choices. There are so many "favorite" flank steak recipes that friends have told me about over the years, for a couple of weeks I tested as many versions as I could manage. This is the one that won the most raves, with a quick marinade that's tangy and sweet. Be sure not to cook the meat beyond the medium stage for the most tender and flavorful results.

For a larger crowed, you can easily double this recipe, marinating two steaks in the same amount of marinade. You might also want to intentionally cook more than needed, so you'll have leftovers for the next few days. A flank steak sandwich is a perfect use for extra meat. I love to slather the bread with some of the new flavored mustards—maybe herbes de Provence or horseradish flavored—and add crisp lettuce and slices of tomato. MAKES 4 SERVINGS

½ cup tomato juice

½ cup soy sauce (regular or reduced-sodium)

½ cup packed dark brown sugar

¼ cup vegetable oil

2 tablespoons red wine vinegar

2 tablespoons steak sauce, such as A.1.

3 cloves garlic, pressed or minced

1 flank steak (about 1½ pounds)

1. Stir together the tomato juice, soy sauce, brown sugar, oil, vinegar, steak sauce, and garlic in a small bowl.

2. Use a fork to poke holes all over both sides of the flank steak, which will help the marinade penetrate the meat. Place the steak in a large resealable plastic bag and pour the marinade over. Press out most of the air and seal the bag. Massage the bag a bit to distribute the marinade evenly. Marinate in the refrigerator for at least 6 hours or up to 24 hours, turning the bag 2 or 3 times.

3. Preheat an outdoor grill. When the grill is hot, lift the steak from the marinade, allowing the excess to drip off; discard the marinade. Grill the steak, turning once, for 10 to 12 minutes, until medium-rare to medium. Transfer the steak to a cutting board, cover loosely with foil, and let sit for 5 to 10 minutes. Cut the steak crosswise into slices about ¾ inch thick, cutting slightly on the diagonal.

Menu Ideas: I like to begin a steak dinner such as this with a flavorful starter, such as Beet and Fennel Salad with Walnut Dressing (page 59) or Curried Red Lentil Soup (page 75). Serve the steak with Roasted Smashed Potatoes with Garlic and Herbs (page 159) alongside, and finish with simple but delicious Sunken Chocolate Cupcakes (page 175).

Do-Ahead Tips: The steak can be marinated up 24 hours in advance and will have the best flavor if given that much time. The steak should be grilled just before serving.

GRILLED RACK OF PORK
WITH MANGO SALSA

Pork benefits mightily from brining prior to cooking, which helps keep the meat juicy. Grilling the chops in a whole rack, rather than individual pieces, also helps control the moistness of the meat. When grilling isn't an option, you can bake the pork: Start the oven at 450°F for the first 20 minutes, then decrease to 350°F and bake for another 20 minutes or so. I like to add a bit of water to the roasting pan to help keep the cooking juices from scorching. MAKES 4 SERVINGS

1 rack of pork (about 2½ pounds)

2 tablespoons olive oil

BRINE

6 cups water

½ cup packed light brown sugar

⅓ cup kosher salt

¼ cup molasses

8 cloves garlic, crushed

3 dried bay leaves, crumbled

10 whole cloves

2 tablespoons freshly ground black pepper

MANGO SALSA

1 medium mango, peeled, seeded, and finely diced

6 tablespoons freshly squeezed lime juice

¼ cup minced red onion

¼ cup minced red bell pepper

1 tablespoon minced ginger

1 tablespoon minced fresh cilantro

1 teaspoon minced jalapeño chile

1 teaspoon light brown sugar

Salt

1. For the brine, stir together the water, brown sugar, and salt in a large bowl and let sit for 10 to 15 minutes, stirring occasionally, until the sugar and salt are dissolved. Stir in the molasses, garlic, bay leaves, cloves, and pepper.

2. Add the rack of pork to the brine and cover the bowl securely with plastic wrap. Or, place the rack in a large resealable plastic bag and pour the brine over, sealing the bag well. Brine the pork in the refrigerator for 4 to 6 hours, turning the pork or bag a couple of times to brine evenly.

3. While the pork is brining, make the salsa. Stir together the mango, lime juice, onion, bell pepper, ginger, cilantro, jalapeño, and brown sugar. Season to taste with salt and let sit for 1 hour. Taste the salsa again for seasoning, adding more jalapeño or salt to taste.

4. If you have a regulated gas grill, preheat one side to medium, the other side to medium-low. For charcoal grilling, prepare the grill for indirect heat, with most of the coals on one side and just 6 to 8 coals on the other.

5. Remove the pork from the brine, rinse under cold water, and thoroughly pat dry with paper towels. Rub the pork with the olive oil and season with a bit of pepper. Set the pork on the hotter side of the grill and cook for about 5 minutes, browning it well on all sides. Move the pork rack to the cooler side of the grill, cover the grill, and continue cooking for 25 to 30 minutes, until an instant read thermometer inserted in the center of the meat registers 135°F. Transfer the rack to a cutting board, cover with aluminum foil, and let sit for 15 minutes (the internal temperature will rise to about 150°F).

6. Use a heavy knife to cut between the ribs into chops and set them on individual plates, spooning the mango salsa alongside.

Menu Ideas: These chops will be delicious with Orzo with Sugar Snap Peas (page 133) or Sautéed Spinach with Mustard Sauce (page 158). Finish with Blueberry Tart (page 184) or Applesauce Cake with Cinnamon–Cream Cheese Frosting (page 168).

Do-Ahead Tips: The salsa can be made up to 4 days in advance and refrigerated (note that the jalapeño heat will develop more over time). The pork can be brined up to 1 day in advance, but longer will make the pork too salty.

CHILI WITH FIRE-ROASTED PEPPERS

I use two types of beef for this chili, cubed round steak and ground beef; each provide different flavor and texture. Since some guests like a little more kick in their chili, I pass a bottle of Tabasco sauce around the table. MAKES 8 TO 10 SERVINGS

4 tablespoons vegetable oil

1¾ pounds top round steak, cut into ¼-inch cubes

1¾ pounds lean ground beef (preferably chili grind)

1 can (12 ounces) beer

2½ cups finely chopped yellow onions

3 stalks celery, finely chopped

4 cloves garlic, pressed or minced

1 green bell pepper, roasted, peeled, seeded, and diced (see page 222)

2 large jalapeño chiles, roasted, peeled, seeded, and diced (see page 222)

2 serrano chiles, roasted, peeled, seeded, and diced (see page 222)

2 tablespoons chili powder

2 tablespoons ancho chile powder

1 tablespoon ground cumin

1 tablespoon dried oregano

1 tablespoon sweet Hungarian paprika

1 tablespoon salt

2 teaspoons freshly ground black pepper

2 teaspoons ground coriander

3 cans (14½ ounces each) diced tomatoes

2 cups top-quality beef broth

1 can (15 ounces) tomato sauce

1 cup water

¼ cup cornmeal

2 cans (16 ounces each) red kidney beans, drained and rinsed

1 can (16 ounces) black beans, drained and rinsed

GARNISHES

Sour cream, chopped onion, grated Cheddar cheese, Tabasco sauce

1. Heat 1 tablespoon of the oil in a large, wide pot over medium heat. In 2 to 3 batches for each, brown the cubed meat and ground beef, 3 to 4 minutes each. As each batch is cooked, scoop it into a large bowl. Add more of the oil to the pan as needed and allow the pan to reheat between batches. Return all the beef to the pot, add the beer, and cook for 10 minutes.

2. Add the onions, celery, and garlic and cook for about 10 minutes, until the vegetables begin to soften. Stir in the roasted pepper and chiles, chili powder, ancho powder, cumin, oregano, paprika, salt, pepper, and coriander. Continue cooking, stirring well so the spices evenly coat the other ingredients, for 1 to 2 minutes, until aromatic. Stir in the tomatoes, broth, tomato sauce, and water. Simmer the chili, uncovered and stirring occasionally, for 1 hour. The chili should not boil; decrease the heat to medium-low if needed.

3. Sprinkle the cornmeal over the chili and stir to blend. Cover the pot and simmer, stirring occasionally, until the chili is quite aromatic and slightly thickened, about 1 hour longer. Stir in the beans and simmer, uncovered, for another 30 minutes. Taste the chili for seasoning, adding more salt or pepper to taste.

4. Place the sour cream, chopped onion, and Cheddar cheese in separate bowls. Spoon the chili into individual bowls, passing the garnishes and Tabasco sauce separately for guests to add to their own taste.

Menu Ideas: I always make this along with a big basket of Classic Cornbread (page 149), to enjoy while watching the Super Bowl. Consider having beef franks or polish sausages and warmed buns on hand, in case a guest has a hankering for a chili dog.

Do-Ahead Tips: If possible, make the chili 1 to 3 days before you plan to serve it and refrigerate. Gently warm over low heat before serving. I sometimes freeze the chili as well.

SESAME-CRUSTED TUNA
WITH SOY-LEMON SAUCE

In this lovely dish, inspired by a lunch I enjoyed in Hawaii years ago, sesame seeds give tuna a wonderful nutty flavor while forming a delicate crust on the fish.

I usually just "grill" these tuna pieces in a heavy grill pan on top of the stove, or simply sauté them in a regular skillet. The crust can be tricky on an outdoor grill—I find much of it tends to fall off during cooking. I typically cook some of the tuna pieces rare, others more medium, so guests can pick the doneness they prefer. Try the crusted tuna in the Salade Niçoise with Grilled Ahi Tuna on page 49. MAKES 6 SERVINGS

½ cup sesame seeds, toasted (see page 222)

2 tablespoons freshly squeezed lemon juice

2 tablespoons soy sauce

2 tablespoons minced fresh chives or green onion tops

2 teaspoons minced or pressed garlic

2 teaspoons minced or grated ginger

1 teaspoon sesame oil

6 (8-ounce) tuna steaks, 1 inch thick

2 tablespoons olive oil

SOY-LEMON SAUCE

1 cup dry white wine

2 tablespoons freshly squeezed lemon juice

2 tablespoons soy sauce

¼ cup sour cream

¼ cup unsalted butter, cut into 4 pieces and chilled

Salt and freshly ground white pepper

1. Stir together the sesame seeds, lemon juice, soy sauce, chives, garlic, ginger, and sesame oil. Set the tuna steaks on a tray or platter, spoon half of the sesame mixture over, and spread evenly, pressing with your fingers to help them adhere. Turn the steaks over and spoon the remaining sesame mixture on the second side. Let sit at room temperature for 20 minutes.

2. For the sauce, combine the wine and lemon juice in a medium saucepan and bring to a boil over high heat. Boil for 8 to 10 minutes, until reduced to ⅓ cup. Decrease the heat to low, whisk in the soy sauce, then whisk in the sour cream. Whisk in the butter, 1 piece at a time, allowing each piece to melt in creamily before adding the next. Season to taste with salt and pepper. Keep warm over very low heat; do not allow the sauce to boil.

3. Preheat the broiler.

4. Heat an ovenproof grill pan or large cast-iron skillet over medium heat (allow enough time for the skillet to fully heat). Add the olive oil, then add the tuna steaks and cook until the sesame crust is set and lightly browned, 1 minute per side. Transfer the skillet to the oven and broil a few inches from the heat for 1 to 2 minutes, until rare, or longer to suit your taste.

5. Cut the tuna steaks into ¾-inch-thick slices. Arrange the slices in a fan on each warmed plate. Spoon the sauce over and serve.

Menu Ideas: This tuna is delicious served with Ginger Asian Slaw (page 47) to start. Alongside the tuna, I like to serve Cauliflower and Tomato Gratin (page 154) or Sautéed Spinach with Mustard Sauce (page 158).

Do-Ahead Tips: The sauce can be prepared up to 1 hour in advance; reheat very gently so the sour cream does not break. The crust can be prepared and the tuna coated up to 30 minutes in advance. The tuna should be cooked just before serving.

MY GRANDMOTHER'S CABBAGE ROLLS

My grandmother made cabbage rolls countless times and I still remember how light they were. She always used homemade sauerkraut that was fermenting in the crock in her basement, but today I am content with the bagged sauerkraut from the deli cold case (which I prefer to the milder jarred type). This recipe has a lot of ingredients, but the results are very much worth the time and effort.

MAKES 4 TO 6 SERVINGS

1 green cabbage (about 2 pounds)

4 tablespoons olive oil

2 medium yellow onions, diced

2 cloves garlic, pressed or minced

½ cup long-grain white rice

2 cups chicken stock (page 83) or top-quality chicken broth

½ pound lean ground pork

½ pound lean ground beef

1 egg, beaten

1 tablespoon chopped fresh thyme or 1 teaspoon dried thyme

3 teaspoons sweet Hungarian paprika, plus more for serving

1 teaspoon caraway seeds

½ teaspoon celery seeds

¾ teaspoon salt

¼ teaspoon freshly ground black pepper

1 pound fresh sauerkraut (about 2 cups)

2 carrots, diced

1 can (14½ ounces) diced tomatoes

Sour cream, for serving

1. Half-fill a large pot with water and bring to a boil. While the water's heating, remove any tough or damaged outer leaves from the cabbage. Use a small, sharp knife to cut out all of the core from the cabbage, leaving the head intact. Line a large baking sheet with several layers of paper towels.

2. Gently slide the whole cabbage head into the boiling water, cored side down. Boil for about 5 minutes (you may need to hold the head down with tongs). Continue simmering, and as the outer leaves become tender and pliable, use the tongs to carefully pull them away from the head and transfer them to the paper towels. You need about 12 leaves in all (1 or 2 of the largest leaves can be halved to make 2 rolls). Blanch what is left of the cabbage head for 5 minutes longer, until tender. Transfer to a bowl to cool, then coarsely chop and set aside.

3. Heat 3 tablespoons of the olive oil in a large skillet over medium heat. Add the onions and garlic and cook for 8 to 10 minutes, until tender and aromatic. Transfer to a bowl with a slotted spoon and set aside to cool. Add the rice to the skillet with the remaining 1 tablespoon olive oil. Cook over medium heat, stirring, for 2 minutes. Add 1 cup of the chicken stock and cook, stirring occasionally, for 2 minutes. Decrease the heat to medium-low and cook for about 5 minutes, or until all the liquid is absorbed. (The rice will still be firm; it will fully cook when baked.)

4. Add the pork and beef to the skillet and cook over medium heat, using the wooden spoon to break the meat into smaller pieces, for 8 to 10 minutes, until no longer pink. Stir in the egg, thyme, 2 teaspoons of the paprika, caraway seeds, celery seeds, salt, and pepper. Cook, stirring, for about 2 minutes, until the egg is cooked and the rice mixture is evenly coated with the spices. Transfer the mixture to a large bowl, stir in half of the onions (about 1 cup), and set aside to cool. Reserve the skillet.

5. When the filling is cool, set one of the cooled cabbage leaves on the work surface and trim away the tough rib portion with a small knife. Spoon about ¼ cup of the filling into the center of the leaf. Fold up the bottom portion of the leaf, then fold in the sides and roll the packet upwards to fully enclose the filling. Use a toothpick or two to secure the roll. Continue with the remaining filling and leaves, making 12 rolls in all.

6. Preheat the oven to 350°F. Place the sauerkraut in a colander and rinse under cold water for a minute or two, then squeeze in your hands to remove the excess water.

7. Combine the reserved onions with the carrots in the reserved skillet and cook over medium heat for 2 to 3 minutes. Stir in the reserved chopped cabbage and cook for 15 minutes, adding 2 or 3 tablespoons water if the mixture becomes dry. Add the sauerkraut and stir well to blend. Stir in the tomatoes and remaining 1 cup chicken stock and 1 teaspoon paprika. Season with salt and pepper.

8. Transfer half of the sauerkraut mixture to a 9 by 13-inch baking dish. Arrange the cabbage rolls evenly in the dish and top with the remaining sauerkraut mixture. Cover the dish securely with foil and bake for 1½ hours. Let sit for 10 minutes before serving.

9. Remove and discard the toothpicks from the cabbage rolls. Arrange the rolls with some of the sauerkraut on individual plates. Top each with a dollop of sour cream and sprinkle of paprika.

Menu Ideas: Starring as the main course, I serve 2 (or 3, for bigger appetites) rolls per person, with just crusty bread alongside. The rolls can also be served as a side dish, 1 per person, alongside The Best Roasted Chicken (page 112) or Veal Chops with Green Peppercorns and Rosemary (page 117).

Do-Ahead Tips: The rolls may be assembled with sauerkraut in the baking dish a day ahead. They should be baked just before serving; allow the dish to come to room temperature before baking.

CLAM AND MUSSEL CATAPLANA
WITH CHORIZO

I first encountered cataplana on a buying trip to Portugal in 1996. A cataplana pan is traditionally made of pounded copper, with two rounded halves hinged together like a clam shell. At the table, the top half flips open, revealing the contents while doubling as a receptacle for discarded shells. The pans come in several sizes. A 10-inch pan is ideal for this recipe, though you can also simply cook the cataplana in a large pot, such as a Dutch oven.

If you're buying the prosciutto custom-cut at the counter, ask for end pieces that you can trim and dice. Otherwise, ask for the prosciutto to be sliced about ¼ inch thick, thicker than it is typically cut. **MAKES 6 TO 8 SERVINGS**

1 tablespoon olive oil

6 ounces chorizo sausage, cut into ¼-inch diagonal slices

3 ounces thick prosciutto slices, diced

1 large yellow onion, diced

1 green bell pepper, cored, seeded, and diced

1 red bell pepper, cored, seeded, and diced

1 shallot, minced

3 cloves garlic, pressed or minced

1 dried bay leaf

2 teaspoons sweet Hungarian paprika

1 teaspoon salt

½ teaspoon freshly ground black pepper

¼ teaspoon dried red pepper flakes

1 can (14½ ounces) diced tomatoes, drained, liquid reserved

½ cup dry white wine

1½ pounds live Manila or other hard-shell clams, rinsed

1 pound live mussels, scrubbed and debearded

⅓ cup minced fresh flat-leaf parsley

2 teaspoons minced fresh cilantro

1. Heat the oil in a large skillet over medium-high heat. Add the chorizo and prosciutto and cook for 2 to 3 minutes, until lightly browned. Scoop out with a slotted spoon and drain on paper towels, reserving the oil in the skillet.

2. Add the onion, bell peppers, shallot, garlic, and bay leaf to the skillet and sauté over medium heat, stirring often, for about 5 minutes, until tender. Stir in the paprika, salt, black pepper, and dried red pepper flakes and stir 2 minutes. Add the tomatoes and ¼ cup of their liquid and the wine. Decrease the heat to medium-low and simmer for about 30 minutes, until the liquid is reduced by about half. Stir in the chorizo and prosciutto.

3. To assemble the cataplana, spoon half of the vegetable mixture into a 10-inch cataplana pan or Dutch oven. Scatter the clams and mussels over and top with the remaining vegetables. Close the cataplana cover, or cover the Dutch oven with its lid. Simmer over medium heat for 15 minutes. Open the lid and gently stir the mussels and clams to distribute the sauce. Re-close the lid and cook for 3 to 5 minutes longer, until all the shells have opened (discard any clams or mussels that do not open). Discard the bay leaf. Sprinkle with the parsley and cilantro.

4. Serve the cataplana from the pan set in the center of the table, ladling the shellfish and sauce into heated shallow bowls. If you prepared the dish in a Dutch oven, provide empty bowls on the table for discarded shells.

Menu Ideas: Serve this centerpiece entrée with a simple crisp salad such as Bibb Lettuce and Grapefruit Salad (page 52) or Frisée Salad with Toasted Hazelnuts (page 50). You'll also want good crunchy bread on hand for mopping up the wonderful sauce. When it's in season, I'll serve fresh corn on the cob with the cataplana instead of a salad. The cataplana can also be served as a first course.

Do-Ahead Tips: The vegetable base can be made up to 2 days in advanced, covered, and refrigerated. Assemble and bake the cataplana just before serving.

MARDI GRAS GUMBO

I first learned about gumbo and other distinctive dishes from the South when I was in my early 30s. A cooking class in the New Orleans kitchen of an outstanding home cook gave me countless insights into classic gumbo and other regional dishes. Making the roux is one of the most important steps. It takes careful attention to watch the slow development of the nut brown color and almost constantly stirring to ensure even cooking. If your roux blackens and burns, the flavor will be too harsh and you'll need to start over.

This gumbo is very spicy with 1 full tablespoon of cayenne in the spice rub; decrease that amount by half or more if you prefer a milder flavor. MAKES 8 SERVINGS

8 boneless, skinless chicken thighs (about 2 pounds total), cut into 1-inch cubes

4 (8-ounce) boneless, skinless chicken breasts, cut into 1-inch cubes

1½ teaspoons salt

6 andouille sausages (about 1¼ pounds total), kielbasa, or other smoked pork sausage

½ cup water

1 large yellow onion, finely chopped

1 green bell pepper, cored, seeded, and chopped

1 red bell pepper, cored, seeded, and chopped

¾ cup chopped celery

2 cloves garlic, pressed or minced

¾ cup plus 2 tablespoons vegetable oil, plus more if needed

6 cups chicken stock (page 83) or top-quality chicken broth

¾ cup all-purpose flour

1 can (14½ ounces) stewed tomatoes

8 ounces fresh or thawed frozen whole okra, stems trimmed, halved crosswise

12 ounces medium or large shrimp, peeled and deveined

4 cups cooked basmati rice

1. For the spice rub, stir together the cayenne, paprika, coriander, oregano, thyme, garlic powder, bay leaves, and pepper in a small bowl.

2. Place the chicken pieces in a large bowl or broad dish and season with the salt. Add half of the spice mixture and stir well to evenly coat. Let sit for 20 minutes (refrigerated, if your kitchen is warm).

3. While the chicken is sitting, place the sausages in a medium skillet with the water, cover, and set over medium-high heat. When the water comes to a boil, steam the sausages for 5 minutes, then uncover and continue cooking, turning the sausages occasionally, for 5 to 7 minutes, until lightly browned. Let cool. Cut into ½-inch pieces and set aside.

4. Stir together the onion, bell peppers, celery, and garlic in a medium bowl. Add the remaining spice rub and toss to evenly mix. Set aside.

5. Heat ½ cup of the vegetable oil in a large nonstick skillet over medium heat. In 3 or 4 batches, brown the chicken pieces on all sides. Set aside; reserve the skillet. Place the chicken stock in a medium saucepan and warm gently over medium-low heat.

6. Measure the oil from the skillet and add enough additional vegetable oil to measure ¾ cup. Transfer to a Dutch oven or other large pan and stir in the flour. Cook over medium-low heat, stirring, until the flour takes on a reddish brown color and nutty aroma. Be patient; this can take 20 minutes or so. Stir often at the beginning, then be sure to stir constantly once the roux begins taking on color to ensure even cooking and no burnt spots.

7. Carefully but quickly add the vegetable mixture to the pot, taking care to avoid splattering the hot roux. (The vegetables decrease the temperature of the roux, to help avoid overcooking.) Cook, stirring constantly to evenly coat the vegetables in the roux, for 5 minutes. Slowly add the warm chicken stock, stirring constantly. Increase the heat to medium. When the liquid comes to a low boil, add the sausages and stewed tomatoes (with their liquid), reduce the heat, and cook uncovered for 30 minutes.

SPICE RUB

1 tablespoon cayenne pepper

1 tablespoon sweet Hungarian paprika

1 tablespoon ground coriander

2 teaspoons dried oregano

2 teaspoons dried thyme

2 teaspoons garlic powder

2 dried bay leaves, crushed

1 teaspoon freshly ground black pepper

8. Heat the remaining 2 tablespoons oil in a medium skillet over medium heat, add the okra, and cook for 5 minutes. Add the okra and chicken pieces to the gumbo and simmer 20 minutes. Taste the gumbo for seasoning, adding more salt to taste. Keep warm over low heat until ready to serve.

9. Shortly before serving, add the shrimp to the gumbo and simmer for 3 to 5 minutes, until the shrimp are just cooked through. Serve the gumbo over rice in shallow soup bowls.

Menu Ideas: I enjoy Spinach and Hearts of Palm Salad with the optional fried oysters (page 44) as a start to this New Orleans meal. As a main course, gumbo can stand alone, with only squares of warm Classic Cornbread (page 149) alongside. Follow up with Lemon Bread Pudding (page 166), by which time you may need a nap.

Do-Ahead Tips: The gumbo can be made to just before the shrimp is added and refrigerated for up to 3 days or frozen for 1 to 2 months. Gently reheat over medium-low heat and add the shrimp shortly before serving.

RACK OF LAMB
WITH ROSEMARY AND GARLIC

Lamb is one of the quintessential centerpieces of a celebration dinner, and this rosemary-marinated rack of lamb is no exception. It is an expensive cut of meat, no denying it, but worth the delicious splurge for a special occasion. Be sure to plan ahead for the 3 days of marinating, so the meat will have the most developed herb-garlic-lemon flavor before roasting.

The sauce is delicious made simply with beef broth (choose a top-quality broth with good flavor that's not too salty), but it will have a more developed flavor if you make the Quick Lamb Stock I recommend here. You'll need lamb trimmings for that; ask your butcher. He should also be able to trim the lamb bones (called *Frenching*) and provide you with the trimmings as well. MAKES 8 SERVINGS

3 (7- to 8-bone) lamb racks, trimmed,
    trimmings reserved

2 tablespoons olive oil

ROSEMARY MARINADE

1 cup olive oil

½ cup freshly squeezed lemon juice

8 cloves garlic, chopped

3 tablespoons finely chopped fresh rosemary

½ teaspoon freshly ground black pepper

SAUCE

1½ teaspoons finely chopped fresh rosemary

1 clove garlic, chopped

1 teaspoon dried oregano

¼ cup red wine vinegar

¾ cup dry red wine

¾ cup Quick Lamb Stock (at right) or top-quality
    beef broth

¾ cup tomato sauce (top-quality canned or
    homemade)

Salt and freshly ground black pepper

1. For the marinade, stir together the olive oil, lemon juice, garlic, rosemary, and pepper in a small bowl.

2. Place the lamb racks in 1 or 2 large resealable bags or in a wide pan. Drizzle the marinade over the meat, turning to coat the racks evenly. Seal the bag(s) or cover the dish tightly and refrigerate for 3 days, turning several times.

3. Preheat the oven to 500°F.

4. Heat the olive oil in a large skillet over medium-high heat. Remove the lamb racks from the marinade and allow the excess to drip off. In batches if necessary, brown the lamb racks well on all sides in the hot oil, about 5 minutes total. Transfer the lamb to a roasting pan, slightly overlapping the racks so they lay evenly in the pan; reserve the skillet for making the sauce. Roast the lamb for 12 to 18 minutes, until a meat thermometer inserted in the thickest part registers 140°F for rare (145°F for medium-rare to medium).

5. While the lamb is roasting, make the sauce. Skim excess fat from the reserved skillet. Add the rosemary, garlic, and oregano to the pan and stir for a few moments over medium-high heat. Add the vinegar to deglaze the pan, scraping up any browned bits. Add the red wine and stock and simmer for about 5 minutes, until reduced by two-thirds. Add the tomato sauce and simmer for about 5 minutes longer, until the sauce thickens. Season to taste with salt and pepper.

6. Cut the racks into individual chops, arrange on plates, and coat lightly with the sauce. Pass the remaining sauce separately.

QUICK LAMB STOCK

If you don't have enough trimmings from the rack of lamb, buy some inexpensive lamb blade or shoulder chops to use for the stock.
MAKES ABOUT 1 CUP

1 tablespoon unsalted butter

1 pound lamb scraps from racks

1 medium yellow onion, diced

1 large carrot, diced

½ cup dry white wine

2 cups top-quality beef broth

Heat the butter in a large saucepan over medium heat, add the lamb scraps, and brown well on all sides, 3 to 5 minutes. Add the onion and carrot and cook, stirring often, for about 5 minutes longer, until the vegetables are browned. Add the wine and cook, stirring often, until the liquid is reduced by half. Add the beef broth and simmer over low heat for about 25 minutes, until the stock is reduced by one-third. Strain.

Menu Ideas: White Bean and Watercress Gratin (page 135) is a particularly ideal accompaniment for this lamb, but I have also served it with Asparagus Salad with Champagne Vinaigrette (page 65) and Ratatouille with Fresh Rosemary (page 152).

Do-Ahead Tips: The lamb will be most delicious with 3 days of marinating, but I wouldn't marinate it any longer than that. You can make the lamb stock up to 3 days in advance. The lamb should be roasted just before serving.

FRESH DUNGENESS CRAB WITH TWO SAUCES

When I was growing up in Oregon, my family frequently went crabbing, often catching our limit of the plump Dungeness crab that are so prolific in Northwest waters. What a treat to eat our fill on those wonderful summer evenings. The crabs can be served hot, warm, or ice cold; the favorite in my family is cold with these two sauces. The first is similar to the traditional dressing for Crab Louis, with a bit of kick from horseradish; the second is a flavorful twist on tartar sauce. My husband still prefers a good classic cocktail sauce, which I'll purchase and embellish with extra horseradish and a squeeze of fresh lemon juice.

If you have enough small dishes, it's nice to serve each person their own portion of each sauce to have on their plate for easy dipping. Be sure to have crab crackers and seafood picks for each guest, to make easy work of picking the meat from the shells. MAKES 6 SERVINGS

6 (2½-pound) cooked Dungeness crabs, cleaned, cracked, and chilled (see below)

LOUIS SAUCE

½ cup chili sauce, such as Heinz

½ cup mayonnaise

¼ cup crème fraîche or sour cream

1 tablespoon prepared horseradish

2 teaspoons freshly squeezed lemon juice

½ teaspoon Tabasco sauce

½ teaspoon Worcestershire sauce

¼ teaspoon garlic powder

TARTAR SAUCE

¾ cup mayonnaise

¼ cup finely chopped cornichons or dill pickles, plus 2 teaspoons juice from the jar

1 tablespoon minced fresh flat-leaf parsley

1 tablespoon minced shallot

2 teaspoons minced capers

1 teaspoon grated yellow or white onion

½ teaspoon green peppercorn mustard or Dijon mustard

Salt

1. For the Louis sauce, stir together the chili sauce, mayonnaise, crème fraîche, horseradish, lemon juice, Tabasco sauce, Worcestershire sauce, and garlic powder in a medium bowl. Refrigerate until ready to serve.

2. For the tartar sauce, stir together the mayonnaise, cornichons and juice, parsley, shallot, capers, onion, and mustard in a small bowl. Season to taste with salt and refrigerate until ready to serve.

3. Mound the chilled crab pieces in large serving bowls or on a large platter to pass at the table. Pass the sauces separately, or serve in individual bowls for each guest. Have 2 large bowls on the table for discarded shells.

COOKING, CLEANING, AND CRACKING DUNGENESS CRAB: I make a point of going to one of the top seafood markets or grocery stores in town for the freshest, most delicious Dungeness crab. I often take advantage of precooked crabs, saving time and effort at home. Most fish vendors will clean and crack the precooked crabs for you as well.

But when I do buy (or a friend gives me) live Dungeness crabs, I simply boil them in a really big pot of well-salted water. The crabs change color from brownish-purple to bright orange as they cook. After 15 minutes, drain the crabs and run cold water over them to cool. Then remove the backs and clean out the innards, removing the feathery gills as well. Rinse well, then remove the legs and break or cut the bodies in half for serving.

Menu Ideas: I like to serve the sweet, luscious crab with a simple green salad. A bit of the Louis sauce can be thinned with olive oil and white wine vinegar to serve as the salad dressing; or just use your favorite vinaigrette. A must alongside is great warm fresh bread, or garlic bread.

Do-Ahead Tips: The sauces can be made up to 3 days ahead and refrigerated, and will be best if made at least 6 hours in advance so the flavors have time to meld. The crab can be cleaned and portioned a day ahead; wrap well and refrigerate until ready to serve.

SEATTLE CIOPPINO

My friend Linda Wyman used to make a version of this cioppino 30 years ago when our close-knit group of friends would get together for casual Sunday dinners. As fresh herbs became more available I added them and fine-tuned the old favorite. Have a large bowl or two at the table for discarded shells. And plenty of napkins! This stew is a messy but delicious treat. Look for fish stock in the freezer section of your fish market or grocery store. **MAKES 8 SERVINGS**

10 sprigs fresh flat-leaf parsley

5 sprigs fresh basil

6 sprigs fresh oregano or thyme

1 dried bay leaf

¼ cup olive oil

2 medium yellow onions, finely diced

4 cloves garlic, pressed or minced

1 green bell pepper, cored, seeded, and diced

1 red bell pepper, cored, seeded, and diced

¾ pound small button mushrooms, trimmed and quartered

¼ cup diced celery

1 can (28 ounces) diced tomatoes

2 cups dry white wine

1 cup fish stock, chicken stock (page 83), or top-quality chicken broth

1 can (6 ounces) tomato paste

1 teaspoon salt

2 pounds halibut or rockfish, skin and bones removed, cut into 1-inch cubes

1¼ pounds large shrimp, peeled and deveined

½ pound sea scallops

1½ pounds live Manila or other hard-shell clams, rinsed

2 (2½-pound) cooked Dungeness crabs, cleaned and cracked (see page 104)

1. Tie together the parsley, basil, oregano, and bay leaf in a piece of cheesecloth, secured with kitchen string.

2. Heat the olive oil in a large soup pot over medium heat. Add the onions and garlic and cook, stirring occasionally, for 8 to 10 minutes, until tender and aromatic but not browned. Add the bell peppers, mushrooms, and celery and cook for about 5 minutes, until softened. Stir in the herb bundle, tomatoes, wine, fish stock, tomato paste, and salt. Bring to a low boil over medium-high heat. Decrease the heat to medium low, cover, and simmer for 1 hour. (The mixture should not boil actively; decrease the heat as needed.)

3. Discard the herb bundle. Add the seafood in this order: fish cubes, shrimp, scallops, clams, and finally crab pieces. Cover the pot, increase the heat to medium, and simmer for about 15 minutes, or until the clams have opened and the fish, shrimp, and scallops are cooked through. Don't stir during cooking to keep from breaking up the fish pieces.

4. Discard any clams that have not opened. Distribute the different seafoods among large, shallow bowls and ladle the flavorful broth over.

Menu Ideas: As a star centerpiece dish, the cioppino needs only crusty garlic bread and a crisp green salad alongside (perhaps Parmesan Cones with Baby Greens and Herb Salad, page 66, with or without the Parmesan Cones).

Do-Ahead Tips: The cioppino base can be made up to 2 days in advance, cooled, and refrigerated. Gently reheat the base over medium-low heat and cook the seafood just before serving.

HALIBUT WITH NUT CRUST
AND APPLE VINAIGRETTE

Halibut takes on great flavor with this hazelnut crust, complemented by the crunch and tang of the apple vinaigrette. In spring, I'll collect some pea vines from our garden to sauté and serve alongside. If you're not able to find halibut, other firm white fish, such as turbot or sea bass, can be used. **MAKES 6 SERVINGS**

¼ cup unsalted butter, melted

¼ cup vegetable oil

6 (6-ounce) skinless halibut fillet pieces

APPLE VINAIGRETTE

6 tablespoons vegetable oil

1 large apple, peeled, cored, and diced (Pink Lady, Fuji, or Gala)

1 tablespoon minced shallot

⅓ cup freshly squeezed lemon juice

2 teaspoons sugar

3 tablespoons apple cider vinegar

3 tablespoons hazelnut or pecan oil (or olive oil in a pinch)

2 teaspoons Dijon mustard

2 teaspoons minced fresh thyme or ½ teaspoon dried thyme

1 teaspoon finely grated lemon zest

½ teaspoon crushed pink peppercorns

Salt and freshly ground black pepper

NUT CRUST

2 cups coarsely chopped toasted hazelnuts or pecans (see page 222)

1 tablespoon finely grated lemon zest

1½ teaspoons minced fresh thyme or ½ teaspoon dried thyme

1¼ teaspoons salt

¾ teaspoon dry mustard

½ teaspoon cayenne pepper

1. Preheat the oven to 425°F. Line a baking sheet with a silicone baking mat or parchment paper.

2. For the vinaigrette, heat 1 tablespoon of the vegetable oil in a medium skillet over medium heat. Add the apple and shallot and cook, stirring, for 2 to 3 minutes, until the shallot is tender. Stir in the lemon juice, sugar, and remaining 5 tablespoons vegetable oil. Transfer half this mixture to a food processor and pulse a few times to finely chop. Combine this with the remaining apple/shallot mixture in a medium bowl. Whisk in the vinegar, nut oil, mustard, thyme, lemon zest, and peppercorns. Season to taste with salt and pepper and set aside. (Refrigerate the dressing if making more than 1 hour in advance; allow it to come to room temperature before serving.)

3. For the nut crust, combine the nuts, lemon zest, thyme, salt, mustard, and cayenne in the food processor. Pulse 10 to 15 times to finely chop the nuts, until they have a texture of bread crumbs; avoid overprocessing. You don't want to make nut paste. Transfer to a shallow dish.

4. Stir together the melted butter and vegetable oil in a shallow dish. Dip the halibut in this to evenly coat, allowing the excess to drip off. Immediately coat the fish evenly with the nut crust and set on the baking sheet. Bake for 8 to 12 minutes, until the crust is nicely browned and the fish is just opaque throughout (the timing will vary depending on the thickness of the fish).

5. To serve, set the halibut pieces on individual warmed plates. Stir the vinaigrette to remix and spoon it over and alongside the fish.

Menu Ideas: Garlic-and-Herb Baked Artichokes (page 150) or Sautéed Spinach with Mustard Sauce (page 158) would be great partners for this entrée, along with Lemon Israeli Couscous (page 161) or Orzo with Sugar Snap Peas (page 133).

Do-Ahead Tips: The apple vinaigrette can be made up to 1 day in advance and refrigerated. The halibut can be coated with the nut crust and refrigerated for up to 4 hours before cooking. The fish should be baked just before serving.

GRILLED HONEY AND MUSTARD RIBS

Baby back ribs have become wildly popular in recent years. I love the rub with its herbal-spicy flavors that complement the sweetness of the "wash." You can serve the flavorful ribs unadorned or with a side of your favorite barbecue sauce. Note that there is a thin membrane on back of the rack of bones that needs to be peeled off before cooking. These ribs are great the next day, reheated or eaten cold. MAKES 6 TO 8 SERVINGS

3 full racks baby back ribs (5 to 6 pounds total)

¼ cup grainy mustard

SPICE RUB

5 tablespoons celery salt

2 tablespoons cumin powder

1 tablespoon cayenne pepper

1 tablespoon seasoned salt, such as Lawry's

1 tablespoon garlic powder

1 tablespoon sweet Hungarian paprika

1 teaspoon dried oregano

½ teaspoon dried sage

RIB WASH

¼ cup honey

2 tablespoons water

2 tablespoons light or dark brown sugar

Menu Ideas: The ribs are great for dinner served with Sweet Onions and Rice (page 153). For a more casual picnic or buffet, I recommend Coleslaw with Lemon-Caper Dressing (page 64) and Watermelon and Red Onion Salad (page 63). For dessert, Rhubarb and Strawberry Crisp (page 170) is always a winner.

Do-Ahead Tips: The spice rub and rib wash can be made up to 2 days in advance, the wash refrigerated. The ribs can be marinated for up to 24 hours. They can also be roasted, covered with foil, and held for several hours before grilling. And they can be grilled up to 4 hours before serving; keep warm in a 200°F oven or gently reheat before serving.

1. For the spice rub, stir together the celery salt, cumin, cayenne, seasoned salt, garlic powder, paprika, oregano, and sage in a small bowl.

2. For the rib wash, stir together the honey, water, and brown sugar in a small bowl.

3. Cut the rib racks in half. To remove the membrane, place the racks meat side down. Using the edge of a knife, loosen a bit of the membrane along the edge of the last rib, grasp the membrane firmly with a paper towel, and pull the membrane away. Continue until all the membrane is removed.

4. Spread the meat side of the ribs with the mustard. Drizzle the wash over both sides of the ribs and sprinkle with the rub. Cover and marinate in the refrigerator for at least 2 hours.

5. Preheat the oven to 300°F. Line a large roasting pan with aluminum foil.

6. Place the rib racks in the pan, meat side up, and roast for 1½ hours. Add about 1 cup of water to the pan after 30 minutes to provide moisture to keep the ribs from drying out.

7. If using a gas grill, preheat it to medium heat. For a charcoal grill, prepare indirect heat: Push the hot coals to one side, place a disposable foil pan of water in the center, and return the grate.

8. Place the roasted rib racks on the grate (opposite the coals, if using charcoal). Lower the lid and cook, turning the racks a couple of times, for about 45 minutes, until the meat begins to shrink from the end of the bones. Transfer the grilled rib racks to a cutting board and cut into individual ribs.

BRAISED BRISKET WITH ONIONS

Brisket is the perfect comfort food for so many people. Like pot roast or beef stew, it's a no-fail winner for a chilly winter night or any time a cozy meal is in order. Long, slow cooking is the key to making lean brisket tender and moist. The flavorful cooking juices reduce to a supremely flavorful sauce that gains a natural sweetness from the carrots and onions. I like to pass a dish of horseradish alongside, for guests to use to their taste; freshly grated horseradish is always a treat. **MAKES 6 TO 8 SERVINGS**

1 (4- to 5-pound) beef brisket

Salt and freshly ground black pepper

6 tablespoons olive oil

4 large yellow onions, halved and cut into ¼-inch
   slices

8 cloves garlic, sliced

1 tablespoon sugar

2 large carrots, chopped

1 cup dry red wine

1 dried bay leaf

1 can (14½ ounces) diced tomatoes

½ teaspoon freshly grated nutmeg

2½ cups top-quality beef broth

Menu Ideas: To accompany this rich, flavorful dish, consider serving Radish and Fennel Salad (page 46), or just crisp greens tossed with Basic Vinaigrette (page 43). Serve the brisket with Braised Red Cabbage (page 138) or Roasted Smashed Potatoes with Garlic and Herbs (page 159). Very Citrus Cheesecake (page 178) will finish off dinner in style.

Do-Ahead Tips: The brisket can be fully cooked and the cooking liquids reduced up to a day in advance. When the meat has cooled, cut it into serving slices and arrange in a baking dish. Spoon the cooled reduced cooking liquids and vegetables over, cover with foil, and refrigerate. Reheat in a 350°F oven for about 30 minutes before serving.

1. Preheat the oven to 325°F.

2. Season the brisket liberally with salt and pepper. Heat 3 tablespoons of the olive oil in a large heavy pot, such as a Dutch oven, over medium-high heat. Brown the meat well on all sides, 5 to 7 minutes total (decrease the heat to medium if necessary). Transfer the meat to a large plate and set aside.

3. Heat another 2 tablespoons of the olive oil in the pot. Add the onions and sauté over medium heat, stirring occasionally, for about 15 minutes, until tender and lightly browned. Add the garlic and sugar, stir well, and cook for 10 to 12 minutes longer, until the onions are richly browned. Scoop the onions into a bowl and set aside.

4. Heat the remaining 1 tablespoon olive oil in the pot. Add the carrots and sauté for 5 to 7 minutes, until tender and lightly browned. Transfer to the bowl with the onions. Pour the wine into the pot and bring just to a boil over medium-high heat, stirring to scrape up the cooked bits from the bottom of the pot. Add the bay leaf, then return the brisket to the pot along with the onions and carrots. Add the tomatoes and season with the nutmeg and another good pinch of salt and pepper. Add the broth and bring to a boil. Cover the pot and braise in the oven for 1 hour.

5. Gently stir the vegetables and cooking liquid. Cover and continue braising in the oven for 2½ to 3 hours longer, until the meat is very tender when pierced with a fork. Carefully turn the meat once halfway through.

6. Lift the brisket onto a cutting board, cover with foil, and let rest. Scoop out most of the vegetables from the pot with a slotted spoon and set aside. Discard the bay leaf. Bring the cooking liquid to a boil over medium-high heat and boil for about 20 minutes, until reduced by about three-quarters and thickened. Return the vegetables to the sauce to reheat for a minute or two.

7. To serve, cut the brisket into 1-inch-wide slices across the grain and arrange them on individual plates, slightly overlapping. Spoon the braised vegetables and sauce over and serve.

FOUR-STAR FRIED CHICKEN

It might look like your standard fried chicken, all perfectly golden and crisp, smelling so good you're willing to risk burned fingertips to get at the first piece. But after your first bite, you'll notice a little something different here: a lingering spicy flavor that comes from a brine with cayenne and other spices. Be sure to plan a day ahead for that brining.

All the chicken pieces should be bone-in and skin-on for best results. A deep fat thermometer is a handy tool here to ensure even cooking at the desired temperature. Note the chicken should not brine for much longer than 24 hours or it may become too salty. The brine would also be good for a whole turkey breast before grilling or roasting. MAKES 8 SERVINGS

4 bone-in chicken breasts, halved crosswise

4 bone-in chicken thighs

4 chicken drumsticks

3 cups all-purpose flour

1 teaspoon salt

1 teaspoon garlic powder

1 teaspoon cayenne pepper

1 teaspoon freshly ground white pepper

Vegetable oil for frying

BRINE

4 cups water

2 tablespoons salt

1 tablespoon soy sauce

2 teaspoons cayenne pepper

2 teaspoons garlic powder

2 teaspoons Worcestershire sauce

1½ teaspoons freshly ground white pepper

1. For the brine, combine the water, salt, soy sauce, cayenne, garlic powder, Worcestershire sauce, and pepper in a large bowl and whisk to mix until the salt is dissolved. Add the chicken pieces, which should be fully covered by the brine; add a bit more cold water if needed. Cover the bowl and refrigerate for 24 hours, gently stirring once or twice.

2. Combine the flour, salt, garlic powder, cayenne, and pepper in a large bowl and whisk to mix. Cover a large baking sheet with a thin layer of flour. Line another baking sheet with a couple layers of brown paper or paper towels.

3. Drain the chicken and pat dry with paper towels, discarding the marinade. Toss 2 or 3 pieces at a time in the flour mixture to evenly coat. Transfer to the floured baking sheet and let sit for 10 minutes. Toss once again in the flour to ensure a thorough coating, which will help reduce splattering when fried. Let sit for 10 minutes again before frying.

4. Meanwhile, pour 2 to 3 inches of oil in a wide, deep heavy pot, such as a Dutch oven (it's important the oil come no more than halfway up the sides of the pan for safety). Heat the oil over medium heat to 365°F to 375°F. Preheat the oven to 275°F.

5. Gently slip 3 or 4 pieces of the dredged chicken into the hot fat, taking care not to crowd them in the pan. Cook, turning the pieces a few times, for about 20 minutes, until the skin is nicely browned and the juices run clear when the thickest part is pierced with a knife. Transfer the fried chicken to the paper-lined baking sheet and keep warm in the oven while frying the remaining chicken.

Menu Ideas: This is delicious hot for dinner with Zucchini Fritters with Fresh Herbs (page 157) and your favorite potato alongside. Cold fried chicken makes a great picnic item with some Coleslaw with Lemon-Caper Dressing (page 64), Classic Cornbread (page 149), and Twenty-Hour Baked Beans (page 143) alongside. Dessert can be as simple as fresh fruit with one or two types of your favorite cookies.

Do-Ahead Tips: Served hot, the chicken will be best fried shortly before serving, while it is hot, juicy, and crisp, though you can reheat it in a 300°F oven if needed. The chicken can be fried up to 2 days in advance and refrigerated before eating cold or reheating. I have also frozen the brined chicken parts for up to a month. After defrosting slowly in the refrigerator, simply coat and fry the chicken as directed.

THE BEST ROASTED CHICKEN

Every cook has their favorite way to prepare the perfect roasted chicken. James Beard was the most outspoken about rotating the whole bird from side to side during the roasting. Julia Child always reminded us to start the oven at 425°F and lower the heat halfway through cooking. A wonderful chef and restaurateur who early on helped us build Sur La Table, the late Carol Nockold, incorporated all these concepts and always produced the perfect bird, very juicy and tender. You may want to add an extra lemon's worth of fresh juice to the cooking juices just before serving, according to your taste. **MAKES 4 SERVINGS**

1 (3½- to 4-pound) whole chicken

2½ teaspoons salt

1 small yellow onion, quartered

1 lemon, halved

4 sprigs fresh flat-leaf parsley

3 tablespoons unsalted butter, at room temperature

1 clove garlic, pressed or minced

2 tablespoons olive oil

Menu Ideas: This chicken can be served hot or cold, a wonderfully versatile recipe. For dinner, it will be perfectly partnered with Beet and Fennel Salad with Walnut Dressing (page 59) and Roasted Smashed Potatoes with Garlic and Herbs (page 159). Wedges of Very Citrus Cheesecake (page 178) would be perfect for dessert. If a picnic is in order, serve the cold chicken with Coleslaw with Lemon-Caper Dressing (page 64) and White Bean and Tuna Salad with Roasted Peppers (page 51); cap off the meal with a tin of Black and White Cocoa Bars (page 173).

Do-Ahead Tips: If serving the chicken cold, you can cook it up to 8 hours in advance. Allow the bird to cool to room temperature before wrapping in foil or plastic wrap to refrigerate until ready to serve. If serving the chicken hot, it should be roasted just before serving, though will stay hot, wrapped in foil, for up to 30 minutes.

1. Preheat the oven to 425°F.

2. Rinse the chicken inside and out under cold running water. Dry well inside and out with paper towels. Sprinkle ½ teaspoon of the salt in the chicken's cavity. Add the onion, lemon halves, parsley sprigs, and 1 tablespoon of the butter to the cavity. Use kitchen string to tie together the leg ends, and then to tie around the opposite end of the bird, securing the wing tips against the side of the chicken. Stir the garlic into the remaining 2 tablespoons butter. Use your fingers to separate the skin from the chicken breast and spread the garlic butter between the skin and flesh. Season the surface of the chicken with ½ teaspoon of the salt.

3. Set the bird breast up on a rack set in a roasting pan. Roast for 20 minutes. Decrease the temperature to 350°F. Turn the chicken onto one side and drizzle 1 tablespoon of the olive oil over. Sprinkle with ½ teaspoon of the salt. Roast for 15 minutes. Turn the bird onto its other side. Drizzle with the remaining 1 tablespoon olive oil and baste the bird with the pan juices. Sprinkle with another ½ teaspoon salt. Roast for 15 minutes longer. Return the chicken to its back and sprinkle with the remaining ½ teaspoon salt. Roast, basting every 10 minutes, for 25 to 30 minutes longer. To check for doneness, the thigh juices should run clear when pierced with a knife or an instant read thermometer will register 175°F when inserted in the thickest part of the thigh. A larger chicken may require up to 20 minutes more cooking time.

4. Use a carving fork or large tongs to tip the onion, lemon, parsley, and juices from the chicken cavity into the roasting pan (these juices should also be clear, not at all pink). Transfer the chicken to a platter, remove the strings, and cover with foil to keep warm.

5. Use a wooden spoon to press on the lemon halves to extract the juice. Set the roasting pan over medium heat and reduce the juices for a few minutes, until thickened. Strain the juices through a fine sieve.

6. Use poultry shears or a large knife to cut the chicken into pieces, arranging them on a serving platter or individual plates. Pour the strained cooking juices over the chicken and serve.

OSSO BUCO
WITH SAGE GREMOLATA

The first time I was served osso buco was while taking a cooking class in New York during my 20s. I fell in love with this beautiful dish and have developed my own version in the years since. Choose large shank pieces of similar size for even portions. The meat should be tied securely around the perimeter so it holds together during cooking; your butcher can often do this for you. The marrow found in the center of each bone is a special luxury. Encourage your guests to use the tip of their knife to lift it out and savor. MAKES 6 SERVINGS

6 veal shank pieces, 1 inch thick (about 4½ pounds total), tied with string

Salt and freshly ground black pepper

½ cup all-purpose flour

2 tablespoons unsalted butter

2 tablespoons olive oil

1 large yellow onion, chopped

1 large beefsteak tomato, chopped

2 stalks celery, chopped

2 medium carrots, chopped

2 tablespoons tomato paste

2 tablespoons chopped fresh flat-leaf parsley

3 cloves garlic, pressed or minced

2 dried bay leaves

1 teaspoon chopped fresh sage

1 teaspoon chopped fresh rosemary

½ teaspoon chopped fresh thyme

2 cups dry white wine

1 cup top-quality beef or veal broth

2 (2-inch) strips lemon zest

SAGE GREMOLATA

1 tablespoon minced fresh sage

1 tablespoon finely grated lemon zest

3 cloves garlic, pressed or minced

1. Preheat the oven to 325°F.

2. Season the shanks with salt and pepper, then coat them with the flour, patting to remove the excess. Heat the butter and olive oil in a large ovenproof sauté pan or deep skillet over medium-high heat. Add the shanks and brown well on both sides, about 5 minutes total. Set the shanks aside on a plate.

3. Add the onion, tomato, celery, carrots, tomato paste, parsley, garlic, bay leaves, sage, rosemary, and thyme to the pan. Decrease the heat to medium and cook, stirring occasionally, for about 10 minutes, until the vegetables are tender. Stir in the white wine, broth, and lemon zest strips. Bring to a boil over medium-high heat. Season with a good pinch each of salt and pepper. Return the shanks to the pan and cover. Transfer to the oven and braise for about 2½ hours, until quite tender but not falling from the bone.

4. Transfer the veal shanks to a heated platter, remove the strings, and cover with foil to keep warm. Place the pan over medium-high heat and discard the bay leaves. Simmer the sauce for about 10 minutes, until reduced by half. Taste for seasoning, adding more salt or pepper to taste.

5. Meanwhile, make the gremolata: Stir together the sage, grated lemon zest, and garlic in a small bowl until well blended.

6. Set the veal shanks on individual warmed plates and spoon some of the sauce over. Sprinkle with the gremolata and serve.

Menu Ideas: The rich veal shanks pair perfectly with a classic risotto with grated Parmesan cheese and minced parsley. You could serve mashed potatoes or soft polenta instead. To start things off, Winter Pomegranate and Endive Salad (page 62) would be ideal. I always love to finish the dinner with a lemon dessert; Lemon Bread Pudding (page 166) would be a great option.

Do-Ahead Tips: The shanks can be braised up to a day ahead, cooled, then refrigerated overnight. Warm them in a 300°F oven for 20 to 25 minutes before serving. The gremolata can also be prepared up to a day ahead and refrigerated.

CHILES RELLENOS WITH POTATOES AND CHEESE

These meatless stuffed chiles have delicate flavor from a potato and cheese filling, with a touch of heat from ancho chile powder. If the chiles are on the small side you may want to cook extra so you'll have seconds available as needed. Take care when peeling and seeding the roasted chiles so that they remain as whole as possible.

1 medium russet potato will provide at least the 1½ cups grated potato needed. Let it cool completely before grating and blending with the cheeses. MAKES 6 SERVINGS

6 large poblano chiles, roasted (see page 222)

1½ cups coarsely shredded cooked russet potato

1 cup grated or crumbled queso fresco cheese

1 cup grated medium Cheddar cheese

⅓ cup minced yellow or white onion

½ teaspoon ancho chile powder

¾ teaspoon salt

Vegetable oil for frying

1 cup all-purpose flour

½ teaspoon freshly ground black pepper

3 eggs, separated

½ cup crème fraîche or sour cream

SAUCE

2 tablespoons vegetable oil

1 cup finely chopped yellow or white onion

3 cloves garlic, pressed or minced

1 can (14½ ounces) stewed tomatoes

1 teaspoon ground cumin

½ teaspoon ground cardamom

Salt and freshly ground black pepper

1. For the sauce, heat the oil in a medium skillet over medium heat. Add the chopped onion and garlic and cook, stirring, for 3 to 5 minutes, until tender and aromatic. Stir in the tomatoes (with their liquid), cumin, and cardamom. Simmer for about 10 minutes, or until the sauce has thickened, crushing any larger tomato pieces with the back of the spoon. Season to taste with salt and pepper. Set aside.

2. Make a small slit lengthwise down the side of each roasted chile and gently scrape out the seeds with a knife, taking care not to pierce the flesh. Toss together the potato, cheeses, minced onion, chile powder, and ¼ teaspoon of the salt in a large bowl until well blended. Spoon the filling down the length of each chile, about ½ cup each, and slightly overlap the sides to fully enclose the filling; don't overstuff the chiles or they'll burst.

3. Preheat the oven to 350°F. Line a baking sheet with paper towels.

4. Pour about 2 inches of vegetable oil into a Dutch oven or other deep pot and heat over medium heat to 370°F. Combine the flour and pepper on a large plate and stir to mix. Roll the chiles in the flour, patting to remove excess, and set aside on a plate. Beat the egg whites until stiff peaks form, adding the remaining ½ teaspoon salt about halfway through. Beat the egg yolks in a small bowl and then fold them gently into the egg whites.

5. When the oil is heated, roll the chiles in the flour, patting to remove the excess. Coat one of the chiles in the egg mixture and very gently slide into the hot oil. Repeat with another chile, cooking two at a time. Fry for about 1 minute until browned, then turn and brown the other side. (I use a flat spatula to gently roll each chile over; be careful not to break the skin of the chile as you do.) Carefully transfer the chiles to the baking sheet and repeat with the remaining chiles.

6. When all 6 chiles have been fried, remove the paper towel from the baking sheet and bake the chiles in the oven for about 5 minutes, or until the cheese is fully melted. Reheat the sauce while the chiles are baking.

7. Spoon the sauce onto warmed plates, top with the chiles rellenos, and serve with dollops of crème fraîche on top.

Menu Ideas: The bright flavors of Ceviche with Papaya and Mint (page 12) will be a great precursor to this slightly rich main course. Then serve Spicy Spanish Rice (page 139) alongside the chiles. You can serve smaller stuffed chiles as a first course before simple grilled fish (with the Spanish rice), or as a side dish to any simple meat.

Do-Ahead Tips: The chiles can be stuffed up to 8 hours in advance, covered with plastic wrap, and refrigerated. They should be coated in egg, fried, and baked just before serving. The sauce can be made up to a day in advance.

CHICKEN TAGINE WITH APRICOTS AND ALMONDS

This tagine is an ideal example of Morocco's vibrant cuisine: chicken braised with warm spices, dried apricots, honey, and vegetables in a stew of incomparable fragrance and flavor. I prefer to use chicken thigh meat; the darker meat stays moist and tender when simmered. You can use chicken breast pieces if you prefer, but avoid overcooking. MAKES 6 SERVINGS

¼ cup all-purpose flour

2 teaspoons ground cinnamon

2 teaspoons ground ginger

1½ teaspoons salt

1 teaspoon ground cumin

1 teaspoon ground turmeric

1 teaspoon freshly ground black pepper

3 pounds boneless, skinless chicken thighs, each cut into thirds

3 tablespoons olive oil

3 tablespoons unsalted butter

1 large yellow onion, chopped

1 large red bell pepper, cored, seeded, and chopped

6 cloves garlic, pressed or minced

1 tablespoon finely chopped shallot

1 cup chicken stock (page 83) or top-quality chicken broth

¼ teaspoon saffron threads

5 sprigs fresh flat-leaf parsley

5 sprigs fresh cilantro

2⅓ cups water

1 cup dried apricots, each halved

¼ cup honey

2 cinnamon sticks

2 cups couscous

¾ cup toasted blanched whole almonds (see page 222)

1. Stir together the flour, cinnamon, ginger, salt, cumin, turmeric, and pepper in a large bowl. In batches, add the chicken and toss well to evenly coat.

2. Heat the oil and butter in a deep sauté pan over medium heat. Working in batches, brown the chicken pieces for a few minutes on each side and transfer to a plate. Set aside.

3. Add the onion, bell pepper, garlic, and shallot to the pan and cook for 3 to 5 minutes, until just beginning to soften. Return the chicken to the pan with the chicken stock and saffron. Tie together the parsley and cilantro sprigs with kitchen string and add to the pan. Cover and cook over medium-low heat for about 30 minutes, until the chicken is tender and cooked through. (The liquids should simmer gently, not boil; decrease the heat if needed.)

4. While the chicken is cooking, combine 1 cup of the water with the apricots, honey, and cinnamon sticks in a small saucepan. Bring just to a boil over medium-high heat. Decrease the heat to medium-low and simmer, stirring occasionally, for about 25 minutes, or until the apricots are plump and the liquid is reduced to a thick glaze.

5. Add the apricot mixture to the chicken and continue simmering for 10 minutes. Check for seasoning, adding more salt or pepper to taste. Discard the cinnamon sticks and herb bundle.

6. Place the couscous in a medium heatproof bowl. Bring the remaining 1⅓ cups water to a boil, pour over the couscous, and stir to mix. Cover the bowl with foil to seal securely and set aside for 5 minutes. Fluff the couscous with a fork and spoon it onto individual plates. Top the couscous with the chicken mixture. Scatter the almonds over and serve.

Menu Ideas: I like to start this tagine dinner with Smoky Moroccan Meatballs (page 11) and a tray of Crudités with Spicy Red Pepper Dip (page 28). Bring everyone to the table with Endive and Radicchio Salad (page 42). Finish the feast with Moroccan-Style Biscotti (page 174) or your favorite store-bought cookies.

Do-Ahead Tips: The tagine can be prepared up to a day in advance and refrigerated. Slowly reheat over medium-low heat before serving.

VEAL CHOPS
WITH GREEN PEPPERCORNS AND ROSEMARY

When brined, green peppercorns take on a surprisingly mild flavor, so don't be shy about using the quantity I call for here. I prefer the more tender veal rib chops, but you can use loin chops as well. **MAKES 6 SERVINGS**

6 cloves garlic, coarsely chopped

1½ tablespoons coarsely chopped fresh rosemary

½ cup extra-virgin olive oil

2 teaspoons salt

3 tablespoons green peppercorns in brine, drained

6 (8- to 10-ounce) veal rib chops, about 1 inch thick

Menu Ideas: This simple but elegant entrée will be wonderful with Roasted Smashed Potatoes with Garlic and Herbs (page 159) and Sautéed Spinach with Mustard Sauce (page 158). Start things off with Choux Puffs with Salmon and Shrimp (page 36) and Endive and Radicchio Salad (page 42). Vanilla Zabaglione in Chocolate Cups (page 181) will finish the dinner in style.

Do-Ahead Tips: The peppercorn oil can be made up to 4 hours in advance and left to sit at room temperature. The chops need to be broiled just before serving.

1. Preheat the boiler. Line a broiler pan with aluminum foil and lightly oil the foil.

2. Pile the garlic and rosemary together on the chopping board and finely chop them together, to help blend their flavors. Heat the olive oil in a small saucepan over medium-low heat. Add the rosemary/garlic mixture and salt and cook, stirring, for 2 to 3 minutes, until the garlic is just softened and aromatic but not browned. Add the peppercorns, warm for about 1 minute, then remove the pan from the heat.

3. Set the veal chops on the broiler pan and spoon half of the peppercorn mixture over them. Broil a few inches from the element for 5 minutes. Turn the chops and top with the remaining peppercorn mixture. Broil for 5 minutes longer, until about medium-rare. Increase the cooking time by 1 to 2 minutes each side if your chops are more than 1 inch thick or if you prefer the veal to be more well done. Let the meat sit on the pan for a few minutes before serving.

CHOUCROUTE MADE SIMPLE
(SAUERKRAUT WITH PORK)

One of my favorite dinners in Paris is a choucroute garni (sauerkraut piled high with a variety of meats). It's a specialty of the Alsatian region of France, where the sauerkraut is spiked with spices and cooked slowly with pork, sausages, and crisp white wine. This version is simpler to make, a one-pot recipe that verges on stew—it's a great savory dinner in a fraction of the time. Look for bulk, fresh sauerkraut in well-stocked delis and some specialty meat shops. It is also available bagged in most grocery stores' deli or meat section. MAKES 8 SERVINGS

8 ounces salt pork, cut into ½-inch pieces

2 medium yellow onions, sliced

3 cloves garlic, pressed or minced

1½ pounds smoked kielbasa, cut into 1-inch pieces

1 pound boneless pork butt, cut into 2-inch pieces

2 dried bay leaves

10 whole black peppercorns

10 juniper berries

6 whole allspice berries

3 pounds fresh sauerkraut

6 tablespoons tomato paste

1 cup dry white wine

1 smoked ham hock, split

2 cups top-quality beef broth

Menu Ideas: Sauerkraut always comes to the table with a large bowl of steamed potatoes. Waxy potatoes like Yukon Golds are perfect. Pass Dijon mustard for guests to add to taste. If you serve a salad, make it a simple green salad with Basic Vinaigrette (page 43). Consider sliced pears and blue cheese to end the meal, with a plate of Mother's Oatmeal Spice Cookies (page 189).

Do-Ahead Tips: The dish can be made up to 2 days in advance and refrigerated. Reheat over low heat or in a moderate oven before serving. If need be, add a little more beef stock when reheating.

1. Cook the salt pork in a large heavy pot, such as a Dutch oven, over medium heat for 5 to 7 minutes, until the meat is browned and the fat is rendered. Use a slotted spoon to transfer to paper towels to drain, reserving the fat in the pot. Add the onions and garlic to the pot and cook, stirring occasionally, for 8 to 10 minutes, until tender. Scoop into a bowl. Add the kielbasa and pork butt to the pot and cook, stirring occasionally, for about 15 minutes, until browned. Add to the bowl with the onions.

2. Preheat the oven to 350°F.

3. Tie together the bay leaves, peppercorns, juniper berries, and allspice in a piece of cheesecloth, secured with kitchen string. Rinse the sauerkraut several times and drain.

4. Add the tomato paste to the pot and cook, stirring, for 2 to 3 minutes, until lightly browned. Stir in the wine, then add the sauerkraut, spice bundle, and ham hock. Simmer moderately for 15 minutes. The mixture should not boil vigorously; decrease the heat if needed. Stir in the salt pork, onions, kielbasa, and pork butt. Add the beef broth and bring to a low boil over medium-high heat. Remove the pot from the heat, cover with foil, and top with its lid. Transfer to the oven and braise for 1½ to 2 hours, until the meat is very tender.

5. Transfer the ham hock pieces to a plate and let cool until easy to handle. Separate the meat from the bone and gristle and add the meat back to the pot. Discard the spice bundle. Spoon the sauerkraut and various meats into individual bowls and serve.

PAELLA
WITH CHICKEN AND SHELLFISH

I have taken many cooking classes over the years to learn the secrets of making the best paella. This recipe, which comes out well for me every time, is a combination of several different recipes I've played around with. Paella is, by nature, an elaborate recipe with many different ingredients to prepare, so I find that when I make it I might as well cook for a crowd; it's an easy recipe to multiply. My "small" paella pan is 16 inches, I often use a 24-inch pan, but have an even larger one that can accommodate double this recipe. For service, I often set the paella pan in the center of the dinner table or on a buffet table, and allow guests to serve themselves.

If you're able to buy prosciutto custom cut rather than prepackaged, ask for it to be cut in ¼-inch slices. MAKES 8 TO 10 SERVINGS

4 cups chicken stock (page 83) or top-quality
    chicken broth

3 cloves garlic, roasted (see page 221)

½ teaspoon ground turmeric

½ teaspoon dried thyme

¼ teaspoon saffron threads

½ cup all-purpose flour

2 teaspoons salt

1½ teaspoons freshly ground black pepper

12 ounces boneless, skinless chicken thighs, cut
    into 1-inch cubes

12 ounces boneless, skinless chicken breasts, cut
    into 1-inch cubes

4 tablespoons olive oil

6 ounces chorizo sausage, cut into ¼-inch slices

4 ounces prosciutto, cut into ¼-inch dice

1 medium yellow onion, finely chopped

2 cups medium-grain rice

1 (4-inch) sprig fresh rosemary

3 tablespoons freshly squeezed lemon juice

2 dried bay leaves

1 red and 1 yellow bell pepper, roasted, peeled,
    and cut into ¼-inch strips (see page 222)

1 pound live Manila or other hard-shell clams,
    rinsed

¼ cup dry vermouth

1. Preheat the oven to 350°F.

2. Warm the stock in a medium saucepan over medium heat. Add the roasted garlic, turmeric, thyme, and saffron. Keep warm over low heat, stirring occasionally, while cooking the chicken.

3. Toss together the flour, 1 teaspoon of the salt, and 1 teaspoon of the pepper in a medium bowl. Evenly coat the chicken pieces with the flour, patting to remove the excess.

4. Heat 2 tablespoons of the olive oil in a 16-inch paella pan or large, deep, ovenproof sauté pan over medium heat. In 2 or 3 batches, cook the chicken pieces for 3 to 4 minutes, until just browned; do not cook through. Set the chicken aside on a plate. Brown the chorizo and prosciutto in the same pan for 3 to 5 minutes; set aside with the chicken. Heat the remaining 2 tablespoons olive oil in the pan and cook the onion for about 5 minutes, until tender and aromatic. Stir in the rice, coating it evenly with the oil, and cook, stirring, for 2 to 3 minutes. Stir in 1½ cups of the warm stock mixture followed by the rosemary, lemon juice, bay leaves, and remaining 1 teaspoon salt and ½ teaspoon pepper. Cook over medium heat, stirring occasionally, for 2 to 3 minutes.

5. Add the browned chicken, chorizo, and prosciutto, and the roasted peppers, stirring to combine. Add the remaining warm stock and cover the pan with aluminum foil. Bake for 15 to 20 minutes, until the rice is about half-cooked and most of the liquid is absorbed. If the pan seems a bit dry after 12 or 15 minutes, drizzle ¼ cup more broth or water over and return to the oven, uncovered, for 3 to 5 minutes.

6. While the paella is cooking, place the clams and vermouth in a large saucepan over medium-high heat. Cover and cook, tossing the pan gently once or twice, for 3 to 5 minutes, until the clams have steamed open. Use a slotted spoon to scoop the clams into a large bowl. Discard any clams that

1½ pounds live mussels, scrubbed and debearded

1 pound large shrimp, peeled (with tail intact) and deveined

1 bunch green onions, chopped

1 cup thawed frozen peas

do not open. Add the mussels to the pan, cover, and cook for 3 to 5 minutes, until they open (discard any that do not open). Scoop them into the bowl with the clams. Strain the cooking liquid.

7. Scatter the shrimp over the paella and pour ⅓ to ½ cup of the clam and mussel cooking liquid over. Replace the foil and bake for 12 to 15 minutes, until the shrimp are nearly cooked through. Scatter the green onions over and tuck about a dozen each of the clams and mussels with their shells into the rice. Remove the rest of the clams and mussels from their shells and sprinkle them over the rice with the thawed peas. Bake, uncovered, 3 minutes longer. Discard the bay leaves and serve.

PAELLA NOTES: I love making paella for dinner parties and have a variety of pan sizes to choose from, to suit different events and group sizes. The French twist on paella making, as I use here, cooks the dish partly in the oven, a bit gentler cooking method using indirect heat.

In Spain, paella is more often made stovetop, or better yet over an outdoor fire. In this case, the direct heat on the bottom of the pan creates a wonderful brown, nutty-tasting "crust" that is one of the prizes of an expertly made paella.

I sometimes cook my paella on the barbecue for this reason, which you can try too. It just takes a bit of experimenting and practice to ensure that the browning is even and doesn't burn or stick, depending on the type of grill you have. Regulating the heat source and turning the pan often help achieve best results. Just keep an eye on the heat level and pay attention to the bottom of the pan, moving it off the heat now and then if it seems to be getting too hot.

Menu Ideas: While paella definitely stands alone as a solo dish for the main course, the fun of menu planning comes in sharing an array of tapas before the paella is served. See page 196 for a full menu plan based on this centerpiece recipe.

Do-Ahead Tips: Some elements of the paella can be prepared in advance and refrigerated for a day or two, such as the roasted garlic and roasted bell peppers. Otherwise, the paella will be at its best prepared just before serving.

LEMON AND SAGE CORNISH GAME HENS

Small game hens are usually found in the frozen food area of the grocery store and need to be defrosted before roasting; allow a couple days for them to thaw slowly in the refrigerator. Their compact size means less brine time needed than with larger birds, which is a bonus. You'll need a large deep bowl or 2 large resealable plastic bags to brine the birds; you can double the brine if you find you need more to cover them. **MAKES 8 SERVINGS**

4 (1¼-pound) Cornish game hens, rinsed

2 lemons, halved

8 large plus 8 small fresh sage leaves

4 tablespoons olive oil

2 teaspoons lemon pepper or freshly ground
    black pepper

BRINE

9 cups water

3 tablespoons salt

3 tablespoons Worcestershire sauce

1 tablespoon garlic powder

1½ teaspoons freshly ground white pepper

GARLIC BUTTER

½ cup unsalted butter, at room temperature

5 cloves garlic, pressed or minced

1 tablespoon finely grated lemon zest

3 tablespoons freshly squeezed lemon juice

⅓ cup minced fresh flat-leaf parsley

1 teaspoon minced fresh sage

Menu Ideas: Sweet Onions and Rice (page 153) is a perfect match for these roasted hens. Add Sautéed Tiny Tomatoes with Chile Flakes (page 144) for vibrant color and flavor.

Do-Ahead Tips: The hens can be brined up to 24 hours in advance. The garlic butter can be made up to 2 days ahead and refrigerated. They can be prepped and stuffed with garlic butter up to 3 hours before roasting, but roast the birds shortly before serving.

1. For the brine, combine the water, salt, Worcestershire sauce, garlic powder, and white pepper in a very large bowl or stockpot large enough to hold the game hens. Let sit, whisking occasionally, until the salt is dissolved. Add the game hens, cover the bowl with plastic wrap, and refrigerate for at least 12 or up to 24 hours. Turn the hens a few times to be sure they brine evenly.

2. For the garlic butter, combine the butter, garlic, lemon zest, lemon juice, parsley, and sage in a small bowl and stir to thoroughly blend. Refrigerate until ready to serve, but allow the butter to come to room temperature before using.

3. Preheat the oven to 425°F.

4. Drain the hens, discarding the brine. Rinse them under cold water and pat dry with paper towels. Place a lemon half in each hen cavity. Rub the large sage leaves between your palms to help release their aroma and add 2 leaves to each hen cavity.

5. Lift the skin on the breasts with your fingers and rub one-quarter of the soft garlic butter between the skin and breast meat of each hen. Slip a small sage leaf into both sides of each hen breast as well. Rub the outside of each hen with the olive oil and sprinkle with the lemon pepper. Tie together the leg ends on each hen with kitchen string.

6. Set the hens in a large roasting pan breast up and roast for 35 minutes. Turn the hens onto their sides and roast for 15 to 20 minutes longer, until the thigh juices run clear when pierced with a knife or an instant read thermometer registers 175°F. Transfer the hens to a platter and scoop out the lemon halves. Cover the hens with foil. Let sit for 10 minutes before serving.

7. Set the roasting pan over medium heat and boil 3 to 5 minutes to reduce the cooking juices by half. Squeeze the juice from 2 of the lemon halves and add them to the cooking juices.

8. Use poultry shears or other heavy kitchen shears to halve each bird, cutting first down the center of the breastbone, then down either side of the backbone (discard the backbone). Set the hen halves on individual plates and spoon some of the roasting juices over.

WINE-BRAISED CORNED BEEF
WITH BROWN SUGAR GLAZE

St. Patrick's Day is a favorite holiday of my good friend, Joe McDonnal. He began creating delicious, elaborate parties in the day's honor many years ago. The party has become a hallmark event every March, with this dish as a centerpiece. Most corned beef recipes simmer the meat fully covered in liquid; Joe braises the meat with red wine in the oven. The aroma is amazing while it cooks, reminiscent of mulled wine.

This recipe will be all the better if you start with a top-quality corned beef. Some butchers and other specialty markets make their own corned beef, which is worth seeking out. I buy mine from Market-House Corned Beef in Seattle, often as much as 10 pounds for a big dinner. If the only corned beef you're able to find is vacuum sealed, drain it well and rinse several times before proceeding. I don't bother with the spice packet that comes with the meat, using more aromatic jarred pickling spices instead. Any leftover corned beef will make phenomenal sandwiches the next day. **MAKES 8 TO 10 SERVINGS**

1 (4-pound) whole uncooked corned beef

3 tablespoons pickling spices

1 bottle (750 ml) dry red wine, or more if needed

BROWN SUGAR GLAZE
½ cup packed dark brown sugar

2 tablespoons dry sherry

2 tablespoons Dijon mustard

Menu Ideas: For ideal side dishes, choose from Cauliflower and Tomato Gratin (page 154), Old-Fashioned Green Beans with Bacon (page 142), Tiny Potatoes with Hot Bacon Dressing (page 132), and Classic Cornbread (page 149). You might also want to pass bowls of Dijon mustard or horseradish.

Do-Ahead Tips: The corned beef can be cooked a day in advance. Let cool in the braising pan, then cover with foil and refrigerate. Let come to room temperature before reheating in a 350°F oven for about 15 minutes before serving.

1. Preheat the oven to 350°F.

2. Set the corned beef fat side up in a baking dish. Sprinkle the spices over. Pour the red wine into the dish to come about halfway up the sides of the meat; add more wine if needed. Cover the pan with foil and braise the meat in the oven for about 4 hours, until the meat is fork-tender.

3. For the glaze, stir together the brown sugar, sherry, and mustard in a small bowl.

4. When the meat is tender, remove the pan from the oven and discard the foil. Scrape the spices off the surface of the meat and carefully ladle off about two-thirds of the wine (too much liquid will wash away the glaze). Drizzle one-quarter of the glaze over the meat. Return the pan, uncovered, to the oven and roast for 40 minutes longer, drizzling another layer of glaze over the meat every 10 minutes.

5. Transfer the corned beef to a cutting board, cover loosely with foil, and let sit 10 minutes. Cut across the grain into slices and serve.

HERB-RUBBED LAMB CHOPS
WITH RAITA

I prefer rib lamb chops for this preparation over loin chops, which are typically thicker and have meat on either side of the bone. But either can be used here. Count on 2 or 3 chops per person, depending on the appetites of your guests and what else is on the menu. Raita, a classic Indian sauce, complements the rich, savory lamb chops with refreshing yogurt and cucumber. You can substitute a timeless classic, mint jelly, for the raita to accompany the lamb chops, or serve both. MAKES 4 TO 6 SERVINGS

¼ cup olive oil

4 cloves garlic, pressed or minced

2 tablespoons chopped fresh flat-leaf parsley

4 teaspoons chopped fresh mint

4 teaspoons chopped fresh oregano

2 teaspoons chopped fresh thyme

12 lamb chops (about 3 pounds)

Salt and freshly ground black pepper

1 lemon, cut into wedges

Fresh mint sprigs, for serving

RAITA

8 ounces plain yogurt (not nonfat)

1 cucumber, peeled, seeded, and finely chopped
    or coarsely grated

1 teaspoon salt

¾ teaspoon ground cumin, toasted (see page 222)

¼ teaspoon cayenne pepper, toasted
    (see page 222)

¼ teaspoon ground coriander, toasted
    (see page 222)

½ cup very thinly sliced sweet or yellow onion

¼ cup chopped fresh mint

½ teaspoon sugar

¼ teaspoon ground cinnamon

1. For the raita, line a small sieve or colander with cheesecloth and add the yogurt. Let sit over a bowl to drain of excess liquid for 1 hour. Toss the cucumber with the salt in a small bowl and let sit for 30 minutes. Rinse the cucumber under cold water and drain on paper towels.

2. In a medium bowl, combine the drained yogurt, cucumber, toasted spices, onion, mint, sugar, and cinnamon. Stir well to mix, then season to taste with salt and pepper. Cover and refrigerate for at least 1 hour before serving.

3. Blend the olive oil, garlic, parsley, mint, oregano, and thyme into a coarse paste in a mini-processor or blender, or with a mortar and pestle. Rub the paste evenly over the lamb chops. Cover and refrigerate for at least 1 hour.

4. Preheat an outdoor grill or the broiler. Season the lamb chops with salt and pepper. Grill or broil, turning once, for 6 to 10 minutes, until medium rare. (Loin chops may need an extra minute or two per side.) Transfer the chops to a plate, cover loosely with foil, and let sit for a few minutes.

5. Arrange the lamb chops on individual plates, with lemon wedges and sprigs of mint alongside. Pass the raita separately.

Menu Ideas: This recipe seems most suited to summertime, when I'll start the meal with Corn Chowder with Roasted Peppers (page 71), or perhaps Radish and Fennel Salad (page 46). Ratatouille with Fresh Rosemary (page 152) and a few spears of simple steamed asparagus are ideal partners for the lamb chops.

Do-Ahead Tips: The raita can be made up to 24 hours in advance. The lamb chops can be marinated up to 8 hours in advance. The lamb chops should be cooked just before serving, though I also serve them at room temperature for a casual buffet or on a picnic, in which case the chops can be cooked a few hours in advance.

LAMB SHANKS TAGINE
WITH PRESERVED LEMON

This tagine recipe is inspired by one shared with me by John Sundstrom, the chef-owner of Lark restaurant in Seattle. I love his adaptation with the generous dose of pungent, tart lemon flavor to contrast the earthy character of the lamb.

The traditional tagine dish is earthenware with a conical shape that draws condensed steam from cooking back down onto the ingredients for maximum moisture. They are typically not large enough for volume cooking such as this. I cook the lamb shanks in a large roasting pan and serve them over the couscous in a colorful tagine, which makes a striking addition to the table. **MAKES 8 SERVINGS**

8 (1- to 1¼-pound) lamb shanks

2 teaspoons salt

1 teaspoon freshly ground black pepper

1 cup all-purpose flour

½ cup olive oil

4 carrots, diced

1 large yellow onion, chopped

1 large fennel bulb, trimmed, halved, and sliced

6 cloves garlic, coarsely chopped

1¼ cups dry white wine

1 can (14½ ounces) diced tomatoes

2 teaspoons coriander seeds, toasted (see page 222)

1½ teaspoons cumin seeds, toasted (see page 222)

2 teaspoons fennel seeds

1 (2-inch) cinnamon stick

8 small preserved lemons

1½ cups pitted green olives

5 cups chicken stock (page 83) or top-quality chicken broth

6 tablespoons freshly squeezed lemon juice

1 cup plain yogurt

2 to 3 tablespoons harissa

¼ cup chopped fresh cilantro

1. Preheat the oven to 325°F.

2. Season the lamb shanks with 1 teaspoon of the salt and the pepper, then coat with the flour, patting to remove the excess. Heat the oil in a large heavy pot, such as a Dutch oven, over medium heat. Brown the lamb shanks well on all sides, 3 or 4 at a time, for about 5 minutes. Transfer to a plate and set aside.

3. Add the carrots, onion, and fennel to the pot. Cook, stirring occasionally, for 5 to 7 minutes, until lightly browned. Stir in the garlic. Add the wine, tomatoes, coriander, cumin, fennel, and cinnamon stick. Cook over medium-low heat, stirring occasionally, for about 15 minutes, until the vegetables are tender and the liquid has thickened.

4. Quarter the preserved lemons, then cut away and discard the soft flesh. Cut the lemon skins into ⅛-inch strips.

5. Return the lamb shanks to the pot. Scatter the lemon and the olives evenly over and around the meat. Add the chicken stock and remaining 1 teaspoon salt. Cover and braise in the oven 3 to 4 hours, until the meat is very tender and begins pulling away from the bones (cooking time will vary with the size of the shanks). Transfer the shanks to a platter. Set the pot over medium-high heat and boil for 10 to 20 minutes to reduce the sauce by one-quarter. Stir in the lemon juice and check for seasoning. Remove the cinnamon stick.

6. Combine the yogurt and harissa in a small bowl and stir to mix. Arrange the lamb shanks on individual plates (on the couscous, if serving). Top with the sauce and sprinkle with cilantro. Pass the harissa/yogurt mixture separately.

PRESERVED LEMONS: Preserved lemons are a staple in Moroccan cuisine and other dishes with North African or Middle Eastern influence. They are made quite simply by curing fresh lemons in lemon juice and salt for about a month. It's not difficult to do at home but does require a certain amount of prior planning. Look for prepared preserved lemon on well-stocked grocery shelves or at gourmet markets.

Menu Ideas: Serve the shanks with Lemon Israeli Couscous (page 138). Aspargus Salad with Champagne Vinaigrette (page 63) is an ideal first course. Mint tea, Oranges with Candied Zest (page 187), and Moroccan-Style Biscotti (page 174) can cap off the meal.

Do-Ahead Tips: The tagine can be made up to 2 days in advance; return the shanks to the sauce, cover, and refrigerate. Warm the shanks gently in a 300°F oven for 10 to 15 minutes before serving.

SALMON
WITH WILD MUSHROOM SAUCE

Wild mushrooms are one of the most distinctive ingredients we're blessed with in the Northwest. It's hard to imagine a more Northwest partnership than wild mushrooms with local wild salmon. The cooking technique here sautés the fish just on the skin side, so the skin gets crispy-brown while the surface of the fish is very tender and delicate.

A dozen or more varieties of wild mushrooms are available throughout the year in well-stocked produce sections and at farmers' markets. During spring I tend to use morel mushrooms for this dish and in the fall the prolific chanterelle, but other types can be utilized as well. You can even use shiitake or other cultivated mushrooms if you're unable to find wild mushrooms. Do not wash wild mushrooms with water. When these delicate mushrooms get wet they become soggy and lose much of their flavor. Instead, use a small mushroom brush to clean off any dirt and leaves. MAKES 6 SERVINGS

2 tablespoons olive oil

2 cloves garlic, coarsely chopped

6 (6-ounce) skin-on salmon fillet pieces, pin bones removed

2 tablespoons finely chopped fresh flat-leaf parsley

WILD MUSHROOM SAUCE

3 tablespoons unsalted butter

3 tablespoons olive oil

½ cup minced shallots or yellow onion

12 ounces wild mushrooms, trimmed and coarsely chopped

1 clove garlic, pressed or minced

¼ cup Cognac or other brandy

¾ cup chicken stock (page 83) or top-quality chicken broth

½ cup whipping cream

1 teaspoon minced fresh thyme

Salt and freshly ground black pepper

1. For the mushroom sauce, heat the butter and 2 tablespoons of the oil in a large skillet over medium heat. Add the shallots and cook, stirring occasionally, for 5 minutes, or until tender and aromatic. Add half of the mushrooms and the garlic and cook, stirring occasionally, for 5 minutes. Add the Cognac and carefully flame the brandy with a long match. When the flames subside, add the chicken stock. Simmer for 5 to 8 minutes, until reduced by one-quarter. Remove the pan from the heat, stir in the cream, and let cool slightly. Purée the mixture in a food processor or blender until smooth; set aside.

2. Chop the remaining mushrooms more finely. Wipe out the skillet and heat the remaining 1 tablespoon olive oil over medium heat. Add the finely chopped mushrooms and sauté for about 5 minutes, until tender. Add the mushroom purée and thyme and season to taste with salt and pepper. Keep the sauce warm over very low heat while cooking the salmon, or gently reheat just before serving.

3. Heat the olive oil in a large skillet, preferably nonstick, over medium heat. Add the garlic, remove the pan from the heat, and let sit to infuse for 5 minutes. Scoop the garlic into a small dish (save for another use) and return the skillet to medium heat. Season the salmon with salt and pepper. Add the pieces to the pan skin side down and cook without turning for about 10 minutes, or until the skin is nicely browned and the flesh is nearly opaque across the top. If the tops are not cooked in that time, cover the skillet loosely with a piece of foil for 1 to 2 minutes, which will help the tops cook.

4. Transfer the salmon pieces to individual plates and spoon the mushroom sauce over. Garnish with a sprinkle of parsley and serve.

Menu Ideas: In the spring, I serve this salmon with Orzo with Sugar Snap Peas (page 133) or Artichoke Risotto with Spring Peas and Mint (page 146). In the fall, I shift to a cool-weather side dish such as Tiny Potatoes with Hot Bacon Dressing (page 132) or Roasted Pepper and Corn Spoon Bread (page 155).

Do-Ahead Tips: The mushroom sauce can be made up to 2 hours in advance and refrigerated. Reheat the sauce gently (stir in another ¼ cup or so of stock if needed) and cook the salmon just before serving.

SALMON WITH LEMON AND DILL: Marilyn Harris, a great cook, author, and radio personality from Cincinnati, taught a class in the Sur La Table store in Berkeley, highlighting ways to cook salmon. I've never forgotten one preparation in particular that cures the salmon in sugar, kosher salt, and a handful of fresh dill. Wrapped tightly in plastic, it adds a surprising amount of flavor to the fish after just 1 hour in the refrigerator. (For 2 pounds salmon, use 2 teaspoons each salt and sugar and ¼ cup chopped fresh dill.) After rinsing off the cure and drying the salmon well, you can proceed with cooking the salmon any number of ways, including simple grilling or pan-frying.

I occasionally spread a thin layer of mayonnaise on the surface of the cured fillets, top with a slice or two of lemon and more fresh dill, then broil or bake. It makes for a rich delicious way to enjoy salmon, with added flavor from Marilyn's initial curing trick. Finish with a squeeze of lemon juice and maybe a dollop of tartar sauce (page 104) alongside.

SIDE DISHES

Sides can take on many different personalities, which is fun when it comes to planning dinner as you have so many options to choose from. By definition, a side is any dish that is served as a complement alongside the main course—which is usually meat, fish, or poultry. Side dishes, however, can be among the most versatile recipes of your repertoire. Many can often also serve as a stand-alone first course (pasta, risotto, fritters) and others can be a vegetarian main course (heartier gratins or robust vegetable dishes such as ratatouille).

There are a few things to consider to help narrow down your side dish choices. Typically, you'll have already chosen a main course, the starting point. Consider then whether you're in the market for a starch side, a vegetable, or both. If your main course has a starch element already—potatoes, rice, or grains—you may want to serve only a vegetable side. If the entrée is on the lighter side, lean toward a richer or starchier side to balance. For many dinners you'll want to have a small serving each of a vegetable and a starch.

If your main course has a saucy element, choose a side dish that will meld well with the sauce, such as couscous, rice, or mashed potatoes. Also think about overall balance, so if your main course is on the rich side, opt for less rich side dishes; or if your entrée has strong flavors of mustard or spice, it will be best to pair it with milder flavors that won't compete.

TINY POTATOES
WITH HOT BACON DRESSING

Fingerling potatoes—the knobby, small potatoes that look vaguely finger-like—are ideal in this recipe. Their slightly nutty, earthy flavor is perfectly matched to the bacon and pecan embellishments. If you're using new potatoes that aren't tiny, halve or quarter them before cooking.
MAKES 6 SERVINGS

½ cup pecan pieces

1 tablespoon unsalted butter, melted

¼ teaspoon salt

¼ teaspoon cayenne pepper

2 pounds fingerling potatoes or small new potatoes, scrubbed

HOT BACON DRESSING

6 strips thick-cut bacon, cut into ¼-inch pieces

1 teaspoon crushed mustard seeds

½ cup minced green onions

¼ cup dry sherry

¼ cup apple cider vinegar

¼ cup vegetable oil

2 tablespoons chopped fresh flat-leaf parsley

1 tablespoon honey

1. Preheat the oven to 350°F.

2. Place the pecan pieces in a small bowl, drizzle the butter over, and add the salt and cayenne pepper. Toss to evenly coat, then scatter in a baking dish. Toast in the oven for 8 to 10 minutes, until lightly browned and aromatic. Set aside to cool.

3. Place the potatoes in a large pan of salted water and bring to a boil over high heat. Decrease the heat to medium and simmer for 10 to 15 minutes, depending on their size, until the potatoes are tender but not falling apart. Drain well, then transfer to a large bowl.

4. For the dressing, fry the bacon in a large skillet over medium heat for 5 to 7 minutes, until browned and crisp. Use a slotted spoon to transfer the bacon to paper towels to drain. Discard all but about 2 tablespoons of the bacon fat from the skillet. Add the mustard seeds and cook for about 1 minute, until lightly toasted, then stir in the green onions, sherry, vinegar, oil, parsley, and honey.

5. Pour the dressing over the still-warm potatoes, add the toasted pecans and bacon, and toss to mix. Set aside for 30 minutes, stirring occasionally, before serving. Serve at room temperature for a salad. The potatoes can also be reheated in the oven to serve as a hot side dish.

Menu Ideas: This recipe can do double duty, served either as a warm potato salad for a casual menu or backyard barbecue, or as a side dish to roasted or grilled meat. The potatoes will also be perfect alongside Grilled Honey and Mustard Ribs (page 108) or Four-Star Fried Chicken (page 110). They also work well as part of a buffet as well, since they are delicious even at room temperature.

Do-Ahead Tips: The recipe can be fully prepared up to a day in advance and refrigerated. Allow to come to room temperature or reheat in the oven before serving, depending on the menu.

ORZO
WITH SUGAR SNAP PEAS

Sugar snap peas and snow peas may both be used in this recipe, and both tend to be available fresh year-round. I particularly love the extra crunch and sweetness that the plumper sugar snap peas have. The peas play well off the rice-shaped orzo pasta, with a fresh dose of herbal flavor from dill as a final accent. **MAKES 8 SERVINGS**

1½ cups orzo

2 tablespoons unsalted butter, cut into pieces

2 tablespoons olive oil

1½ pounds sugar snap peas, trimmed and
    halved crosswise on the bias

6 cloves garlic, pressed or minced

2 tablespoons chopped fresh dill

Salt and freshly ground black pepper

Menu Ideas: This dish may be served hot or cold, a great side dish option for a buffet or picnic with Four-Star Fried Chicken (page 110) and Coleslaw with Lemon-Caper Dressing (page 64).

Do-Ahead Tips: You can prepare the recipe 4 to 5 hours in advance and refrigerate. Serve warmed or at room temperature.

1. Bring a medium pan of salted water to a rolling boil. Add the orzo and cook over medium-high heat for about 8 minutes, until al dente. Drain the pasta well, then return to the empty pan. Add the butter, tossing gently so that it melts and evenly coats the orzo. Set aside.

2. Heat the olive oil in a large skillet over medium heat. Add the peas and garlic and cook, stirring, for 4 to 5 minutes, until the peas are cooked but still crisp and the garlic is lightly browned. Take care that the garlic doesn't burn; decrease the heat to medium-low if needed.

3. Add the orzo to the skillet and toss gently to blend with the peas. Stir in the dill with salt and pepper to taste.

ASPARAGUS WITH GARLIC

Though asparagus is now available year-round, I still thrill when the first local spears appear each spring, plump, tender, and full of flavor. Unless the spears are thin, I peel away the tough outer skin from the lower portion of the spears before cooking. Depending on the thickness of the spears, I serve 6 to 10 per person.

For a little added flavor, sprinkle the asparagus with minced fresh herbs or grated Parmesan cheese just before serving.
MAKES 8 SERVINGS

2 pounds asparagus, trimmed

2 tablespoons unsalted butter

1 tablespoon olive oil

2 cloves garlic, pressed or minced

Salt and freshly ground black pepper

1. Bring a deep skillet or large saucepan of lightly salted water to a boil and fill a large bowl with ice water. Add the asparagus and blanch for 1 to 2 minutes. With a slotted spoon, transfer the asparagus to the ice water until cool, then drain well on paper towels.

2. Heat the butter and olive oil in a large skillet or sauté pan over medium heat. Add the garlic and cook, stirring, for 1 to 2 minutes, until beginning to soften but not browned. Add the asparagus and roll gently back and forth in the pan to evenly coat with the garlic mixture. Cook for 2 to 3 minutes, until the asparagus is well heated. Season to taste with salt and pepper and serve.

Menu Ideas: This is an ever-pleasing side dish that can be paired well with a wide range of entrées, from Grilled Honey and Mustard Ribs (page 108) to Salmon with Wild Mushroom Sauce (page 128).

Do-Ahead Tips: The asparagus can be blanched up to 24 hours in advance, cooled quickly in a cold water bath, and dried well. Wrap the asparagus in a damp kitchen towel and refrigerate until needed. Sauté the garlic and asparagus just before serving.

WHITE BEAN AND WATERCRESS GRATIN

Peppery, vibrant watercress with creamy white beans is a delicious combination that pairs well with many main courses. Cooking with dry beans often means an overnight soak in cold water before cooking them. But I use a shortcut that allows you to complete the dish in the same day. **MAKES 10 TO 12 SERVINGS**

1 pound dry white beans (Great Northern or navy)

1 large yellow onion, finely chopped

3 sprigs fresh thyme

2 dried bay leaves

2½ teaspoons salt

¼ teaspoon freshly ground black pepper

3 tablespoons olive oil

1 tablespoon white wine vinegar

4 cloves garlic, pressed or minced

2 cups well packed watercress sprigs, stems removed (about 2½ ounces)

1½ cups grated Gruyère or Emmenthaler cheese

1 cup plain dried bread crumbs

Menu Ideas: One of my favorite dinners starts with Bibb Lettuce and Grapefruit Salad (page 52), followed by Rack of Lamb with Rosemary and Garlic (page 102) with this gratin and Asparagus with Garlic (page 134) alongside. Cap things off with Chocolate Espresso Pots de Crème (page 167).

Do-Ahead Tips: The bean mixture can be prepared up to 2 days in advance. Stir in the watercress and bake the dish just before serving.

1. To quick-soak the beans, place in a large saucepan with enough cold water to cover by 2 inches. Bring to a boil over high heat. Decrease the heat to medium and simmer, uncovered, for 2 minutes. Let sit for 1 hour.

2. Drain the beans well and return to the pan. Add the onion, thyme, bay leaves, 1 teaspoon of the salt, and the pepper. Add cold water to cover by about 1 inch (about 5 cups). Bring to a boil over high heat, then decrease the heat to medium-low. Simmer for 45 minutes to 1 hour, until the beans are tender. Drain the beans over a bowl to retain the cooking liquid; discard the thyme sprigs and bay leaves. Set aside 1 cup of the beans and place the rest in a large bowl. Return the cooking liquid to the pan and boil over medium-high heat for 15 minutes, until reduced to about 1½ cups.

3. Preheat the oven to 375°F.

4. In a blender, purée the 1 cup reserved beans with the reduced cooking liquid, olive oil, vinegar, half of the garlic, and the remaining 1½ teaspoons salt. Add the purée to the whole beans, stirring gently to blend.

5. Stir the watercress (reserving a small handful of leaves for garnish), ¾ cup of the cheese, and ½ cup of the bread crumbs into the bean mixture. Scrape into a 12-inch gratin dish. In a small bowl, stir together the remaining garlic, ¾ cup cheese, and ½ cup bread crumbs. Sprinkle over the beans. Bake the gratin for about 25 minutes, until bubbly and golden. Spoon the beans onto individual plates and garnish with the remaining watercress sprigs.

MINI CORN MUFFINS
WITH ROASTED GARLIC AND FRESH HERBS

These muffins are so flavorful they don't need butter or any other embellishment. They make a great accompaniment to a salad or simple meat dish, but also can be a nibble served on a cocktail table. I also bake the muffins in madeleine pans for a classy shell-like shape for variation. **MAKES 36 MINI MUFFINS**

1 cup buttermilk

⅛ teaspoon baking soda

1¼ cups all-purpose flour

1 cup plus 2 tablespoons yellow cornmeal

1 teaspoon minced fresh rosemary

½ teaspoon minced fresh thyme

½ teaspoon salt

½ teaspoon baking powder

½ cup sugar

6 tablespoons unsalted butter, at room temperature

2 teaspoons mashed roasted garlic (see page 221)

1 egg

Menu Ideas: These little muffins can accompany any salad (in place of more traditional bread) or main course. I also like to serve them at a buffet, particularly one showcasing a spiral-cut ham or roasted turkey. The muffins can be split and a small piece of ham or turkey slipped in for a delightful mini sandwich.

Do-Ahead Tips: The muffins are at their best if baked no more than a few hours before serving. They can, however, be frozen for a couple of weeks, in a resealable plastic bag or well wrapped in foil.

1. Preheat the oven to 350°F. Spray a 36-cup mini muffin pan with nonstick spray.

2. Combine the buttermilk and baking soda in a small bowl and set aside for 1 to 2 minutes. Combine the flour, cornmeal, rosemary, thyme, salt, and baking powder in a medium bowl and stir with a whisk to evenly blend.

3. In a large bowl, cream together the sugar and butter with an electric mixer at medium speed until well blended and fluffy, then blend in the roasted garlic. Add the egg and the buttermilk mixture and continue blending on low until smooth. With the mixer at low speed, slowly add the dry ingredients, working just until blended (do not overmix or the muffins will be heavy).

4. Spoon the batter into the muffin tins, filling each about three-quarters full. Bake for about 15 minutes, until the muffins are puffed and the tops spring back lightly when pressed. Let cool for a few minutes in the pan before un-molding onto a wire rack. Serve warm or at room temperature.

BRAISED RED CABBAGE

My grandmother often made red cabbage in a similar preparation to this. The memory of the sweet and tart flavors on fall evenings reminds me of all the meals I was able to share with her. I rinse the cabbage in cold water as soon as I've sliced it, then shake away the excess water. This refreshes the cabbage and just enough water clings to it to help it wilt as it cooks.

Choose apples for this recipe that will hold together during cooking, preferably not-too-sweet apples that will complement the savory flavors of the dish. I find Fuji or Braeburn apples work well. **MAKES 8 SERVINGS**

6 strips thick-cut bacon, cut into ¼-inch pieces

2 tablespoons unsalted butter

1 sweet onion, halved and thinly sliced

1 (2-pound) head red cabbage, cored, thinly sliced, and rinsed with cold water

1 Fuji or Braeburn apple, cored, peeled, and diced

½ cup red wine vinegar

¼ cup packed light brown sugar

1 tablespoon molasses

1½ teaspoons salt

1 teaspoon minced fresh thyme

½ teaspoon freshly ground black pepper

1. Fry the bacon in a large skillet over medium heat for 8 to 10 minutes, until browned and crisp. Use a slotted spoon to transfer the bacon to paper towels to drain, reserving the bacon fat in the skillet. Add the butter to the skillet and, when it has melted, add the onion. Cook, stirring occasionally, for 10 to 12 minutes, until tender and aromatic (the onion shouldn't brown; decrease the heat to medium-low if needed).

2. Shake excess water from the cabbage and add to the skillet, a couple of handfuls at a time. Stirring frequently, allow each addition to cook down for 1 minute or so to make room before adding the next. Stir in the apple, vinegar, brown sugar, molasses, salt, thyme, and pepper. Cover the skillet loosely with its lid or a piece of foil. Cook over medium-low heat, stirring occasionally, for about 1 hour, until the cabbage is tender.

3. Spoon the braised cabbage onto individual plates and sprinkle with the bacon.

Menu Ideas: This is an ideal dish to serve alongside Wine-Braised Corned Beef with Brown Sugar Glaze (page 124), with steamed red potatoes as well. The cabbage would also pair nicely with the flavors of Braised Brisket with Onions (page 109) and Roasted Smashed Potatoes with Garlic and Herbs (page 159).

Do-Ahead Tip: The cabbage can be cooked up to 1 day in advance and reheated gently on the stovetop just before serving.

SPICY SPANISH RICE

Growing up, I loved Spanish rice, although it's become something of a forgotten side dish in the last couple of decades. But this wonderful, aromatic, comforting recipe deserves to have a comeback. Don't shy away from using canned tomatoes (drained of their juice) in place of diced fresh tomatoes when vine-ripened, flavorful tomatoes are not available. You can omit the bacon and use 1 tablespoon corn oil in place of the bacon fat for cooking the vegetables. **MAKES 6 TO 8 SERVINGS**

2 strips thick-cut bacon, finely diced

½ cup finely diced red bell pepper

½ cup finely diced green bell pepper

½ cup finely diced onion

1 jalapeño chile, cored, seeded, and finely diced

3 cloves garlic, pressed or minced

1 teaspoon minced fresh oregano or ½ teaspoon dried oregano

¾ teaspoon salt

¼ teaspoon freshly ground black pepper

1 cup long-grain white rice

¾ cup finely diced plum tomatoes

1¾ cups chicken stock (page 83) or top-quality chicken broth, or more if needed

1. Fry the bacon in a large skillet over medium heat for 3 to 5 minutes, until browned and crisp. Use a slotted spoon to transfer the bacon to paper towels to drain, reserving the bacon fat in the skillet.

2. Add the bell peppers, onion, and jalapeño to the skillet and cook, stirring, for 3 minutes, until tender and aromatic. Stir in the garlic, oregano, salt, and pepper until well blended. Add the rice and stir 3 minutes, until evenly coated and lightly toasted (some of the rice grains will begin turning opaque).

3. Stir in the tomatoes, followed by the chicken stock. Bring just to a boil over medium-high heat. Decrease the heat to low, cover, and cook for 20 minutes, or until the rice is tender and all liquid is absorbed. (If the rice is dry before it is tender, stir in another ¼ cup of the stock and cook about 5 minutes longer.) Stir with a fork, cover, and let sit off heat for 5 minutes. Stir in the bacon and taste the rice for seasoning, adding more salt or pepper to taste.

Menu Ideas: This is a nice contribution to any menu with south-of-the-border appeal, including Chiles Rellenos with Potatoes and Cheese (page 114) or your favorite soft tacos. Start things off with Radish and Fennel Salad (page 46) or, when fresh corn is at its best, Roasted Corn Salad (page 53). Finish your piquant meal with something refreshing, such as the Pomegranate Sorbet (page 183) or a simple scoop of vanilla ice cream with Mother's Oatmeal Spice Cookies (page 189).

Do-Ahead Tips: The rice can be cooked up to 3 hours in advance, reserving the bacon. Reheat in a low oven and stir in the bacon just before serving. Undercook the rice a bit if making in advance; it will continue to absorb liquid and will also cook more when reheated.

CHEESE-STUFFED TOMATOES
WITH LINGUINE

Every time I make this for family and friends, I smile as I remember all the fantastic meals shared with Lydie Marshall and her husband Wayne. Lydie, who has a wonderful cooking school in Nyons, France, inspired this dish, which I have enjoyed adapting over the years.

Rather than making a tomato sauce for this pasta dish, you stuff fresh tomatoes with a quick and easy blend of cheeses, herbs, and garlic, then roast the tomatoes until they're tender. Perched on a bed of linguine that's been tossed with seasoned buttery bread crumbs, the tomatoes and their cheesy stuffing create an instant sauce as your guests cut into them. Because it makes a bit of a delicious mess in doing so, it's best to serve the dish alone, in a shallow pasta or soup bowl, rather than on the same plate with other items. You can use Boursin in place of some or all of the goat cheese in the stuffing, if you like. **MAKES 6 SERVINGS**

6 (5-ounce) medium vine-ripened tomatoes

Salt

6 ounces herbed goat cheese

4 ounces mascarpone

⅓ cup whole milk

1 tablespoon minced fresh chives

1 tablespoon minced fresh thyme

1 clove garlic, pressed or minced

PASTA

8 ounces linguine or thin spaghetti

2 tablespoons unsalted butter

1 tablespoon olive oil

1 clove garlic, pressed or minced

½ cup plain dried bread crumbs

⅓ cup chopped fresh flat-leaf parsley

6 tablespoons freshly grated Parmesan cheese

6 tablespoons chopped fresh basil

1. Preheat the oven to 425°F.

2. Cut the top ½ inch from each tomato, reserving the tops. Using a melon baller or serrated grapefruit spoon, remove the seeds and flesh from the insides, leaving just the tomato shells. Lightly salt the interior of each tomato. Drain them upside down on a few layers of paper towels for 15 minutes.

3. Stir together the goat cheese, mascarpone, milk, chives, thyme, and garlic in a small bowl. Spoon the mixture into each tomato, top with the reserved tomato "lids," and set in a shallow baking dish. Bake the tomatoes until tender, about 25 minutes.

4. While the tomatoes are baking, bring a large pan of salted water to a boil over high heat. Add the pasta, stirring to separate the strands, and cook for 10 to 12 minutes, until al dente. While the pasta is cooking, heat the butter and oil in a small skillet over medium heat. Add the garlic and cook for a few seconds, then add the bread crumbs and continue to cook for 2 to 3 minutes, stirring often, until lightly toasted. Remove the skillet from the heat and stir in the parsley; set aside.

5. Drain the pasta well and toss it with the bread crumb mixture in a large bowl. Divide the pasta among 6 warmed pasta bowls, making a nest in each for a tomato. Sprinkle the pasta with the Parmesan cheese and set the stuffed tomatoes on top. Sprinkle the basil over and serve. Encourage your guests to cut into their tomato right away to allow the cheese to blend with the pasta.

Menu Ideas: This is best served as a solo course, whether a light main course with a salad beforehand, or as a precursor to a simple grilled meat entrée, such as rib eye steaks rubbed with minced fresh oregano.

Do-Ahead Tips: The tomatoes can be prepared and stuffed up to 6 hours in advance and refrigerated. They should be baked, and the pasta cooked, just before serving.

OLD-FASHIONED GREEN BEANS
WITH BACON

When I was young, I had a summer job of picking buckets of Blue Lake pole beans in fields not far from where we lived in Oregon. We also grew beans in our family garden, so summer beans were plentiful and enjoyed fresh or canned and frozen to eat throughout the year. This is one favorite preparation that I learned from my mother and grandmother. It's certainly not the mode today to cook beans as long as is called for here. But unless the green beans will end up in a salad where crunch is called for, I prefer to cook them to the point that they're tender.

You can use fresh or canned tomatoes; I tend to use fresh only when they're at their summertime best. When they aren't at their peak, a 14½-ounce can of diced tomatoes, drained, will give you the 1½ cups needed here. **MAKES 6 TO 8 SERVINGS**

2 pounds green beans, trimmed

6 strips thick-cut bacon, diced

½ cup finely chopped yellow onion

1 clove garlic, pressed or minced

1½ cups diced tomatoes (about ¾ pound)

Salt and freshly ground black pepper

Menu Ideas: These beans will be delicious alongside Braised Brisket with Onions (page 109), Barbecued Flank Steak (page 91), or Halibut with Nut Crust and Apple Vinaigrette (page 106). A scoop of Roasted Pepper and Corn Spoon Bread (page 155) will be an ideal accompaniment.

Do-Ahead Tips: You can cook the beans a few hours ahead, drain well, cover, and refrigerate. The onion-tomato mixture can also be prepared an hour or two in advance. Assemble and finish the dish just before serving.

1. Bring a large pan of salted water to a boil. Add the green beans, decrease the heat to medium, and cook, stirring occasionally, for 20 to 25 minutes, until the beans are soft but not mushy. The water shouldn't boil; decrease the heat to medium-low if needed. Drain the beans well and return to the empty pan.

2. While the beans are cooking, fry the bacon in a large skillet over medium heat for 8 to 10 minutes, until crisp and browned. With a slotted spoon, scoop the bacon onto paper towels to drain, reserving the fat in the skillet. Add the onion to the skillet and sauté over medium heat for 2 to 3 minutes, until tender and aromatic. Stir in the garlic and cook 1 minute longer.

3. Add the tomatoes to the skillet, decrease the heat to medium-low, and cook, stirring occasionally, for 5 minutes, until the tomato juices have thickened. Add the tomato mixture and the bacon to the green beans, toss well over medium heat to warm through, and season to taste with salt and pepper.

TWENTY-HOUR BAKED BEANS

Canned baked beans were the norm for so long, particularly when I was growing up. We'd happily sop up the sweet sauce with the brown bread my mother always served alongside. I created this version for the wonderful barbecues that we host, or go to, all year-round. The slow baking helps blend the flavors of molasses and spices. If you have enough ramekins, serve the beans in them so the sauce doesn't run all over the plate. **MAKES 10 TO 12 SERVINGS**

1 pound dry navy beans

4 strips thick-cut bacon, cut into ½-inch pieces

1 large yellow onion, finely chopped

1 red bell pepper, cored, seeded, and finely chopped

6 cloves garlic, pressed or minced

1 tablespoon water

2 teaspoons dry mustard

1 can (14½ ounces) stewed tomatoes

1 cup packed light brown sugar

½ cup ketchup

½ cup molasses

½ cup pure maple syrup

2 tablespoons white vinegar

1 tablespoon Worcestershire sauce

2 dried bay leaves

2 teaspoons salt

1 teaspoon freshly ground black pepper

8 ounces salt pork, cut into 3 pieces

Menu Ideas: These beans will make a great addition to most any potluck supper or picnic. When slabs of Grilled Honey and Mustard Ribs (page 108) or Four-Star Fried Chicken (page 110) are on the menu, plan on this to accompany, along with Coleslaw with Lemon-Caper Dressing (page 64) and Watermelon and Red Onion Salad (page 63).

Do-Ahead Tips: You can make the baked beans up to 2 days ahead. Reheat in a low oven; it's difficult to reheat on the stovetop without scorching the bottom.

1. Place the beans in a large bowl, add cold water to cover by about 2 inches, and soak at least 12 hours or overnight. You can also quick-soak the beans (see page 135).

2. Drain the soaked beans thoroughly, place in a Dutch oven or other large pot, and add fresh cold water to cover by about ½ inch (about 5 cups). Bring the water to a low boil over medium-high heat, then decrease the heat to medium. Simmer uncovered for 30 minutes; do not let the beans boil, and decrease the heat to medium-low if needed.

3. Preheat the oven to 300°F.

4. Cook the bacon in a medium skillet over medium heat, stirring occasionally, for 2 to 3 minutes, until tender and translucent but not crisp. Add the onion, bell pepper, and garlic and cook 2 to 3 minutes longer, until the onion is tender.

5. Add the onion mixture to the beans. Stir together the water and dry mustard in a small dish, then add to the beans, along with the tomatoes, brown sugar, ketchup, molasses, syrup, vinegar, Worcestershire sauce, bay leaves, salt, and pepper. Stir to mix well, then add the salt pork, poking it down into the beans. The liquid should just barely cover the beans at this point; gently boil the mixture for about 10 minutes to thicken slightly if needed.

6. Cover the pot and bake in the oven for 3 hours. Stir the beans, re-cover, and return to the oven. Decrease the temperature to 250°F and continue baking for 5 hours longer, until the beans are tender and the mixture has a thick saucy consistency. Discard the bay leaves. The beans can be served hot or at room temperature.

SAUTÉED TINY TOMATOES
WITH CHILE FLAKES

In recent years we've seen a great variety of tomatoes available, no longer just big beefsteaks and plum tomatoes, but a range of sizes, shapes, and colors that are wonderful in countless different recipes. For this easy, colorful side dish, small grape tomatoes are best. They are conveniently bite-sized, with a slightly firmer texture than cherry tomatoes, so they hold up well to pan frying. If you can only find cherry tomatoes, be sure to sauté them for just a minute or so, to ensure that they hold their shape. **MAKES 6 TO 8 SERVINGS**

2 tablespoons olive oil

1 small yellow or sweet onion, diced

5 cloves roasted garlic (see page 221), with its roasting oil

1½ pounds grape or cherry tomatoes

2 tablespoons minced fresh flat-leaf parsley

½ teaspoon dried red pepper flakes

¼ cup chopped mixed fresh herbs (oregano, thyme, chives, and/or tarragon)

Salt

1. Heat the olive oil in a large skillet over medium heat. Add the onion and roasted garlic and cook, stirring often, for about 5 minutes, until the onion is tender and aromatic (mash the garlic a bit to help break it up and distribute it evenly). Add the tomatoes, parsley, and pepper flakes. Increase the heat to medium-high and sauté, stirring occasionally, for about 3 minutes, until the tomatoes are heated through and you see that a handful of the tomatoes' skins have begun to split.

2. Remove the skillet from the heat and sprinkle with the garlic oil, mixed herbs, and salt. Transfer to a warmed serving bowl or individual plates and serve immediately.

Menu Ideas: The bright red color of these little tomatoes is beautiful on a buffet sideboard or alongside Lemon and Sage Cornish Game Hens (page 122) served with Orzo with Sugar Snap Peas (page 133). They are also the ideal partner to a simple grilled steak or hamburger.

Do-Ahead Tips: You can sauté the onion and garlic up to 1 hour in advance. The tomatoes should be sautéed just before serving.

ARTICHOKE RISOTTO
WITH SPRING PEAS AND MINT

After so many trips to Italy over the years, I've come to love risotto in all its variations. What makes the cooking method distinct is the slow addition of hot liquid and nearly constant stirring, creating risotto's creamy texture.

Risotto is an incredibly versatile dish to which countless vegetables, herbs, seafood, and even meats can be added. I often blanch our garden peas for this recipe, but frozen peas work perfectly year-round. For a shortcut, you can omit the artichokes, or replace them with blanched, chopped asparagus. **MAKES 8 SERVINGS**

½ lemon

2 large artichokes or 10 baby artichokes

7 to 8 cups chicken stock (page 83) or top-quality chicken broth

¼ cup olive oil

1 medium yellow onion, finely chopped

1 clove garlic, pressed or minced

2 cups Arborio rice

½ cup dry white wine

2 cups fresh or thawed frozen peas

2 tablespoons finely grated lemon zest

3 tablespoons freshly squeezed lemon juice

1 cup grated Parmesan cheese

½ cup mascarpone

Salt and freshly ground black pepper

2 tablespoons minced fresh mint

1. Squeeze the juice from the lemon half into a medium bowl of cold water and then drop the half into the water as well.

2. For large artichokes, use a sharp, heavy knife to cut the top off each artichoke, about 2 inches up from the base. Use your fingers to pull away a few layers of the tough outer green leaves, snapping them off at the base. Use a small paring knife to cut away the stem where it meets the base of the artichoke and trim away the remaining tough green outer skin. Also trim away any remaining tough leaf bases along the top edge, so that you're left with a disk of artichoke bottom, evenly trimmed and pale. Use a small spoon to scoop out the fuzzy choke from the base, being careful to not remove the flesh of the artichoke bottom. Cut the artichoke bottom across in half, then cut each half into ¼-inch wedges. Drop them in the lemon water right away to avoid discoloring.

3. For baby artichokes, peel away a few layers of the tough outer leaves until you're left with a core of tender, pale green leaves. Cut off the top inch from the artichoke and trim the stem. Cut each artichoke into quarters and drop them into the lemon water.

4. Warm the stock in a medium saucepan over medium heat. It should not boil; decrease the heat to low as needed.

5. Drain the artichoke pieces and dry well with paper towels.

6. Heat the olive oil in a large saucepan over medium heat. Add the onion and garlic and cook, stirring often, for 2 to 3 minutes, until tender and aromatic. Add the artichoke pieces and cook 6 minutes for the smaller wedges, 10 minutes for the quartered whole artichokes, until about halfway cooked (partly translucent on the surface). The onion should not brown; decrease the heat to medium-low if needed.

Menu Ideas: In Italy, risotto is often served as a solo course, between the antipasti and meat course. I often serve it as a side dish, the starch accompaniment for most any meat or fish. A heavy, rich dish like Osso Buco with Sage Gremolata (page 113) is a perfect choice for risotto, as is Salmon with Nasturtium Butter (page 90). You can also serve this as a vegetarian main course (using vegetable stock in place of the chicken stock).

Do-Ahead Tips: The artichokes can be trimmed, cut, and partially sautéed up to 3 hours in advance and left to sit, covered, at room temperature. The rice should be added and the risotto cooked just before serving, as the rich creamy texture is rather fleeting.

7. Add the rice and stir to evenly coat with the oil, about 1 minute. Add the wine and stir 1 to 2 minutes, until it is fully absorbed by the rice. Add 2 cups of the warm stock and cook, stirring often, for 3 to 4 minutes, until it is fully absorbed. Add 1 cup more of the stock and cook, stirring, for 2 or 3 minutes longer, until it is absorbed. Stir in the raw peas (thawed frozen peas should be added later), 1 tablespoon of the lemon zest, and the lemon juice. Continue adding the stock 1 cup at a time, allowing it to be absorbed before adding the next, and stirring constantly to assure even cooking and prevent sticking. It will take 25 to 30 minutes in all; later additions of stock will take longer to absorb than earlier ones. If using thawed frozen peas, stir them in with the last addition of stock. The liquid should be creamy and thick, the rice tender but still firm.

8. Remove the pan from the heat and stir in the Parmesan and mascarpone. Season to taste with salt. Spoon the risotto into individual shallow bowls and top each with a sprinkling of the mint, remaining 1 tablespoon lemon zest, and a grind or two of black pepper.

COUSCOUS
WITH VEGETABLES AND HERBS

Most people think couscous is a grain, but it is actually made from a semolina flour dough formed into small, grain-like shapes. It comes in such small beads that it cooks in a flash; just a few minutes with hot stock and the couscous becomes tender and fluffy. The couscous used here is the traditional North African type, as compared to Israeli couscous, which comes in larger, pearl-sized spheres.

For an added dose of color, I'll sometimes use ½ red bell pepper and ½ yellow bell pepper rather than just the red, and stir in finely chopped green onions just before serving. If you are using shelled fresh spring peas, blanch them in boiling water for 1 minute before adding to the skillet. **MAKES 4 TO 6 SERVINGS**

2 tablespoons unsalted butter

1 red bell pepper, cored, seeded, and finely diced

½ cup finely chopped sweet onion

1 medium zucchini, coarsely grated

½ cup fresh or thawed frozen peas

¼ cup minced fresh flat-leaf parsley

3 tablespoons freshly squeezed lemon juice

1 teaspoon minced fresh savory or thyme,
    or ½ teaspoon dried savory or thyme

½ cup chicken stock (page 83) or top-quality
    chicken broth

¾ cup couscous

2 tablespoons minced fresh basil

1 teaspoon finely grated lemon zest

Salt and freshly ground black pepper

1. Heat the butter in a large skillet over medium heat. Add the bell pepper and onion and cook, stirring occasionally, for 8 to 10 minutes, until tender and aromatic. Add the zucchini and cook for 5 minutes longer, stirring to blend. Stir in the peas, parsley, lemon juice, and savory. Set aside.

2. Bring the stock just to a boil in a medium saucepan over medium-high heat. Stir in the couscous, cover, and let sit off the heat for 5 minutes.

3. Fluff the couscous with a fork and add to the vegetables, stirring to evenly mix. Stir in the basil and lemon zest with salt and pepper to taste.

Menu Ideas: This wonderful side dish is particularly versatile; it can be served hot or cold, on a buffet or plated, and can even stand in for a salad. Couscous is classic with a tagine (pages 116 and 126) or similar dishes with a rich sauce that the couscous can absorb. Lemon and Sage Cornish Game Hens (page 122) will be great with the couscous as well.

Do-Ahead Tips: The couscous can be made up to 1 day in advance and refrigerated. Reheat over medium heat, drizzled with a tablespoon or two of water to remoisten.

CLASSIC CORNBREAD

A friend and creative chef in Seattle, Joe McDonnal, has not only served us wonderful meals in his own home over the years, but he has also created parties and events for us by way of his catering company and dinner club, The Ruins. This cornbread is one that all of Joe's patrons have enjoyed and I'm grateful to him for allowing me to share the recipe with you. You can use either white or yellow cornmeal here; I sometimes use half of each. Any leftovers are great the next day, toasted and lightly buttered. **MAKES 12 SERVINGS**

1 cup unsalted butter, melted

¾ cup sugar

4 eggs

2 cups buttermilk

1 teaspoon baking soda

2 cups fine cornmeal

2 cups all-purpose flour, sifted

1 teaspoon salt

Menu Ideas: You'll find that I've recommended this cornbread as a partner to many dishes in this book, including Chili with Fire-Roasted Peppers (page 94) and Mardi Gras Gumbo (page 100). With a dish of honey-butter alongside, it is hard to eat just one piece!

Do-Ahead Tips: I prefer to bake the cornbread shortly before serving, so it is at its most moist and tender. Wrap any leftover cornbread well in foil and toast the next morning, or freeze for up to 30 days. Thaw the bread, still wrapped, at room temperature.

1. Preheat the oven to 350°F. Butter a 9 by 13-inch baking dish.

2. Whisk together the butter and sugar in a bowl until the sugar is dissolved. Add the eggs and whisk until smooth. In another bowl, stir together the buttermilk and baking soda and set aside for 1 minute. Stir this into the butter mixture until evenly blended.

3. Stir the cornmeal, flour, and salt into the wet ingredients just until fully combined; avoid overmixing or the cornbread will be tough.

4. Pour the batter into the prepared baking dish, spreading evenly. Bake for about 30 minutes, or until a toothpick inserted in the center comes out clean. Let cool slightly before cutting into pieces to serve warm or at room temperature.

GARLIC-AND-HERB BAKED ARTICHOKES

This recipe makes a generous first course of one whole artichoke per person, if you have a simpler main course to follow. But I most often serve the artichokes in halves, for either a smaller first course or a side dish to any number of meat or pasta dishes. Be sure to serve the artichokes on a plate large enough to accommodate the discarded leaves, or have a bowl on the table for the leaves.

MAKES 4 TO 8 SERVINGS

4 artichokes, trimmed (see below)

½ cup unsalted butter

4 cloves garlic, pressed or minced

⅔ cup plain dried bread crumbs

⅔ cup freshly grated Parmesan cheese

¼ cup olive oil

2 teaspoons minced fresh thyme or ½ teaspoon dried thyme

2 teaspoons minced fresh marjoram or ½ teaspoon dried marjoram

½ teaspoon salt

½ teaspoon freshly ground black pepper

Menu Ideas: This is a great start to any menu that has Italian touches, such as Osso Buco with Sage Gremolata (page 113) or Fresh Summer Tomato and Crab Pasta (page 26) served as an entrée. As a vegetable side dish, I recommend the artichokes alongside Grilled Rack of Pork with Mango Salsa (page 83).

Do-Ahead Tips: The artichokes can be precooked and stuffed up to 6 hours in advance and refrigerated. They'll be best baked shortly before serving, though they can be reheated if necessary.

1. Bring 3 to 4 inches of water to a boil in the bottom of a steamer. Set the artichokes upright on the steamer rack and set the rack above the water. Cover and steam for 40 to 45 minutes, until the base of an artichoke is tender when pierced with the tip of a knife. Be sure the water doesn't boil away; add more boiling water as needed. Set the artichokes aside to cool.

2. While the artichokes are steaming, melt the butter in a medium saucepan over medium heat. Pour ¼ cup into a small dish and set aside. Add the garlic to the remaining butter in the pan and cook for 1 to 2 minutes, until tender and aromatic but not browned. Add the bread crumbs, cheese, olive oil, thyme, marjoram, salt, and pepper and stir until well mixed. Set aside.

3. Preheat the oven to 350°F.

4. Pull out and discard the small leaves from the center of each artichoke, revealing the fuzzy choke. Scoop out the choke with a small spoon, being careful not to remove the tender artichoke bottom underneath. Gently spread out the leaves of each artichoke and spoon some of the bread crumb mixture down between the layers of leaves. Spoon the remaining stuffing in the center cavities.

5. Set the artichokes in a small baking dish and drizzle with the reserved butter. Bake until heated through and the tips of the artichoke leaves begin to brown, 20 to 25 minutes. Transfer to individual plates and serve.

TRIMMING ARTICHOKES: If you don't cook artichokes often, it can be a little intimidating to tackle them, but they really are easy to prepare. It's good to have a halved lemon on hand to rub over the cut surfaces as you go, to avoid discoloration.

First, check to see how pronounced the thorns are at the ends of the leaves; some will be almost nonexistent, others worth your attention. If the latter, use kitchen shears to snip off the ends so neither you nor your guests are surprised by a prick from a thorn.

To expose the choke and make it easier for removing later, I cut off the top 1½ inches or so of the artichoke (none of which is edible anyway). Because the leaves are rather tough, I find a serrated knife easiest for this task. Trim the stem of the artichoke to the base and you're ready to proceed with cooking.

RATATOUILLE
WITH FRESH ROSEMARY

My friend Lydie Marshall taught me a trick she uses when making ratatouille to give it wonderful flavor. She drains the juices from the cooked vegetables, reduces them, then stirs them back in to the vegetables to add concentrated flavor. To do so, scoop the vegetable mixture into a fine mesh strainer placed over a bowl and let the juices drip out on their own for 20 to 30 minutes; don't be tempted to press on the vegetables. Return the juices to the skillet and boil until they are reduced to a thick syrup. Pour this back over the vegetables and quickly toss to blend.

When fresh plum tomatoes are at their summertime best, use them in place of the year-round canned plum tomatoes called for here; you'll need about 2 cups of peeled, seeded, and diced tomato. **MAKES 8 SERVINGS**

½ cup olive oil

1 red bell pepper, cored, seeded, and diced

1 green bell pepper, cored, seeded, and diced

1 yellow bell pepper, cored, seeded, and diced

1 large yellow onion, diced

Salt

1 medium eggplant, diced

2 medium zucchini, diced

6 cloves garlic, pressed or minced

¼ cup chopped fresh flat-leaf parsley

2 tablespoons minced fresh rosemary

1 can (28 ounces) whole plum tomatoes, drained and diced

1 cup lightly packed slivered fresh basil leaves

Freshly ground black pepper

1. Heat ¼ cup of the olive oil in a large skillet or sauté pan over medium heat. Add the bell peppers and onion with a pinch of salt. Cook, stirring occasionally, for 8 to 10 minutes, until tender and aromatic. Spoon the mixture into a large bowl.

2. Heat 2 tablespoons of the remaining olive oil in the skillet. Add the eggplant and cook, stirring often, for 5 to 7 minutes, until tender. Add the eggplant to the bell peppers.

3. Heat 1 tablespoon of the remaining olive oil in the skillet, add the zucchini with a pinch of salt, and cook for 3 to 5 minutes, until tender. Transfer to the bowl with the other vegetables.

4. Heat the remaining 1 tablespoon olive oil in the skillet. Add the garlic, parsley, and rosemary and sauté for about 1 minute, until the garlic is aromatic but not browned. Stir in the tomatoes (with their liquid) and cook for about 5 minutes, until slightly thickened. Stir in the basil, then return all the vegetables to the pan. Cook gently, stirring often, for 20 to 25 minutes, until the flavors are well blended. The vegetables should be tender but not mushy. (Strain the vegetables and reduce the cooking liquid, if you like; see above.) Season to taste with salt and pepper.

Menu Ideas: Ratatouille is not only a great side dish for everything from Herb-Rubbed Lamb Chops with Raita (page 125) to The Best Roasted Chicken (page 112), it can also be a delicious filling for an omelet or spooned over a bowl of freshly cooked pasta and tossed with Parmesan cheese. You can serve ratatouille hot, at room temperature, or chilled.

Do-Ahead Tips: I think this dish is even better the next day, so by all means consider making the ratatouille a day or two before you plan to serve it.

SWEET ONIONS AND RICE

This easy baked side dish has graced our dinner table for years; I'm sure your family will love it too. Sweet onions are, thankfully, available nearly year-round now, between Walla Wallas from my corner of the country, Vidalias from Georgia, Maui sweets from Hawaii, and sweet onions from south of the equator as well.

One characteristic of sweet onions is that they are typically higher in water content than regular onions, so they often produce juicy results when sautéed (particularly in the volume here). This water content will vary with the season and different varieties, however. After sautéing, you should have about 1 cup of liquid in the pot, which will be needed to ensure enough moisture for the rice to bake. Add water as needed to reach 1 cup liquid before you add the half-and-half and cheese. **MAKES 12 SERVINGS**

½ cup unsalted butter

4 large (1-pound) sweet onions, quartered and cut into ¼-inch slices

1 cup long-grain white rice

8 ounces Jarlsberg or other Swiss-style cheese, grated

⅔ cup half-and-half

1½ teaspoons salt

½ teaspoon freshly ground black pepper

1. Preheat the oven to 325°F. Lightly butter a 9 by 13-inch baking dish.

2. Melt the butter in a very large saucepan over medium heat. Add the onions and cook, stirring often, for about 30 minutes, until the onions are tender and translucent but not browned, and they have released quite a bit of liquid. (The volume will have reduced by about half.)

3. While the onions are cooking, bring a medium saucepan of salted water to a boil over medium-high heat. Add the rice and boil for 5 minutes, just to partly soften. Drain.

4. Remove the onion pan from the heat and eyeball the amount of liquid at the bottom; add water as needed so there is about 1 cup of liquid. Add the drained rice, all but ½ cup of the cheese, the half-and-half, salt, and pepper. Stir until well blended. Pour the mixture into the prepared baking dish and cover with foil. Bake for about 1 hour, until the rice is fully tender. Remove the foil and sprinkle with the remaining ½ cup cheese. Continue baking, uncovered, about 20 minutes longer, until the cheese is fully melted. Let sit for 15 minutes before serving.

Menu Ideas: This dish will be a winner on any buffet spread, a wonderful accompaniment to a wide range of meat entrées, from simple grilled steak to Rack of Lamb with Rosemary and Garlic (page 102), serving Asparagus with Garlic (page 134) alongside. Consider starting dinner with Spinach and Hearts of Palm Salad (page 44; with or without the fried oysters) and wrapping things up with a light dessert, such as the Blueberry Tart (page 183) or Ginger Cake with Lemon Cream (page 176). This recipe is a particularly good option when you're feeding a crowd.

Do-Ahead Tips: You can prepare the onions and par-cook the rice up to 6 hours in advance and refrigerate. Assemble and bake shortly before serving.

ZUCCHINI FRITTERS
WITH FRESH HERBS

Anyone who's ever had abundant zucchini in their garden (or been the recipient of overflow from such a garden) knows the creative challenge of coming up with enough ideas for using them up. This is one tasty option I devised for our garden's output. I like to use both regular bread crumbs and the flakier, crisper panko bread crumbs for the different textures they provide. But you can omit the panko and simply use more regular crumbs, if you prefer. The optional sour cream sauce adds a bit of tangy richness. **MAKES 6 TO 12 SERVINGS**

1½ pounds zucchini, trimmed and coarsely grated

1½ teaspoons salt

2 eggs

½ cup minced sweet onion

½ cup plain dried bread crumbs

½ cup panko bread crumbs

½ cup finely chopped fresh flat-leaf parsley

2 tablespoons minced fresh basil

2 tablespoons whipping cream or half-and-half

1 tablespoon minced jalapeño chile

1 tablespoon minced fresh mint

2 cloves garlic, pressed or minced

3 to 4 tablespoons olive oil

Freshly ground black pepper

SOUR CREAM SAUCE (OPTIONAL)

½ cup sour cream (light or regular)

1 teaspoon finely grated lemon zest

2 tablespoons freshly squeezed lemon juice

1 teaspoon minced fresh mint

¼ teaspoon garlic salt or regular salt

1. For the sour cream sauce, whisk together the sour cream, lemon zest, lemon juice, mint, and garlic salt in a small bowl. Refrigerate until ready to serve. (Best if made at least 2 hours in advance so the flavors can meld.)

2. Place the zucchini in a colander or sieve, add 1 teaspoon of the salt, and toss to mix evenly. Set the colander in a bowl or on a dish and let drain for 30 minutes. Squeeze the zucchini in your hands to remove excess water.

3. Preheat the oven to 170°F.

4. Whisk the eggs in a large bowl until frothy. Add the onion, both bread crumbs, parsley, basil, whipping cream, jalapeño, mint, garlic, and remaining ½ teaspoon salt. Stir until well blended, then stir in the zucchini.

5. Heat 3 tablespoons olive oil in a large skillet, preferably nonstick, over medium heat. When hot, form 3 or 4 fritters in the pan, spooning about ¼ cup of the mixture for each and flattening them to 3-inch circles. Fry for 4 to 6 minutes, until browned and crisp, turning once. Transfer to a baking sheet and keep warm in the oven while cooking the rest. Add additional oil if needed.

6. Arrange the fritters on individual plates, top with a grinding or two of black pepper, and add a drizzle of the sour cream sauce over the tops.

Menu Ideas: These fritters are perfect accompanying Halibut with Nut Crust and Apple Vinaigrette (page 106) or Osso Buco with Sage Gremolata (page 113). Depending on how much else is on the menu, 1 fritter per person may be enough, or serve 2 per person if your menu is simpler. I sometimes also serve them—2 per person—as a plated first course with a drizzle of the sauce on top. Or I also may cook the fritters in smaller rounds and serve them as an appetizer, passed on platters with the sauce alongside for dipping.

Do-Ahead Tips: The sauce can be made up to 2 days in advance and refrigerated. The zucchini fritters can be fried up to 30 minutes in advance, though they are at their best served directly from the skillet. Reheat in a 325°F oven before serving if needed.

SAUTÉED SPINACH
WITH MUSTARD SAUCE

When preparing spinach, just pinch off long tough stems and give the leaves a thorough rinse in a sink of cold water. Spin or shake as much water from the leaves as you can, then pat dry with paper towels or roll up in a kitchen towel to dry further before cooking. Excess water clinging to the leaves will make for watery results in the skillet, washing away the delicious olive oil and garlic coating. Because spinach is so voluminous before wilting in the heat of the pan, I use a Dutch oven for this recipe so I can cook it all at once. You can instead use a large skillet or sauté pan, though you'll need to add the spinach a handful at a time so each batch can wilt to make room before adding the next.

You can use fresh spinach that comes in bags rather than bunches, if you prefer; you'll need three 12-ounce bags. **MAKES 6 TO 8 SERVINGS**

2 tablespoons Dijon mustard

2 teaspoons freshly squeezed lemon juice

3 tablespoons olive oil

2 cloves garlic, pressed or minced

3 (1-pound) bunches spinach, tough stems removed, rinsed, and dried

Salt and freshly ground black pepper

¼ cup toasted pine nuts (see page 222)

Menu Ideas: This spinach preparation is the perfect side dish for a wide range of main courses, including Halibut with Nut Crust and Apple Vinaigrette (page 106) and Veal Chops with Green Peppercorns and Rosemary (page 117). Start the meal with Five-Onion Soup (page 82) or Tomato and Roasted Red Pepper Soup with Chile Cream (page 87).

Do-Ahead Tips: The spinach can be trimmed and rinsed up to 4 hours in advance, wrapped in a kitchen towel or paper towels, and refrigerated. The mustard sauce can be made up to 8 hours in advance; refrigerate, but allow to come to room temperature before serving. The spinach should be cooked just before serving.

1. Stir together the mustard, lemon juice, and 1 tablespoon of the olive oil in a small dish; set aside.

2. Heat the remaining 2 tablespoons oil in a large pan, such as a Dutch oven, over medium heat. Add the garlic and cook for 10 to 15 seconds, stirring constantly. Add the spinach (in batches, if needed) and stir carefully to evenly coat with the oil. Continue to cook, stirring often, for 3 to 5 minutes, until the spinach is evenly wilted and bright green. Remove the pan from the heat and season to taste with salt and pepper.

3. Arrange the spinach on individual plates, drizzle the mustard sauce over, and sprinkle with pine nuts.

SWISS CHARD: Swiss chard, which I love, makes a delicious alternative to spinach in this recipe. When I was growing up, my dad's garden always supplied huge armloads of chard from late summer into fall, sometimes even early winter. I find many people just aren't quite sure how to cook Swiss chard; it's often undercooked, or when the center stem is not removed before cooking you may end up with a mouthful of tough, stringy bits.

It's important to cut away chard's thick stem where it meets the leaf, since the two portions cook very differently. The leaves can then be cooked like spinach, though require a few more minutes. If you care to use the stem portion, thinly slice it and sauté separately, to stir into the cooked leaves later.

ROASTED SMASHED POTATOES
WITH GARLIC AND HERBS

These twice-cooked potatoes take on a delicious combination of textures, creamy-soft on the inside, crispy on the outside. Be sure to pick the smallest potatoes you can find, I like the baby red potatoes, but small yellow or white thin-skinned potatoes will work as well. This definitely isn't the place to use bigger russet baking potatoes. **MAKES 6 SERVINGS**

⅓ cup olive oil

3 cloves garlic, pressed or minced

2 pounds small red potatoes, scrubbed

Coarse sea or kosher salt

½ cup sour cream

¼ cup minced mixed fresh herbs (tarragon, parsley, chives, thyme, and/or oregano)

Menu Ideas: These potatoes will be a great complement to Grilled Scallops with Red Pepper–Harissa Coulis (page 8) served as a main course, with Sautéed Spinach with Mustard Sauce (page 158) alongside.

Do-Ahead Tips: You can boil and flatten the potatoes and make the garlic oil up to 3 hours ahead. The potatoes should be roasted just before serving.

1. Stir together the olive oil and garlic and warm gently in the microwave or over low heat for 1 minute. Set aside at room temperature to infuse for 1 hour, stirring once or twice.

2. Preheat the oven to 400°F. Line a large baking sheet with a silicone baking mat or parchment paper.

3. Place the potatoes in a large pan of cold salted water and bring to a boil over high heat. Decrease the heat to medium and simmer for 15 to 18 minutes, until the potatoes are quite tender but not falling apart. Drain the potatoes and let cool slightly.

4. While the potatoes are still warm, use the side of a heavy cleaver or the bottom of a small skillet to evenly smash the potatoes to about ¾ inch thick, keeping them intact. Set the potatoes in a single layer on the baking sheet. Drizzle the garlic oil over and sprinkle with salt to taste. Roast the potatoes for about 25 minutes, until nicely browned and crisp, turning the potatoes halfway through.

5. Arrange the smashed potatoes in small piles on individual plates, topping each serving with a dollop of sour cream and a sprinkling of herbs.

LEMON ISRAELI COUSCOUS

Israeli couscous is different from the North African version, which has a more fine-grained, fluffy texture. Also known as Middle Eastern couscous, Israeli couscous has larger, pearl-like balls that cook up with a chewy texture that is similar to pasta. **MAKES 8 SERVINGS**

1 tablespoon olive oil

⅓ cup finely chopped yellow onion

1½ cups Israeli couscous

2 cups chicken stock (page 83) or top-quality chicken broth, or more if needed

1 cup frozen petite peas

3 tablespoons finely chopped fresh mint

1 tablespoon finely grated lemon zest

2 tablespoons freshly squeezed lemon juice

1 tablespoon minced fresh flat-leaf parsley

1 tablespoon extra-virgin olive oil

Salt and freshly ground black pepper

Menu Ideas: This is my favorite accompaniment to Lamb Shanks Tagine with Preserved Lemon (page 126), though its bright, lemony-minty flavor would also be delicious alongside Halibut with Nut Crust and Apple Vinaigrette (page 106).

Do-Ahead Tips: The couscous continues to absorb liquid after cooking, so will be at its best made not more than an hour in advance. You may need to add a little more stock or water to keep it from clumping together. Reheat gently over low heat before serving.

1. Heat the olive oil in a medium saucepan over medium heat. Add the onion and cook, stirring, for 2 to 3 minutes, until tender and aromatic. Stir in the couscous and cook for 2 to 3 minutes longer, until evenly coated with oil and lightly toasty in aroma. Add the stock and bring to a boil. Cover, decrease the heat to low, and simmer for 12 to 14 minutes, until tender.

2. Stir the peas, mint, lemon zest, lemon juice, parsley, and extra-virgin olive oil into the couscous, then season to taste with salt and pepper. Cook the couscous, stirring, over medium-low heat until the mint and lemon are aromatic, 2 to 3 minutes longer. The couscous should be tender and the mixture fluffy, not soupy. If it is too dry, add a few tablespoons more stock or water.

DESSERTS

For many people, a meal just isn't complete until there has been some sort of sweet finale. The American ideal of dessert includes cake, pie, an ice cream sundae, but in other countries desserts are often lighter: simple cookies, refreshing sorbet, fresh fruit, or maybe a plate of delicious cheese.

I, too, tend to prefer less-sweet options for the end of a meal most nights of the week, but of course can't resist indulging in richer options when entertaining friends. Since dessert is the last thing you serve and is what your guests may remember most, pick one that will leave a lingering impact. For a larger dinner party, I may make two or three desserts, offering a small sampling of each on a beautiful plate. Or I may include different treats on a buffet so guests can sample as their tastes and appetite dictate.

In the following pages, you'll find quite an array of dessert options that will fit any type of meal you're planning. Many of these recipes, you'll be pleased to see, can be made in advance and take only a bit of attention before serving. That far into the meal, it's important that you're not pulled away from the table for extensive preparations.

BERRY GALETTE

Everyone loves pies and tarts, but sometimes they can be a little more work than you want to do for dessert. The galette style of pie comes to the rescue with the disk of flaky pastry simply folded up around a fresh berry filling, with no shaping into a pie pan or crimping needed. It's the easiest way to make "pie" that I know. For a quicker version, you can replace the homemade pastry dough with a sheet of thawed puff pastry.

Many types of berries make outstanding pies, but strawberries don't hold up nearly as well as blackberries, blueberries, and other berry options. Unless you've got a strawberry-rhubarb pie in mind, I recommend skipping the strawberries. Frozen berries can be used off-season, but allow them to thaw in advance and drain off excess liquid before using. You can even use sliced apples, pears, or other fruit.

MAKES 8 TO 12 SERVINGS

6 cups (about 1½ pounds) blackberries or a mix
    of blackberries, blueberries, and raspberries
¾ cup plus 2 teaspoons vanilla sugar (right)
    or regular granulated sugar
3 tablespoons all-purpose flour
2 tablespoons quick-cooking tapioca
1 tablespoon freshly squeezed lemon juice
½ teaspoon ground cinnamon
¼ teaspoon freshly grated or ground nutmeg

PASTRY DOUGH
½ cup unsalted butter
1 cup all-purpose flour
¼ teaspoon salt
3 to 4 tablespoons cold water

EGG WASH
1 egg
1 teaspoon water

1. For the pastry dough, cut the butter into small cubes and freeze for 5 minutes. Combine the butter, flour, and salt in the bowl of a food processor. Process for 10 to 15 seconds, until the butter is finely chopped. Add 3 tablespoons of the water and pulse for another 10 seconds, or until the mixture looks like cornmeal. Pinch some of the dough between your fingers; it should hold together, not feel crumbly or dusty. If necessary, add more water, a teaspoon at a time, pulsing once or twice after each addition. Turn the dough out onto a clean work surface. Gather about one-quarter of the dough into a small pile and use the heel of your hand to push the dough away from you two or three times, which helps thoroughly blend the butter and flour for a flakier crust. Don't overwork the dough or it will produce a tough crust. Repeat with the remaining dough. Use a pastry scraper to gather the dough, and then form it into a disk about 5 inches across. Wrap in plastic and refrigerate for at least 30 minutes.

2. Preheat the oven to 400°F. Line a baking sheet with a silicone baking mat or parchment paper.

3. Combine the berries, ¾ cup of the sugar, the flour, tapioca, lemon juice, cinnamon, and nutmeg in a large bowl. Toss very gently to evenly coat the berries in the sugar mixture, being careful not to crush the berries.

4. Roll out the dough on a lightly floured work surface to a 14-inch circle. Set it on the baking sheet and spoon the berries into the center, spreading them out slightly and leaving a 2½-inch border bare. Fold in the dough edges to partly cover the filling, pleating 4 or 5 times around the perimeter.

5. For the egg wash, beat the egg in a small bowl until frothy, then beat in the water. Lightly brush the egg wash on the dough, and sprinkle with the remaining 2 teaspoons sugar.

Menu Ideas: Serve this galette after a dinner of simple grilled salmon or Four-Star Fried Chicken (page 110). The rustic tart goes casual with ease, but you can also serve slices on elegant plates for a fancy dinner party.

Do-Ahead Tips: The pastry dough can be made up to 1 month in advance and frozen, or 4 days in advance and refrigerated. Allow it to thaw slowly in the refrigerator for a day before using. The galette can be assembled and baked up to 5 hours before serving.

6. Bake the galette for 15 minutes. Decrease the temperature to 350°F and continue baking for about 30 minutes, until the crust is nicely browned and the filling is bubbling around the edge.

7. Let the galette cool on the baking sheet for at least 30 minutes. Using 2 large spatulas, carefully lift it to a serving platter or a cutting board. Let cool another hour or so before cutting into wedges to serve.

PEACH AND CARDAMOM GALETTE: For a peachy variation to this berry galette, peel (see page 220) and pit 2 pounds of peaches and cut into ¾-inch slices. Use in place of the berries with just ½ cup sugar for tossing. Omit the cinnamon and nutmeg from the sugar mixture, using ¾ teaspoon ground cardamom instead.

VANILLA SUGAR: In this galette recipe, and in many dessert recipes, you can use vanilla sugar in place of regular sugar. Vanilla sugar is simply regular granulated sugar that has been infused with vanilla essence, so the sugar imparts extra flavor when you use it. To make vanilla sugar, plunge 2 or 3 split vanilla beans into 2 to 3 cups of granulated sugar in an airtight container. (You can use beans that you've scraped the seeds out of for another use.) Cover and store in a cool, dark place for a couple weeks before using. As you use sugar from the container, add more sugar to replace it, so you'll always have a good supply. The vanilla beans will impart their flavor and aroma to the sugar for many months.

LEMON BREAD PUDDING

Bread pudding must be one of the most universally loved desserts, all rich and rustic with a triad of comfort-food foundations: bread, milk, and eggs. For this ever-popular recipe, I prefer flaky croissants (though 6 cups of cubed day-old baguette can be used) and embellish the pudding with fresh lemon. If you're using bread that is still soft and fresh, dry the cubes as noted for the croissants here, scattering them on a baking sheet. **MAKES 8 SERVINGS**

6 large croissants

2 tablespoons unsalted butter, at room
    temperature

1½ cups whole milk

1½ cups whipping cream

5 eggs

⅔ cup packed light brown sugar

⅔ cup granulated sugar

2 teaspoons finely grated lemon zest

1 teaspoon pure vanilla extract

½ teaspoon ground cinnamon

½ cup chopped toasted pecans (see page 222)

LEMON CURD

3 egg yolks

1 whole egg

2 tablespoons finely grated lemon zest

¾ cup freshly squeezed lemon juice

½ cup granulated sugar

Menu Ideas: This bread pudding is an ideal way to cap off a dinner of Lamb Shanks Tagine with Preserved Lemon (page 126). Or serve after a casual buffet dinner of Chili with Fire-Roasted Peppers (page 94) and Crudités (page 28).

Do-Ahead Tips: The bread pudding can be baked up to a day in advance and refrigerated. Reheat, covered with foil, in a 300°F oven before serving. The lemon curd can be made up to 3 days in advance and refrigerated.

1. For the lemon curd, whisk together the egg yolks, whole egg, lemon zest, lemon juice, and sugar in the top of a double boiler or in a medium metal bowl. Set over a pan of simmering, not boiling, water and cook over medium-low heat, stirring, for about 10 minutes, until the mixture is thickened. Transfer the lemon curd to a bowl, which helps avoid overcooking, and lay a piece of plastic wrap directly on the surface to keep a skin from forming. Let cool to room temperature, then refrigerate until fully chilled.

2. Preheat the oven to 300°F. Butter an 8-inch square baking dish (2-quart capacity).

3. Cut the croissants in half lengthwise and lightly butter them. Set on a baking sheet and bake for 15 to 20 minutes, until lightly browned. Let cool. Increase the oven temperature to 350°F.

4. Break the croissants into bite-sized pieces and place half of them in the prepared baking dish. Spread about ½ cup of the lemon curd over the croissants, then top with the remaining croissants.

5. Combine the milk and cream in a small saucepan and bring just to a low boil over medium-high heat. Beat the eggs in a large bowl until frothy, then beat in the brown and granulated sugars, lemon zest, vanilla extract, and cinnamon. In a slow stream, whisk in the hot milk mixture. Pour over the croissants and let sit for about 30 minutes, until the custard is well absorbed by the croissants, pressing down on them with the back of a spoon now and then to assure even absorption. (All the custard may not fit into the dish at first, but more can be added as it is absorbed by the croissants.)

6. Set the baking dish in a larger roasting pan and add enough hot water to the larger pan to come about halfway up the sides of the baking dish. Carefully transfer the pan to the oven and bake for 30 minutes. Increase the temperature to 400°F and continue baking for about 10 minutes, until the bread pudding is browned and puffy and the custard is set. Carefully transfer the baking dish to a wire rack to cool the pudding to room temperature (or just slightly warm) before serving.

7. To serve, spoon the remaining lemon curd onto individual plates and set a scoop of the bread pudding on top. Sprinkle the pecans over or pass separately.

CHOCOLATE ESPRESSO POTS DE CRÈME

There is a decadent, silky texture to these rich custards, thanks to cream, egg yolks, and elegant chocolate. I like to serve the dessert in espresso cups, which come in such a range of styles and colors; they make such a whimsical presentation. Top-quality chocolate will really shine in this simple dessert. Simple, crisp cookies would be ideal alongside, which I buy from a favorite bakery if I don't have time to make my own. MAKES 8 SERVINGS

6 ounces top-quality semisweet chocolate, chopped

2 cups whipping cream

2 tablespoons instant espresso powder

4 egg yolks

2 tablespoons sugar

1½ teaspoons pure vanilla extract

Whipped cream, for serving

Chocolate-covered coffee beans, for serving

Menu Ideas: These small pots of wonderful silky chocolate are great following most any meat dish, such as Lemon and Sage Cornish Game Hens (page 122) or Wine-Braised Corned Beef with Brown Sugar Glaze (page 124). Because the pots de crème are made in advance and ready to serve after adding a dollop of whipped cream, this is an easy option for capping off an elaborate or large dinner party.

Do-Ahead Tips: The pots de crème can be made up to 2 days in advance and refrigerated, securely covered with plastic wrap to avoid a skin from forming on the tops.

1. Preheat the oven to 300°F.

2. Place the chopped chocolate in a medium bowl. Bring the cream just to a boil in a heavy saucepan over medium-high heat. Remove the pan from the heat and stir in the espresso powder. Pour the cream slowly over the chocolate. Let sit for a few minutes, then gently whisk to blend the melting chocolate and cream into a smooth mixture.

3. Whisk the egg yolks in a large bowl, gradually adding the sugar. Continue whisking until the yolks are smooth and lightened in color. Whisk in the vanilla extract. Pour a bit of the warm chocolate mixture into the yolks, whisking to thoroughly blend, then gradually whisk in the remaining chocolate. Whisk gently to avoid incorporating air bubbles into the custard.

4. Pour the custard into eight 4-ounce ramekins or espresso cups, filling them by about three-quarters full. Set the ramekins in an oblong baking dish and add boiling water to the pan to come about halfway up the sides of the ramekins. Loosely cover the dish with foil. Carefully transfer the pan to the oven and bake for about 30 minutes, until the custard is set.

5. Transfer the baking dish to a wire rack and let sit until the ramekins are cool enough to handle. Remove them from the water bath and let cool completely. Cover the dishes with plastic wrap and refrigerate for at least 2 hours before serving.

6. To serve, top each pot de crème with a dollop of whipped cream and a chocolate-covered coffee bean.

APPLESAUCE CAKE
WITH CINNAMON–CREAM CHEESE FROSTING

I first tasted this applesauce cake—without the frosting—when it was served as part of breakfast, a nice change from coffee cake and other breakfast breads that are so common. The moist cake, with its warm spices and walnuts, reminds me a little of that old standby carrot cake, but I like this recipe much better! My coauthor, Cynthia, loved the cake just as much and came up with the cinnamony cream cheese frosting to top it off. **MAKES 8 TO 10 SERVINGS**

2½ cups all-purpose flour

1½ teaspoons salt

1½ teaspoons baking soda

1¼ teaspoons baking powder

¾ teaspoon ground cinnamon

½ teaspoon ground cloves

½ teaspoon ground allspice

1½ cups chopped toasted walnuts (see page 222)

1 cup raisins

1 cup granulated sugar

½ cup unsalted butter, at room temperature

2 eggs

1½ cups unsweetened applesauce

½ cup water

CINNAMON–CREAM CHEESE FROSTING

8 ounces cream cheese, at room temperature

¼ cup unsalted butter, at room temperature

4 cups confectioners' sugar

1 teaspoon ground cinnamon

1 teaspoon pure vanilla extract

1. Preheat the oven to 350°F. Butter and flour a 10-inch loaf pan, tapping to remove the excess.

2. Sift together the flour, salt, baking soda, baking powder, cinnamon, cloves, and allspice into a large bowl. Stir in the walnuts and raisins. Cream together the granulated sugar and butter with an electric mixer at medium speed until well blended and fluffy. Add the eggs, 1 at a time. With the mixer at low speed, blend in the dry ingredients in 3 parts, alternating with the applesauce (all at once) and water, to form a smooth batter.

3. Pour the batter into the prepared loaf pan. Bake for about 1 hour, until a toothpick inserted in the center comes out clean. Let cool slightly in the pan, then turn the cake out onto a wire rack and cool to room temperature.

4. For the frosting, cream together the cream cheese and butter until smooth and well blended. Add the confectioners' sugar, 1 cup at a time, blending at low speed. Add the cinnamon and vanilla extract and continue blending until thoroughly incorporated.

5. When the cake is fully cooled, spread the frosting over the top and side. Cut the cake into slices and serve.

Menu Ideas: This moist cake is a perfect dessert for any casual gathering. And you may want to serve it for a weekend brunch as well, with or without the frosting. Unfrosted, it will travel well to a picnic or beachside barbecue.

Do-Ahead Tips: You can make the cake up to 3 days in advance. Wrap in plastic wrap and refrigerate, or wrap well and freeze for up to 1 month. The frosting can be made up to 1 day in advance. The cake should be frosted not more than a few hours before serving.

CAPPUCCINO ICE CREAM

As an alternative to an espresso at the end of a meal, serve this wonderful, strong coffee ice cream with a few chocolate-covered coffee beans on the top. If you prefer a bit lighter coffee flavor, use regular instant coffee powder in place of the instant espresso. This no-egg, no-cook ice cream recipe is a snap to make. You'll be surprised at just how delicious it is. **MAKES 2 QUARTS**

2 cups sugar

⅓ cup instant espresso powder

2 tablespoons unsweetened cocoa powder

½ teaspoon ground cinnamon

1½ cups boiling water

2 cups half-and-half

2 cups whipping cream

¼ cup Cognac or other brandy

Menu Ideas: This rich but easy ice cream partners well with many desserts, such as Sunken Chocolate Cupcakes (page 175) or Mother's Oatmeal Spice Cookies (page 189). Served solo, you may want to top the ice cream with some of the chocolate sauce from the Individual Chocolate Fondues (page 192).

Do Ahead Tips: The ice cream can be made up to 1 week in advance and frozen in a well-sealed container. Ice cream tastes best when it's allowed to warm slightly from the freezer's deep chill. If the ice cream has been made far enough in advance that it is rock hard, let it sit at room temperature for 15 to 20 minutes before serving. Otherwise, I love to time the churning just right so I can serve the ice cream straight from the machine while it's still soft.

1. Combine the sugar, espresso powder, cocoa powder, and cinnamon in a large bowl and stir to mix. Add the boiling water and stir until the sugar dissolves. Set aside until cooled to room temperature.

2. Stir the half-and-half and whipping cream into the sugar mixture, then add the Cognac. Freeze the mixture in an ice cream maker according to the manufacturer's directions.

CHURNING ICE CREAM: I have a nice large ice cream maker that is able to churn 2 quarts at a time. It also has a built-in freezing system that means I can add the ice cream base at room temperature and it will freeze with no problem. Other ice cream makers may be smaller, in which case you may want to halve this recipe or freeze the ice cream in 2 batches. Also, some ice cream makers work best if the ice cream mixture is first fully chilled in the refrigerator before churning. Amend this recipe as needed to suit your ice cream maker's characteristics.

RHUBARB AND STRAWBERRY CRISP

This is a favorite late spring dessert, bright with the vivid, tart flavor of rhubarb, which grows in abundance in the Northwest. My husband is partial to this version of the traditional rhubarb crisp: The addition of early-season strawberries adds flavor, color, and a little more sweetness to the dessert. In this case, slightly firmer strawberries work better than more delicate, fully ripe strawberries, which tend to become mushy when baked. Off season, when there is no fresh rhubarb available, frozen rhubarb works very well.

For the nutty-spiced topping, I use granola, which just adds a bit more character to the topping. Any type of oat-based granola will work. Of course, a scoop of great vanilla ice cream would be ideal alongside. MAKES 12 SERVINGS

2 pounds rhubarb, trimmed and cut into 1-inch
    pieces

3 cups coarsely chopped strawberries

1 cup granulated sugar

¼ cup all-purpose flour

1 teaspoon finely grated lemon zest

1 tablespoon freshly squeezed lemon juice

Pinch of salt

TOPPING

1 cup all-purpose flour

¾ cup chopped toasted pecans or walnuts
    (see page 222)

¾ cup your favorite granola

¼ cup rolled oats (not instant)

½ cup packed light brown sugar

½ cup dried cranberries or raisins (optional)

1 tablespoon granulated sugar

½ teaspoon ground cinnamon

⅛ teaspoon ground allspice

½ teaspoon salt

½ cup unsalted butter, cut into pieces, at room
    temperature

1. Preheat the oven to 375°F.

2. Toss together the rhubarb, strawberries, granulated sugar, flour, lemon zest, lemon juice, and salt in a large bowl and let sit, tossing gently once or twice, for 10 minutes. Spoon into a 9 by 13-inch or similar volume baking dish.

3. For the topping, stir together the flour, pecans, granola, oats, brown sugar, dried cranberries, granulated sugar, cinnamon, allspice, and salt in a medium bowl until well blended. Add the butter pieces and stir well to evenly distribute the butter with the dry ingredients.

4. Scatter the topping evenly over the fruit. Set the baking dish on a baking sheet to catch any drips and bake for 30 to 35 minutes, until the edges are bubbly and the topping is lightly browned. Let sit for at least 10 minutes before serving; serve warm or at room temperature.

Menu Ideas: This is a late spring/early summer treat that will be wonderful after a dinner of Halibut with Nut Crust and Apple Vinaigrette (page 106), Sesame-Crusted Tuna with Soy-Lemon Sauce (page 95), or main-course portions of Artichoke Risotto with Spring Peas and Mint (page 146).

Do-Ahead Tips: You can make the topping 1 day in advance and store in an airtight container in the refrigerator. You can prepare the fruit and bake the crisp the morning of your dinner, although I prefer to bake it just a couple of hours in advance, so it's still warm when served.

RED WINE–POACHED PEARS
WITH RICOTTA STUFFING

When late summer begins to bring us those cooler evenings the pear takes center stage once again. I like to use Bosc pears here, although Bartlett or Anjou will work as well. Choose pears with their stems intact, if possible. The pears should be "medium" on the ripeness scale: ripe enough to have good flavor but not so ripe as to be too tender. The poaching time will vary with the firmness of the pears.

I prefer to poach just two pears at a time (or sometimes three, if I'm doubling the recipe), to keep a better eye on how each pear is cooking. Aside from turning the pears occasionally so they poach evenly, it's no work at all and I fill that time doing other preparations for dinner. But if you're in a hurry, you can poach all six pears at once, in a larger pan using two bottles of wine. **MAKES 6 SERVINGS**

2 tablespoons freshly squeezed lemon juice

6 Bosc pears, with stems

1 bottle (750 ml) hearty red wine, such as
    Cabernet Sauvignon

½ cup sugar

1 cinnamon stick

2 strips lemon zest

3 tablespoons Kirsch (clear cherry brandy) or
    regular brandy

RICOTTA STUFFING

½ cup ricotta cheese (preferably whole milk)

2 tablespoons minced candied ginger

2 tablespoons chopped toasted pine nuts (see
    page 222, optional)

1 tablespoon minced candied orange zest
    (homemade, see page 187, or store-bought)

1 tablespoon dried currants or chopped raisins

Menu Ideas: These pears will be a hit after a dinner of Osso Buco with Sage Gremolata (page 113) or Seattle Cioppino (page 105).

Do-Ahead Tips: The ricotta filling can be made up to 1 day in advance. You can poach the pears and reduce the poaching liquid in the morning and refrigerate. The pears should be stuffed no more than 1 hour before serving.

1. Add the lemon juice to a large bowl of cold water. Slice a bit of the rounded bottom from one of the pears so that it sits upright. Use a melon baller to remove the core from the bottom. Peel the pear, leaving the stem intact, then slip it into the lemon water right away to avoid discoloring. Repeat with the remaining pears.

2. Combine the wine, sugar, cinnamon stick, and zest strips in a saucepan just large enough to hold 2 pears. Bring to a boil over medium-high heat, stirring to help the sugar dissolve. Add 2 pears, decrease the heat to medium, and simmer for about 25 minutes, until the pears are tender when pierced with a knife. Turn the pears occasionally as they poach to ensure even cooking. Lift out the pears with a slotted spoon (preferably rubber, to avoid marring the pears) and set upright in a muffin pan or on a platter to cool. Repeat with the remaining pears. If you don't have enough liquid to cover the last 2 pears, add water as needed.

3. Set the poaching liquid over medium-high heat and boil for 12 to 15 minutes, until reduced to about ¾ cup. Strain the liquid into a small bowl, discarding the cinnamon stick and lemon zest. Stir in the Kirsch and set aside to cool.

4. For the stuffing, stir together the ricotta, candied ginger, pine nuts, candied orange zest, and currants. Refrigerate until needed.

5. Use a small spoon to stuff the ricotta mixture into the core cavities of the cooled pears. Set the pears upright on individual serving plates, drizzle the reduced cooking liquid over and around, and serve.

CITRUS ZEST: When peeling or grating citrus fruit zest, strip away only the colored outer layer of the peel, where the intense citrus flavor is most prominent. Avoid the white pith that lies underneath, which has a more bitter flavor. Use a simple vegetable peeler to peel away the strips.

BLACK AND WHITE COCOA BARS

When I was a teenager, a friend of my mother made a version of these cookie bars. I loved them because they were light compared to so many brownies and bar cookies, so I could always eat two. You can use any type of nuts, such as walnuts or hazelnuts, in place of the pecans I use here. The neighbor who inspired this recipe had a huge walnut tree in the yard, so all the cookies made in their house had walnuts.
MAKES 16 TO 20 BARS

1¾ cups all-purpose flour

1½ cups confectioners' sugar

1 cup unsalted butter, cut into pieces and chilled

½ cup unsweetened cocoa powder

8 ounces cream cheese, at room temperature

1 can (14 ounces) sweetened condensed milk

1 egg

2 teaspoons pure vanilla extract

¾ cup chopped, toasted pecans (see page 222)

½ cup semisweet chocolate chips

1. Preheat the oven to 350°F.

2. Combine the flour, sugar, butter, and cocoa powder in a food processor and pulse until the mixture has the texture of coarse crumbly sand. Scoop 2 cups into a medium bowl and set aside.

3. Press the remaining flour/cocoa mixture evenly across the bottom of a 9 by 13-inch baking dish. Bake for 15 minutes. Set aside to cool. Keep the oven set at 350°F.

4. Beat the cream cheese in a standing electric mixer with the paddle attachment until fluffy. Working at medium-low speed, gradually beat in the condensed milk until smooth. Add the egg and vanilla extract and mix well. Pour into the cooled crust.

5. Add the nuts and chocolate chips to the reserved flour/cocoa mixture and stir to evenly mix. Sprinkle over the cream cheese mixture and press it gently into the cream cheese (or I sometimes swirl it in gently with a small spoon). Bake for about 30 minutes, until firm to the touch and lightly browned around the edges. Let cool before cutting into squares.

Menu Ideas: These cookie bars are enjoyed by everyone, young and old. They go with most any lunch or dinner.

Do-Ahead Tips: These can be made 1 to 2 days in advance. Because of the cream cheese, they should be refrigerated if made more than a couple hours in advance. The flavor will be best if allowed to come to room temperature before serving.

MOROCCAN-STYLE BISCOTTI

There are so many wonderful bakeries in Morocco that it is easy for home cooks to buy special cookies in their neighborhood bakery to serve after dinner. This is just one of the many types I've enjoyed on trips there. Unlike traditional Italian biscotti, these cookies are baked just once (rather than twice) and are treated to a dose of leavening from baking powder, which gives them a light, very crisp texture. I like to pack them in a pretty tin to offer as a hostess gift. **MAKES 24 COOKIES**

6 tablespoons unsalted butter, melted and cooled

1 egg

1 teaspoon pure vanilla extract

1½ cups all-purpose flour

⅔ cup sugar

1 tablespoon baking powder

⅓ cup sesame seeds (untoasted)

Menu Ideas: These wonderful cookies are great passed with chocolates, sweet mint tea, and Oranges with Candied Zest (page 187) after a Moroccan meal or any menu that features bold spices.

Do-Ahead Tips: The biscotti can be made up to 1 week in advance and stored in an airtight container at room temperature.

1. Preheat the oven to 350°F. Line a baking sheet with a silicone baking mat or parchment paper.

2. Whisk together the melted butter, egg, and vanilla extract in a small bowl until well blended. Stir together the flour, sugar, and baking powder in a large bowl. Add the butter mixture and stir to mix well and form a cohesive dough.

3. Form the dough into a log that is ¾ inch thick, 2 inches wide, and about 12 inches long. Use a sharp knife to cut across the log to make ½-inch-thick slices. Spread the sesame seeds on a plate and press both cut sides of each cookie into the seeds. Set them seed side up on the baking sheet about 1 inch apart.

4. Bake the cookies for 18 to 20 minutes, until lightly browned and firm. Let cool on the sheet for a few minutes, then transfer to a wire rack to cool completely.

SUNKEN CHOCOLATE CUPCAKES

Cupcakes are a timeless favorite, so everyone will love these treats. The barely sweet flourless cakes are deeply chocolaty, with a bit of added crunch from the sugar that coats the muffin cups before baking. The better the quality of the chocolate you use, the better the cakes will be—this is a perfect time to splurge. I have baked these in 4-ounce ramekins, making eight slightly larger portions that can be served directly from the ramekins. You may need to increase the cooking time by a few minutes if doing so.

If you don't have a double boiler for gently melting the chocolate and butter, you can set a heatproof bowl over a saucepan that has a couple inches of water in it. The water should not touch the bottom of the bowl and it should only gently simmer, not boil, to avoid overheating the chocolate. **MAKES 12 CUPCAKES**

½ cup sugar, plus more for muffin tin

1 cup unsalted butter, cut into pieces

10 ounces top-quality bittersweet chocolate, coarsely chopped

4 eggs, separated

4 egg yolks

Menu Ideas: I like serving these with the wonderfully easy Cappuccino Ice Cream (page 169), but the versatile cakes can be served a number of other ways, with fresh berries and whipped cream in summer or with rich caramel sauce anytime.

Do-Ahead Tips: You can make the batter an hour or two in advance and spoon it into the prepared muffin tin and refrigerate. The cakes will be at their best baked just before serving.

1. Preheat the oven to 350°F. Butter the cups of a 12-cup muffin pan and coat each with sugar, gently tapping the pan upside down to remove the excess sugar.

2. Combine the butter and chocolate in the top of a double boiler set over (but not touching) simmering water. Cook, stirring occasionally, until the chocolate and butter are fully melted and well blended. Set aside to cool.

3. Whisk together the 8 egg yolks with ¼ cup of the sugar in a large bowl until the yolks are pale yellow in color and slightly thickened. Whisk in the cooled chocolate mixture until evenly blended.

4. Use an electric mixer to beat the egg whites until soft peaks form. With the beaters running, slowly add the remaining ¼ cup sugar and continue beating until the egg whites are shiny and firm. Fold the egg whites into the chocolate mixture in 2 or 3 batches.

5. Spoon the batter into the muffin cups, filling them just to the rim. Bake for 20 to 25 minutes, until the cakes are nicely puffed, set around the edges, and just slightly jiggly in the center. Let the cakes cool in the pan on a wire rack for 15 minutes, then unmold and set upright until ready to serve, warm or at room temperature.

GINGER CAKE WITH LEMON CREAM

Ginger reminds me of Christmas and those gingerbread man cookies we kids got for sitting on the lap of the Cinnamon Bear (in place of Santa) at the Lipman Wolfe department store in Portland. This is an extra-moist, extra-aromatic variation of gingerbread, with a triple dose of ginger: fresh, candied, and ground. The lemon cream alongside is essentially a homemade lemon curd (which you can buy premade for a shortcut) lightened with whipped cream. **MAKES 12 SERVINGS**

1 cup sugar

1 cup vegetable oil

1 cup molasses

2 eggs

2½ cups all-purpose flour, sifted

1 teaspoon ground ginger

½ teaspoon ground cinnamon

½ teaspoon ground cloves

¼ teaspoon ground cardamom

¼ teaspoon freshly ground black pepper

¼ teaspoon ground allspice

1 cup boiling water

2 teaspoons baking soda

5 tablespoons minced candied ginger

¼ cup minced fresh ginger

LEMON CREAM

2 teaspoons finely grated lemon zest

½ cup freshly squeezed lemon juice

½ cup sugar

½ cup unsalted butter

2 teaspoons water

3 eggs

4 egg yolks

1 cup whipping cream

1. Preheat the oven to 350°F. Butter a 9-inch springform pan and dust with flour.

2. Beat the sugar, oil, molasses, and eggs in a standing electric mixer fitted with the paddle attachment until smooth. Combine the flour, ground ginger, cinnamon, cloves, cardamom, pepper, and allspice in a medium bowl and stir to blend. With the mixer at low speed, slowly add the flour mixture and beat until well blended. Combine the boiling water and baking soda in a small bowl; slowly add to the batter, then blend in the candied and fresh ginger.

3. Pour the batter into the prepared pan and bake for about 1 hour, until a toothpick inserted in the center comes out clean. Let cool on a wire rack for 15 minutes. Remove the side of the pan, invert the cake, and remove the bottom of the pan. When completely cooled, turn the cake right side up.

4. For the lemon cream, combine the lemon zest, lemon juice, sugar, butter, and water in a medium saucepan. Cook over medium heat, stirring, until the butter is melted. Remove from the heat. Whisk together the whole eggs and yolks in a medium bowl until well blended. Slowly add one-third of the warm lemon mixture in a stream, whisking constantly. Add the egg mixture to the saucepan and cook over medium-low heat, whisking, for about 5 minutes, until thickened. Transfer the lemon curd to a bowl, lay a piece of plastic wrap directly on the surface, and let cool. Refrigerate until chilled.

5. Beat the cream with a whisk or electric mixer to soft peaks. Whisk the cooled lemon curd gently to soften, then whisk in about one-quarter of the whipped cream. Gently fold in the remaining whipped cream. Refrigerate, covered, until ready to serve.

6. To serve, cut the ginger cake into wedges, arrange on individual plates, and spoon a generous dollop of lemon cream on top of each.

Menu Ideas: The warm flavors of this cake make it an ideal finish for a winter menu of cozy braised dishes such as Wine-Braised Corned Beef with Brown Sugar Glaze (page 124) or Osso Buco with Sage Gremolata (page 113).

Do-Ahead Tips: The lemon cream can be made up to 2 days in advance and refrigerated. Whisk well before serving as the cream can separate a bit. The cake will be at its best served the day it is baked, though it can be made up to 2 days in advance and refrigerated.

VERY CITRUS CHEESECAKE

This is a tangier version of a cheesecake recipe I've been making for many years, a timeless classic. The bright vivid flavor of citrus zest is a wonderful complement to the rich creaminess of cheesecake. Though delicious as is, I adore it with the candied zest garnish for its special added flourish of color and flavor. And during the brief season for fresh rhubarb each spring, I top the cheesecake slices with a rhubarb sauce (at right). **MAKES 16 SERVINGS**

1 large lemon

1 navel orange

1 grapefruit

2½ cups sugar

2½ pounds cream cheese, at room temperature

3 tablespoons all-purpose flour

1 teaspoon pure vanilla extract

¼ teaspoon salt

5 whole eggs

2 egg yolks

½ cup whipping cream

½ cup water

1. Preheat the oven to 500°F. Line a 10-inch springform pan with parchment paper, a round on the bottom and a long strip around the edge.

2. Use the fine teeth of a citrus zester to remove about half the zest from the lemon, orange, and grapefruit. Set this aside for the candied garnish. With a grater, finely grate enough of the remaining citrus zest so that you have 2 teaspoons each of grated lemon, orange, and grapefruit zest. Place in a medium bowl and stir in 1¾ cups of the sugar until well blended. This helps keep the zest from clumping together when it is added to the batter.

3. Beat the cream cheese in an electric mixer fitted with the paddle attachment until light and fluffy. At low speed, gradually add the sugar-zest blend followed by the flour, scraping down the side as needed. Add the vanilla extract and salt and blend until smooth. Add the eggs, one at a time, blending well after each addition, then add the egg yolks. Gently stir in the cream by hand, scooping well across the bottom of the bowl to ensure all the ingredients are very well blended.

4. Pour the batter into the prepared pan. Bake for 8 to 10 minutes, until the top begins to brown. Decrease the oven temperature to 200°F and continue baking for about 1 hour, until the center of the cheesecake no longer jiggles when you gently shake the pan. Transfer the cheesecake to a wire rack to cool to room temperature. Cover and refrigerate at least 6 hours before serving.

5. While the cheesecake is baking, make the garnish. Combine the remaining ¾ cup sugar with the water in a small saucepan. Bring to a boil over medium-high heat, stirring to help the sugar dissolve. Add the reserved zest strips, decrease the heat to medium-low, and simmer for 8 to 10 minutes, until the zest is translucent and the syrup has been fully absorbed. Let cool to room temperature.

6. To serve the cheesecake, remove the sides of the springform pan, cut the cheesecake into serving pieces, and set on individual plates. Spoon a small tuft of the candied zest on each piece and serve.

Menu Ideas: Since the cheesecake makes a lot of servings (you can even squeeze out 20 or more servings, cutting smaller slices that are still satisfying), it is a great option for a larger dinner party. Its richness would be a good complement to a lighter meal of seafood, such as Seattle Cioppino (page 105) or Fresh Dungeness Crab with Two Sauces (page 104).

Do-Ahead Tips: The cheesecake can be baked up to 3 days in advance and refrigerated, well-wrapped in plastic. You can prepare the candied zest up to 3 days prior to baking the cheesecake. Store in an airtight container at room temperature. This is a sturdy cake that can travel well.

QUICK RHUBARB SAUCE: One optional embellishment you might want to add to the cheesecake is this simple rhubarb sauce: Trim and chop 4 or 5 stalks of fresh rhubarb (if large stalks, I peel away some of the tough outer portion). Bring about 1 cup freshly squeezed orange juice and sugar to taste (I usually start with ½ cup) to a simmer over medium heat. Add the chopped rhubarb and bring to a full boil. Decrease the heat to medium low and simmer about 10 minutes, until the rhubarb is very soft. I sometimes add chopped fresh strawberries as well, a great complement of flavor to the rhubarb, and they add a more vivid red to the sauce.

In fall or winter, you can follow the same steps with about 3 cups fresh cranberries for another delicious seasonal sauce to accompany the cheesecake.

PEANUT BUTTER CREAM PIE

This simple pie is perfect for the little kid in all of us. Plan ahead, as it needs to refrigerate for a few hours before serving. If you feel up to making your own chocolate sauce for serving with the pie, try the one from Individual Chocolate Fondues (page 192). Use a top-quality peanut butter for this recipe, preferably natural style, which has the best peanut flavor. **MAKES 12 TO 16 SERVINGS**

1½ cups top-quality peanut butter
　　(crunchy or smooth)

12 ounces cream cheese, at room temperature

1¼ cups sugar

3 tablespoons unsalted butter, melted

2½ cups whipping cream

1 tablespoon pure vanilla extract

Chocolate curls, for serving (see below)

Chocolate fudge sauce, for serving

GRAHAM CRACKER CRUST

1½ cups fine graham cracker crumbs

6 tablespoons unsalted butter, melted

¼ cup sugar

Menu Ideas: Because this is such a rich way to end your evening, consider serving the pie after a lighter entrée, such as Sesame-Crusted Tuna with Soy-Lemon Sauce (page 95).

Do-Ahead Tips: This pie is great for entertaining, since it can be made up to 24 hours in advance. It's best to make the pie the morning of your dinner at the latest so it will have plenty of time to set. Then you'll have only to whip the cream, cut the pie, and garnish before serving.

1. For the graham cracker crust, preheat the oven to 375°F. Stir together the graham cracker crumbs, butter, and sugar in a medium bowl until well blended. Press the crumbs evenly onto the bottom and up the side of a 9- or 10-inch pie pan. Bake the crust for 6 to 8 minutes, until lightly browned. Set aside to cool completely.

2. Cream together the peanut butter, cream cheese, sugar, and melted butter in a large bowl with an electric mixer. Whip 1½ cups of the whipping cream in another bowl until soft peaks form, then whip in the vanilla extract. Fold the whipped cream into the peanut butter mixture in 3 or 4 batches. Pour the filling into the cooled pie shell. Refrigerate for at least 12 hours or overnight.

3. Just before serving, whip the remaining 1 cup whipping cream until soft peaks form. Cut the chilled pie into individual pieces and top each piece with a generous dollop of whipped cream. Finish with a sprinkle of chocolate curls and/or a drizzle of fudge sauce.

MAKING CHOCOLATE CURLS: They look fancy—and I suppose they kind of are—but chocolate curls are a snap to make and add easy flair to any number of desserts. Choose a piece of top-quality chocolate that's at least ¾ inch thick. Scrape a vegetable peeler down the length of the side of the chocolate bar, allowing the curls to fall onto a plate or piece of parchment paper. Try not to handle the curls too much, or they may melt from the heat of your fingers. You can scatter them directly from the plate or paper onto the pie. The curls can be made up to a day in advance and stored in an airtight container.

VANILLA ZABAGLIONE
IN CHOCOLATE CUPS

One of the best shortcuts to an elegant dessert is using the chocolate cups or shells that are available in well-stocked grocery stores and gourmet shops (Sur La Table included). One of my favorite fillings for the shells is zabaglione, the Italian custard I've had on many visits to Italy. The blend of egg yolks, sugar, and sweet wine is commonly served as is or with fresh berries. This version in chocolate cups makes for an almost embarrassingly easy way to serve a fun and impressive dessert. You can also fill them with chocolate mousse (page 190), ice cream, fresh berries topped with dollops of crème fraîche, or any number of quick embellishments that make for a sophisticated dessert.
MAKES 6 SERVINGS

5 egg yolks

⅓ cup sugar

½ teaspoon pure vanilla extract

½ cup sweet Marsala

6 chocolate cups or shells (about ¼-cup capacity each)

Freshly grated nutmeg, cocoa powder, or ground cinnamon

1. Combine the egg yolks, sugar, and vanilla extract in a medium stainless steel mixing bowl and whisk for 2 to 3 minutes, until thick and pale yellow. Alternatively, use a handheld electric mixer to beat for 1 to 2 minutes.

2. Choose a saucepan into which the bowl sits comfortably, with the bottom of the bowl perched a few inches above the bottom of the pan. Pour about 2 inches of water into the bottom of the saucepan and bring to a boil over medium heat. Decrease the heat to low and set the bowl over (not in) the gently simmering water (the water should not boil or the zabaglione may curdle). Whisking constantly, slowly drizzle in the Marsala. Continue whisking for 8 to 10 minutes (a few minutes less if using an electric mixer), until the zabaglione has nearly doubled in bulk and is quite thick with a velvety texture.

3. Remove the bowl from the pan and let cool to about room temperature, whisking occasionally. Spoon the cooled zabaglione into the chocolate cups. Just before serving, top the zabaglione with a sprinkle of nutmeg, cocoa powder, or cinnamon, and serve.

Menu Ideas: Serve this traditional Italian dessert after main-course servings of Cheese-Stuffed Tomatoes with Linguine (page 141) and a salad of crisp greens with a splash of oil and vinegar.

Do-Ahead Tips: I always prepare and serve the zabaglione at the last minute, though it can be made and spooned into the chocolate cups up to 2 hours in advance. Cover the cups loosely with plastic wrap to prevent the surface from drying out and refrigerate until ready to serve.

ORANGE CAKE

This is a wonderfully simple but delicious cake that I serve many different ways. Be sure to use a top-quality pure orange extract, one that tastes of natural orange, rather than having an orange "flavor." The glaze adds a beautiful sheen and additional flavor to the cake. A black metal loaf pan can brown the surface of the cake too much during baking; ideally use a heavyweight aluminum loaf pan, not a glass pan.
MAKES 8 TO 10 SERVINGS

Plain dried bread crumbs, for loaf pan

Finely grated zest of 2 large oranges
    (about ¼ cup)

1 cup plus 1 tablespoon sugar

½ cup blanched almonds (whole or slivered)

1½ cups all-purpose flour

1 teaspoon baking powder

¾ teaspoon salt

½ cup unsalted butter, melted

2 eggs

½ cup whole milk

2 tablespoons pure orange extract

GLAZE (OPTIONAL)

⅓ cup sugar

⅓ cup freshly squeezed orange juice

½ teaspoon pure orange extract

Menu Ideas: This cake is perfect alongside a cup of tea in the afternoon, catching up with a friend. For desserts, I'll serve the cake slices topped with summer berries and a dollop of whipped cream. I also use this cake—cut into slender fingers—as one of the dippers for Individual Chocolate Fondues (page 192).

Do-Ahead Tips: The cake can be made up to 2 days before serving, wrapped well and refrigerated. It also freezes quite well for up to a few weeks; just be sure the cake is fully cooled before wrapping.

1. Preheat the oven to 350°F. Butter an 8½ by 4½ by 2¾-inch loaf pan and dust with the bread crumbs, tapping the pan upside down to remove the excess.

2. Combine the orange zest and 1 tablespoon of the sugar in a small bowl and stir, pressing the mixture with the back of the spoon to draw the flavor from the zest into the sugar. Set aside. Grind the almonds with 2 tablespoons of the flour in the food processor until very fine. Set aside.

3. Sift together the remaining flour, baking powder, and salt in a medium bowl. Place the melted butter in the bowl of a standing mixer. Add the remaining 1 cup sugar and beat to mix. On low speed, beat in the eggs one at a time. Add the flour mixture in 3 additions, alternating with the milk in 2 additions, scraping down the side of the bowl as needed. Beat in the orange extract, then remove the bowl from the mixer. Stir the zest-sugar mixture into the batter, followed by the ground almonds.

4. Pour the batter into the prepared loaf pan. Bake for 65 to 75 minutes, until a toothpick inserted deeply into the center of the cake comes out clean.

5. Shortly before the cake is done, make the glaze. Combine the sugar, orange juice, and orange extract in a small saucepan and warm over medium-low heat, stirring occasionally, for about 10 minutes, until the sugar is just dissolved. Do not allow the mixture to boil.

6. Transfer the cake in the pan to a wire rack and let sit for 2 to 3 minutes. Use a pastry brush to brush a thin layer of glaze onto the cake (still in its pan), allowing it to be slowly absorbed into the cake. Gradually add another thin layer of glaze and repeat. It should take several applications and about 5 minutes to apply all the glaze.

7. Let the cake cool until tepid. Invert the cake onto the wire rack, then turn it upright. (If the cake sticks in the pan, cover it loosely with foil or wax paper, turn it upside down onto your right hand and tap the bottom of the pan with your left hand; the cake will slide out.)

8. When the cake is completely cool, wrap in plastic wrap or foil and let stand for at least 4 hours before serving.

POMEGRANATE SORBET

Now that wonderful pomegranate juice is readily available year-round, this recipe is a snap. You can omit the Campari—a bitter Italian apéritif—if you don't have it on hand, but the addition gives the sorbet a real hit of flavor. Sometimes I'll sprinkle each serving with a few fresh pomegranate seeds and perhaps a bit of fresh chopped mint. **MAKES 1 QUART**

1½ cups water

⅓ cup sugar

⅓ cup light corn syrup

1 cup pure pomegranate juice

2 tablespoons Campari (optional)

1 teaspoon finely grated lemon zest

2 tablespoons freshly squeezed lemon juice

1. Combine the water, sugar, and corn syrup in a small saucepan and warm over medium heat, stirring occasionally, for about 5 minutes, until the sugar dissolves. Set aside to cool completely.

2. Stir the pomegranate juice, Campari, lemon zest, and lemon juice into the sugar syrup. Refrigerate until well chilled.

3. Pour the chilled sorbet base into an ice cream maker and freeze according to the manufacturer's instructions. Transfer the sorbet to an airtight container and freeze until set, at least 2 hours. The sorbet may need to sit at room temperature for 15 to 20 minutes to be soft enough to scoop.

Menu Ideas: This tangy sorbet is wonderful as a small taste between courses or at the end of a meal with a few fresh rasp berries or sliced pitted black Bing cherries on top. Add a few sugar cookies from your favorite bakery alongside and you have a delightful and incredibly easy way to finish any meal.

Do-Ahead Tips: The sorbet can be made up to 3 weeks in advance and frozen in an airtight container. It can become quite hard in the freezer; let sit at room temperature for 10 to 15 minutes if needed. Often I'll simply scrape the sorbet with a spoon to serve, rather than scooping it as I do for ice cream.

BLUEBERRY TART

When I was growing up, we all picked berries in the summer to earn money. There was a blueberry farm in our neighborhood and most of July was spent picking the wonderful plump berries. While fresh berries give the best results here, you can make an admirable tart with frozen berries as well. **MAKES 12 SERVINGS**

5 cups (about 1¼ pounds) blueberries

3 tablespoons all-purpose flour

1 tablespoon freshly squeezed lemon juice

½ teaspoon freshly grated or ground nutmeg

¼ teaspoon ground cinnamon

Vanilla ice cream or whipped cream, for serving

SWEET PASTRY DOUGH

½ cup unsalted butter

1 cup all-purpose flour

2 tablespoons sugar

½ teaspoon salt

1 egg yolk

2 to 3 tablespoons ice water

PASTRY GLAZE

1 egg yolk

2 tablespoons water

1 tablespoon sugar

BERRY GLAZE

5 tablespoons top-quality blueberry jam

1 tablespoon Grand Marnier or other orange liqueur

1 tablespoon finely grated orange zest

1 tablespoon finely grated lemon zest

1. For the pastry dough, cut the butter into small cubes and freeze for 5 minutes. In the bowl of a food processor, combine the butter, flour, sugar, and salt. Process for 10 to 15 seconds, until the butter is finely chopped. Add the egg yolk and 2 tablespoons of the water and pulse for another 10 seconds, or until the mixture looks like cornmeal. Pinch some of the dough between your fingers; it should hold together, not feel crumbly or dusty. If necessary, add more water, a teaspoon at a time, pulsing once or twice after each addition. Turn the dough out onto a clean work surface. Gather about one-quarter of the dough into a small pile and use the heel of your hand to push the dough away from you two or three times, which helps thoroughly blend the butter and flour for a flakier crust. Don't overwork the dough or it will produce a tough crust. Repeat with the remaining dough, then use a pastry scraper to gather the dough and form it into a disk about 5 inches across. Wrap in plastic and refrigerate for 30 minutes.

2. Preheat the oven to 400°F.

3. For the pastry glaze, whisk together the egg yolk and water in a small dish. For the berry glaze, stir together the jam, Grand Marnier, orange zest, and lemon zest in a small saucepan. Warm over medium-low heat, stirring, for 2 to 3 minutes. Set aside.

4. Roll the chilled pastry dough out on a lightly floured work surface to a 12-inch circle about ⅛ inch thick. Use the dough to line a 10-inch tart pan with a removable base. Brush the bottom and sides of the tart shell with the pastry glaze and sprinkle with the sugar.

5. Toss together the blueberries, flour, lemon juice, nutmeg, and cinnamon in a large bowl, being careful not to crush the berries. Scrape the mixture into the tart shell, spreading it evenly. Brush the berry glaze over the berries.

6. Set the tart pan on a baking sheet to catch any drips (don't use an insulated baking sheet) and bake for 35 to 40 minutes, until the crust is nicely browned and the filling is bubbly around the edge. Transfer the tart to a wire rack to cool for at least 1 hour. Remove the sides of the tart pan. Cut the tart into wedges and serve at room temperature with scoops ice cream or dollops of whipped cream on top.

Menu Ideas: I enjoy this simple tart after a dinner of Halibut with Nut Crust and Apple Vinaigrette (page 106) or Fresh Dungeness Crab with Two Sauces (page 104), served with the Parmesan Cones with Baby Greens and Herb Salad (page 66).

Do-Ahead Tips: The pastry dough can be made up to 1 month in advance and frozen, or 4 days in advance and refrigerated. Allow it to thaw slowly in the refrigerator for a day before using. The tart can be assembled and baked up to 5 hours before serving.

BLUEBERRY TARTLETS: You can make blueberry tartlets, using 2- to 4-inch tartlet pans (you'll get between 8 and 16 tartlets depending on the pan size). Double the pastry dough to be sure of having enough to line the small pans, and decrease the baking time to 15 to 20 minutes.

PUFF PASTRY TART WITH PLUMS

I use puff pastry as a quick and easy alternative to homemade pie dough for a number of tarts; it puffs up deliciously during baking for an elegant appearance. Choose a top-quality jam for this tart, it's a good time to splurge. Too-sweet jams don't allow the fruit flavor to shine through. I really like to use red currant all-fruit jelly, but have also tried this with a plum and walnut jam a friend made with good results. The rectangular shape of this tart makes for a fun, elegant presentation. Try to arrange the fruit pieces in even bands to make cutting tidy pieces easier. **MAKES 8 SERVINGS**

¼ cup slivered almonds

5 tablespoons sugar

2 tablespoons all-purpose flour

2 tablespoons unsalted butter,
    at room temperature

1 egg

¼ teaspoon pure almond extract

1 sheet (about 8 ounces) frozen puff pastry,
    thawed

⅓ cup currant or plum jam

1½ pounds ripe plums, pitted and each
    cut into eighths

Menu Ideas: This is slightly rich, with a soft tang from the fruit, so it is a well-balanced dessert that can top off any meal in style. Try it after a dinner of Herb-Rubbed Lamb Chops with Raita (page 125) or Fresh Dungeness Crab with Two Sauces (page 104).

Do-Ahead Tips: You can cut up the plums a few hours in advance and store, well wrapped, in the refrigerator. The tart should be assembled and baked not more than a few hours before serving; it can sit at room temperature in that time.

1. Preheat the oven to 400°F. Line a baking sheet with a silicone baking mat or parchment paper.

2. Place the almonds in a food processor with 3 tablespoons of the sugar and the flour; process until very finely ground. Add the butter, egg, and almond extract and pulse a few times to evenly blend, scraping down the side as needed. Transfer the mixture to a bowl and set aside.

3. Unfold the puff pastry sheet on a lightly floured work surface and roll gently just to even out the dough (you don't need to make it much thinner than it is already); trim if needed to make a tidy rectangle 14 inches by 10 inches. Use the tip of a small knife to make a 1-inch cut diagonally in from each corner of the dough. Roll the edges in just a bit, forming a rim around the perimeter of the dough, and pinch to seal at the corners.

4. Transfer the pastry to the lined baking sheet and spread the jam over the base of the dough. Top the jam with the almond mixture, spreading evenly. Arrange the plum wedges in even rows the length of the pastry. Sprinkle the remaining 2 tablespoons sugar over the plums.

5. Bake the tart for about 30 minutes, until the plums are tender and the pastry is well puffed and browned. Let the tart cool on the baking sheet, then carefully transfer to a cutting board. Cut into rectangles to serve.

PUFF PASTRY: Premade puff pastry—available in the freezer section of most grocery stores today—is one of the best boons to the busy cook. In fact, I tend to have a few boxes in my freezer at all times, ready for a quick dessert, as a flaky topping for a meat pie, or wrapped around a piece of cheese for a quick tapas. See Savory Puff Pastry Bites (page 23), for other puff pastry ideas for the cocktail hour.

MOTHER'S OATMEAL SPICE COOKIES

These cookies were a frequent treat in my house when I was growing up. In fact, they're the first cookies I learned to bake, after the classic Toll House cookies. I've always baked the cookies on an ungreased baking sheet, but you can use a silicone baking mat or parchment paper to line the sheets if you prefer. **MAKES 36 COOKIES**

6 tablespoons whole milk

1 teaspoon baking soda

2 eggs

1 cup packed light brown sugar

1 cup unsalted butter, melted

1 teaspoon pure vanilla extract

2 cups all-purpose flour

2 cups rolled oats

¾ cup raisins

½ cup chopped toasted walnuts (see page 222)

½ cup chopped dates

1 teaspoon salt

1 teaspoon ground cinnamon

1 teaspoon freshly ground or grated nutmeg

¼ teaspoon ground allspice

¼ teaspoon ground cloves

1. Preheat the oven to 325°F. Set 2 oven racks toward the center of the oven.

2. Stir together the milk and baking soda in a small dish. Whisk the eggs in a large bowl until well blended, then whisk in the brown sugar, melted butter, vanilla extract, and milk-soda mixture. Whisk until smooth and evenly blended. Use a wooden spoon to stir in the flour, oats, raisins, walnuts, dates, salt, cinnamon, nutmeg, allspice, and cloves.

3. Drop the cookie dough by tablespoons onto 2 ungreased baking sheets about 2 inches apart. Bake for 15 to 17 minutes, until puffed and nicely browned, switching the baking sheets halfway through. Transfer the cookies to a wire rack to cool.

Menu Ideas: Cookies like this are nearly all-occasion. Serve them any time the mood strikes, with ice cream for a casual dinner, or with coffee after a fancy dinner party.

Do-Ahead Tips: The cookies can be made up to 4 days in advance and stored in an airtight container. They also freeze well for up to 2 months.

DESSERT CHOUX DUO

Here I offer just a couple of many options for filling choux puffs, proving they're just as versatile for dessert as they are at the start of the meal (see Choux Puffs with Salmon and Shrimp, page 36). I think it's fun to offer a few different puffs to guests—each with a different filling. Variations on the Chantilly filling are endless; it can be flavored with coffee powder, any number of fresh fruits, liqueurs, and/or chopped toasted nuts.

Although I offer two fillings here, I often will add a third to the mix, my little secret: a small scoop of top-quality purchased ice cream. In fact, fill the puffs with ice cream and top with the chocolate fondue sauce on page 192 and you'll have the ever-popular dessert, profiteroles. Note that the chocolate mousse must be made 24 hours in advance, so plan ahead. **MAKES 18 SERVINGS**

CHOUX PASTRY

½ cup whole milk

½ cup water

7 tablespoons unsalted butter, cut into pieces

1 tablespoon granulated sugar

⅛ teaspoon salt

1½ cups all-purpose flour

5 or 6 eggs, at room temperature

Confectioners' sugar, for serving

EGG WASH

1 egg

1 teaspoon water

CHOCOLATE MOUSSE

2 tablespoons boiling water

2 teaspoons instant espresso powder

3 ounces top-quality semisweet or bittersweet chocolate, coarsely chopped

2 eggs, separated

3 tablespoons granulated sugar, or more if needed

½ cup whipping cream

Pinch of salt

1. Preheat the oven to 400°F. Line 2 baking sheets with silicone baking mats or parchment paper.

2. For the pastry, combine the milk, water, butter, granulated sugar, and salt in a medium saucepan and warm over medium heat until the butter is melted. Add the flour all at once and stir continuously until the flour is thoroughly incorporated and the dough begins to pull together into a ball; it will be quite stiff at this point.

3. Remove the pan from the heat and beat in the eggs 1 at a time, stirring well with a wooden spoon to fully incorporate each egg before adding the next. The first couple of eggs are the hardest to mix in; as the dough softens, it gets easier. After you have incorporated 5 eggs, the dough should be smooth and satiny. If the dough detaches from the spoon in a few seconds' time when you lift it up, it is perfect and you do not need the extra egg. Otherwise beat in a sixth egg.

4. Transfer the dough to a large pastry bag with a ½-inch plain tip. Pipe the dough onto the baking sheets in 1½-inch mounds at least 2 inches apart.

5. For the egg wash, beat the egg with a fork in a small bowl until frothy, then beat in the water. Use a soft pastry brush to brush the top of each mound lightly with egg wash, gently patting down any tails of dough sticking up.

6. Bake the puffs for 18 to 20 minutes, until the pastry is nicely puffed and deep brown. It's best to bake 1 sheet at a time, so pop the first in the oven while piping the second (which will be fine sitting to wait its turn). Allow the puffs to cool on the baking sheet, then transfer to a wire rack to cool completely before filling.

7. For the chocolate mousse, combine the boiling water and espresso powder in the top of a double boiler set over simmering water, stirring to dissolve. Add the chocolate and stir constantly until fully melted and smooth. Take the pan from the heat and set the bowl aside.

GRAND MARNIER CHANTILLY

¾ cup whipping cream

3 tablespoons Grand Marnier or other orange liqueur

3 tablespoons confectioners' sugar

½ teaspoon finely grated orange zest

> **Menu Ideas:** This is such a fun, universally enjoyed dessert—I can't think of any meal that wouldn't end well with filled puffs.
>
> **Do-Ahead Tips:** The fully cooled puffs can be stored for up to 3 days in the refrigerator in an airtight bag, or up to 1 month in the freezer. The chocolate mousse can be made up to 1 day in advance and the Chantilly made a few hours in advance. The puffs will be at their best filled shortly before serving.

...he egg yolks with the granulated sugar in a large bowl until well ... Whisk in the warm chocolate until smooth. Let cool completely.

9. Beat the cream in another bowl until medium peaks form. Fold the whipped cream into the chocolate mixture. Beat the egg whites with salt in a clean bowl (and be sure you've cleaned the beater very well!) until they form medium peaks. Fold the egg whites into the chocolate-cream mixture a few spoonfuls at a time until thoroughly incorporated. Refrigerate until ready to use.

10. For the Chantilly, whip the cream until medium peaks form. Continue beating while slowly drizzling in the Grand Marnier until stiff peaks form. Beat in the sugar and orange zest. Refrigerate the cream until ready to serve.

11. Shortly before serving, use a serrated knife to cut off the top third of each puff. Spoon the chocolate mousse filling into about 18 of the puffs and the chantilly filling into another 18 or so puffs (don't overfill). Top each puff with its lid and arrange on a serving platter. Sprinkle with a light dusting of confectioners' sugar and serve.

INDIVIDUAL CHOCOLATE FONDUES

For those dinner parties when you want to give yourself a break come dessert time, look no further than simple chocolate fondue. Your guests will love the hands-on fun of picking their favorite dippers to dunk into rich chocolate and it's a great way to end the evening on a dynamic note.

Alter the selections of fruits, cookies, and other dippers to suit the season and your tastes. Other options include most any fresh fruit, dried fruit such as mango or apricots, shortbread cookies, and ladyfingers. When time is really tight, buy a top-quality chocolate fudge sauce to warm for dipping. The recipe below is a silky homemade sauce you'll want to make for countless different uses. It can be embellished with any number of flavorings, including different liqueurs or even a dash of cinnamon or finely ground black pepper. **MAKES 6 SERVINGS**

8 ounces strawberries, hulled, halved if large

2 large ripe bananas, peeled and sliced

1 large navel orange, peeled and sectioned

3 slices (¾-inch-thick) Orange Cake (page 182) or purchased pound cake, cut into fingers

CHOCOLATE SAUCE

1 cup whipping cream

8 ounces top-quality bittersweet or semisweet chocolate, chopped

⅓ cup sugar

2 tablespoons unsalted butter, cut into pieces

2 teaspoons pure vanilla extract or 1 tablespoon brandy or Grand Marnier

Menu Ideas: This tasty fondue would be a welcome finish to most any dinner. Consider serving it as part of a slightly retro meal that starts with Clam and Chive Dip with Pita Chips (page 17) and Olive Pecan Bites (page 10), then continues to Braised Brisket with Onions (page 109), Spicy Spanish Rice (page 139), and steamed green beans.

Do-Ahead Tips: The chocolate sauce can be made up to 2 days in advance and gently reheated in the top of a double boiler. Some fruits can be prepared in advance, if they won't discolor; bananas should be sliced just before serving.

1. For the chocolate sauce, warm the cream in a small saucepan over medium heat. Decrease the heat to low and add the chocolate, sugar, and butter. Stir for 2 to 3 minutes, until evenly melted with a silky texture. Stir in the vanilla extract and set aside until ready to serve. (Refrigerate if making more than 1 hour in advance.)

2. Arrange the fruit and cakes on individual plates or on a large platter for passing. Reheat the chocolate sauce if needed and pour it into individual butter warmers (see below). Set one at each place setting and ask your guests to light the candle underneath.

SERVING FONDUE: There are, of course, fondue pots made just for this task but when there are more than a few people at the dinner table, it becomes challenging for everyone to have easy access. What I use is ceramic "butter warmers"—of roughly ½-cup capacity—meant to keep melted butter warm when serving steamed crab or lobster. They make ideal individual fondue pots, with a votive candle underneath to keep the chocolate melted. I keep matches on hand so if the chocolate begins to bubble (which will scorch the chocolate) you can blow out the candle, then relight it as needed to keep the chocolate warm.

MENU IDEAS

In the following pages, I offer suggestions to help you craft full dinner parties using the recipes and entertaining tips featured in this book. As you'll see, I always approach my dinner parties with a specific theme in mind, a great foundation from which you can build the menu selections, décor, beverage choices, even music options. Each of these themed menu plans outlines the selected recipes, offers a timeline of preparation, and gives you specific ideas of how to decorate the table and set the ambiance for the evening. My good friend Dan McCarthy, a well-respected wine expert and co-owner of McCarthy & Schiering Wine Merchants in Seattle, provides detailed wine recommendations for each menu. With these plans in hand, you'll be able to host wonderful dinner parties with less stress than you might imagine.

An Evening in Spain

When creating a Spanish dinner, I immediately start thinking of the little plates of tapas that start off the evening, followed later by hearty roasted meat or the famous paella. This generous dish—overflowing with scented rice, vegetables, seafood, and/or meat and packed with colors, aromas, and flavors—makes for a most festive dinner party centerpiece.

Greet your guests with glasses of cava (Spanish sparkling wine) or fruit-laden sangria in tall glasses. Tapas can be served pre-plated for each guest, or set the various bowls and platters out on a buffet for guests to serve themselves on small (4-inch) plates as they mingle and visit. I make picks available, too, for spearing a meatball or mushroom, for easy finger food.

You will need to be cooking your paella while your guests mingle and watch. When it is time to allow the paella to rest for a few minutes, invite everyone to the table. Or, you may choose to allow guests to serve themselves from the pan while it is in the kitchen, then they can proceed to the table. I typically serve the salad after the paella, as a palate cleanser before dessert, but you can serve it alongside the paella if you like. I serve the cheesecake on large plates, with the rose-colored rhubarb sauce as an accent.

Keep the music going—preferably hot flamenco music—and enjoy the evening at a leisurely pace. In Spain, dinner is never served until after 10 P.M., so there is no reason to rush.

⌗ MENU ⌗

Minty Meatballs (page 5)

Mushrooms à la Grecque (page 22)

Savory Puff Pastry Bites (page 23)

Toasted Marcona almonds

Party Sangria (page 197) or dry Cava sparkling wine

Paella with Chicken and Shellfish (page 120)

Albariño from the region of Rias Baixas or a joven (young) red from Rioja

Bibb Lettuce and Grapefruit Salad (page 52)

Very Citrus Cheesecake (page 178) with Rhubarb Sauce

Bodegas Gutiérrez de la Vega Casta Diva Cosecha Miel

THIS MENU WILL SERVE 8 GUESTS.

DAN MCCARTHY'S WINE NOTES

Cava is the wonderful sparkling wine made on the east coast of Spain. It is a great way to begin any Spanish meal. The wines range in flavor from very dry to slightly sweet. Try to find a drier style to match the flavors of the marinated meatballs and pork kebabs.

There are many wines that will work with the paella. On the white side, try an albariño from the region of Rias Baixas in Galicia on Spain's Atlantic Coast. These wines have hints of orange and nectarine, yet they are fully dry. If you prefer to serve a red wine, try a joven (young) red from Rioja. A blend of tempranillo and garnacha, this will marry well with a myriad of flavors in the dish.

Spain has many dessert wines, but with this cheesecake I would recommend a wine from the Alicante area called Bodegas Gutiérrez de la Vega Casta Diva Cosecha Miel. It has a long name but it is a popular wine. Cosecha miel translates as "honey harvest," which gives you an idea of the flavor of this gem.

GAME PLAN

Two Days Ahead

Marinate mushrooms and refrigerate

Make meatballs and freeze

Make cheesecake and rhubarb sauce

One Day Ahead

Prepare all paella ingredients to point just before rice gets cooked: sauté chicken and sausages; roast peppers; dice onions and garlic; store in separate containers and refrigerate

Morning of

Make sangria; do not add soft fruit (such as peaches) or club soda until ready to serve

Thaw meatballs in refrigerator

Wash lettuce for salad, wrap in towels, and refrigerate; section grapefruit and reserve; make dressing

Steam clams and mussels for paella; refrigerate

Make puff pastry bites, store in airtight container

Two to Three Hours before Guests Arrive

Cook meatballs

Prepare salad ingredients for quick assembly just before serving

Shortly before Serving

Finish sangria

Assemble, dress, and plate salad

Cook paella

DÉCOR

Red and black are the hot colors of Spain. A tablecloth of red or white with polka dot napkins would be fun. Arrange red candles down the center of the table, under hurricane glasses if you have them. I like to buy red roses a few days early and allow them to fully open. The day of the party, I'll cut the stems short and arrange them in low vases for great impact.

Don't forget the small bowls for discarded clam and mussel shells.

PARTY SANGRIA

You can substitute diced apple for the pear. And in the fall when peaches are passed, you might find lovely purple plums to use in their place.
MAKES 8 TO 10 SERVINGS

1 bottle (750 ml) dry red wine

⅓ cup sugar

⅓ cup Cointreau or other orange liqueur

⅓ cup lemon or orange vodka

1 pear, cored, peeled, and diced

1 small orange, thinly sliced and seeded

1 small lemon, thinly sliced and seeded

1 lime, thinly sliced and seeded

1 cup club soda or plain sparkling water

1 peach or nectarine, peeled (page 221), pitted,
    and thinly sliced

Combine the wine, sugar, Cointreau, vodka, pear, orange, lemon, and lime in a large pitcher and stir to mix. Refrigerate at least 8 hours or overnight.

Just before serving, stir the soda into the sangria and add the peach. Serve in wineglasses or tall glasses, adding a few pieces of fruit to each glass.

Celebrate Italy

I find that the most memorable aspect of a dinner table in Italy is all the wineglasses, empty plates, passionate music, and lively conversation that drives the energy of the evening. In this vein, I tend to keep my table setting simple for an Italian feast, letting the food and wine be the decorations and the centerpiece.

When guests arrive, have your crudités and meats set out in large bowls or on decorative plates. Pile it high, you are going for impact! (Leftover prosciutto and salami will keep well for a week or two.) I recommend passing the pinwheels and baked clams, as they are both best served warm. You can bring them out in waves rather than all at once. Just remember not to overindulge your guests with the hors d'oeuvres. You want them to still be hungry for the grand dinner that awaits.

✠ MENU ✠

Baked Clams with Bacon and Rosemary (page 29)

Prosciutto Pinwheels (page 15)

Bread sticks

An assortment of sliced Italian salamis and prosciutto

Crudités with Roquefort Dip (page 28)

Negroni cocktails or Vernaccia di San Gimignano

Cheese-Stuffed Tomatoes with Linguine (page 141)

Vernaccia di San Gimignano or Orvieto Classico

Veal Chops with Green Peppercorns and Rosemary (page 117)

Sautéed Spinach with Mustard Sauce (page 158)

Sautéed Tiny Tomatoes with Chile Flakes (page 144)

Chianti Classico, Brunello di Montalcino, and Vino Nobile di Montepulciano

Vanilla Zabaglione in Chocolate Cups (page 181)

Vin Santo di Chianti Classico

**THIS MENU CAN EASILY BE ADJUSTED TO SERVE EITHER 6
FOR A MORE INTIMATE DINNER, OR 12 FOR A LARGER GATHERING.**

DAN MCCARTHY'S WINE NOTES

If you serve Negronis to start the evening, be sure the next wine has no oak flavor that would conflict with the bitter note of the Campari. I suggest a Vernaccia di San Gimignano, the dry white wine made from Vernaccia grapes in the vineyards surrounding this charming hill town. Look for a young vintage; the wine should be crisp and fresh. This wine will also work with the linguine and stuffed tomatoes, but you can also try an Orvieto Classico from the beautiful hill town of the same name in Umbria. Again, whites should be as young as possible.

The green peppercorns and rosemary add a spicy nature to the otherwise mild veal. I suggest comparing two or three Tuscan reds, all made with variations of the sangiovese grape. Chianti Classico is a hearty, well-liked sangiovese wine; selections from the regions of Greve, Castelnuovo Berardenga, and Radda have extra concentration that will stand up to the seasonings. For a comparison, try wines from two different areas of southern Tuscany: Brunello di Montalcino, made from Brunello grapes around the village of Montalcino, and Vino Nobile di Montepulciano, made from Prugnolo Gentile from the vineyards behind Montepulciano. They make excellent choices to match with veal.

For dessert, try a sip of a sweet Vin Santo di Chianti Classico. This wine is made from air-dried grapes that are aged in small barrels for a minimum of 5 years. It will add a spark to the rich zabaglione.

GAME PLAN

One Day Ahead

Make Roquefort dip; trim and prepare crudités, wrap in damp paper towels, and refrigerate

Make pinwheels and freeze on baking sheets

Make garlic oil for veal chops

Morning of

Arrange the sliced meat on a tray, cover with plastic wrap, and refrigerate

Clean and trim spinach; wrap in towels to refrigerate until ready to cook

Make mustard sauce for spinach

Stuff tomatoes with cheese and refrigerate

Make clam stuffing, wash shells and store separately

One to Two Hours before Guests Arrive

Stuff clams, arrange on baking sheets, and refrigerate

Bake pinwheels (allow about 10 minutes extra if baking from frozen state)

Arrange crudités on plates or platters around bowl for dip (added just before serving)

Sauté onion/garlic mixture for tomatoes

Shortly before Serving

Cook spinach

Bake clams

Cook linguine and bake tomatoes

Season veal chops and broil

Sauté and finish tiny tomatoes

Make zabaglione and fill chocolate cups

DÉCOR

Again, this is a meal for which I like to keep table decorations to a minimum. I'll often place a runner of fabric or several place mats down the center of the table and top with 8 or 10 tall pillar candles (I prefer candles with 3-inch diameters). Place each candle on a glass trivet, saucer, or large leaf. You can arrange many votives around the table as well, depending on the size of your space.

Using several wine coasters, place the two or three red wines you'll be serving with the main course on the table, so guests can taste and compare. Be sure to use large bowled red wineglasses. Think Italy! Tall glasses with bread sticks or breadbaskets full of crunchy bread will fill the spaces. The light from all the candles will set your table aglow as it reflects off the glasses.

GAME PLAN

Three Days Ahead

> Marinate lamb and refrigerate
>
> Make lamb stock and refrigerate

One Day Ahead

> Assemble bean gratin and refrigerate
>
> Make salmon filling and refrigerate
>
> Seed pomegranate for salad; make croutons; make vinaigrette
>
> Make lemon cream for ginger cake and refrigerate

Morning of

> Assemble phyllo packets
>
> Bake ginger cake
>
> Blanch asparagus, wrap in towels, and refrigerate

One to Two Hours before Guests Arrive

> Prep salad ingredients; combine in large bowl, top with damp paper towels, and refrigerate
>
> Place olives and nuts in small bowls

Shortly before Serving

> Stir watercress into gratin and bake (cover and set aside while roasting lamb)
>
> Bake phyllo packets
>
> Sear and roast lamb, and make sauce
>
> Sauté asparagus
>
> Spread salmon mixture on crackers
>
> Toss and plate salad
>
> Reheat bean gratin

DÉCOR

This is a great time to set your table with a lot of votives. You may be sampling a number of special wines, so the impact of wineglasses lined up with all the candles is always wonderful. Your mats and napkins should have darker color tones, though white napkins contrasting with dark mats can be dramatic.

The centerpiece can easily vary with the seasons. In fall, it could be gorgeous autumn leaves, gourds, and assorted winter squash interspersed with the votives, or your favorite holiday décor if this is a holiday celebration. In springtime, when I'm most inspired to serve this menu, I love to create a mass of primroses down the center of the table. I remove the plants from their boxes and set them on a piece of aluminum foil, which I wrap up around the dirt. Cover the outside of the foil with moss. You can then plant the primroses in your garden after the party.

DAN MCCARTHY'S WINE NOTES

For the appetizers, try a dry white wine from the Northwest. Sémillon—whether on its own or in a Bordeaux-style blend with the Sauvignon Blanc grape—is a wonderful food-friendly wine that can have a touch of elegance as well. For this meal, I recommend you carry through with the same white wine from the appetizers to the salad course.

When it comes to the main course, why not stick with the Northwest theme by serving a lush Syrah wine from Washington State? For the ginger cake, it's an ideal time to sip one of the special late-harvest Rieslings that are made so well in Washington.

An Exotic Moroccan Soirée

My husband and I made a most memorable trip to Morocco in 1997, renting a house in Marrakech that we shared with a group of friends. Immediately our senses were enlivened, not only by the colorful hues decorating the home, but by the smells of the garden, the sounds of many colorful birds, and of course the flavors of the exotic North African cuisine. I like to try to re-create that multi-sensory experience when preparing a Moroccan dinner in my home, serving food that's delightfully aromatic, decorating with splashes of bold color, and creating a warm glow with lots of candles. As soon as guests walk in the front door, smell the spices wafting from the kitchen, and see the vivid colors of the dinner table, they know they are in for a treat.

¤ MENU ¤

Smoky Moroccan Meatballs (page 11)

Roasted almonds

Moroccan dry-cured olives

Lemon Spritzers (page 208)

Frisée Salad with Toasted Hazelnuts (page 50)

Spanish Verdejo wine, preferably from the Rueda region

Lamb Shanks Tagine with Preserved Lemon (page 126)

Couscous with Vegetables and Herbs (page 148)

Spanish Garnacha (Grenache) red wine

Oranges with Candied Zest (page 187)

Moroccan-Style Biscotti (page 174)

Moroccan Mint Tea (page 208)

THIS MENU SERVES 8 GUESTS.

DAN MCCARTHY'S WINE NOTES

There are many wines produced in Morocco, but very few are exported so it can be difficult to find a bottle to serve. Instead, I recommend the white wines of Rueda, Spain, for before dinner. They are made from Verdejo grapes and are crisp, light, and very refreshing. There is a faintly salty nature to Rueda whites that complements the lightly salty appetizers and the salad.

Spanish wines made from Garnacha (or Grenache, as the grape is known in France) are perfect for matching with the lamb shanks with preserved lemon. The faintly earthy nature of the wines is perfect to accent the preserved lemon flavor. Wines from Spain's Navarra region are a fine complement.

GAME PLAN

Two Days Ahead

Make tagine and refrigerate

Make biscotti and store in airtight container

Make candied orange zest and store in airtight container

One Day Ahead

Cook meatballs and refrigerate

Make couscous and refrigerate

Make dressing for salad and refrigerate

Three to Four Hours before Guests Arrive

Prep salad ingredients and store separately, vegetables topped with damp paper towels

Make lemon syrup for spritzers

Place almonds and olives in small bowls

One Hour before Guests Arrive

Mix pitcher of spritzers and refrigerate

Shortly before Serving

Reheat meatballs

Assemble and dress salad

Reheat tagine

Reheat couscous

Assemble oranges

Make Moroccan tea

DÉCOR

To welcome your guests, you may want to display some flowers in the entry that have a sweet smell, like a few stalks of tuberose or freesia to help set the sensory scene. It's easy to embellish your dining room table with color, using deep jewel-toned fabric and place mats (think reds, purples, blues, greens). I like to dot the table with many small glass votives set in colorful or clear glass holders. These can be offset with taller candlesticks with simple white tapers if you like. This is an occasion to dim the lights a bit and let the glow of candles help set the mood for the exotic meal.

Moroccan meals are often served on low tables, with dinner guests perched on pillows on the floor. One night we used an old door set on cinder blocks as our "table," which I covered with a deep green sheet that I'd found on sale as a stand-in tablecloth. We then took all the cushions off the couches and chairs and sat on the floor in a room full of candles. (The dogs were thrilled to be on the same level as the table for once.) I didn't use fragrant candles or flowers on the dinner table, so nothing competed with the aromas of the meal.

If you have them, this is a fun time to use a mix of solid-colored napkins and plates. Vibrantly hued traditional tagine dishes are worthy of bringing to the table for serving, but if you don't have a tagine dish, you can simply plate the main course from the pot in the kitchen. The after-dinner tea is commonly served in small brightly colored tea glasses for extra panache.

LEMON SPRITZERS

The tart, refreshing character of this sparkling drink makes it an ideal accompaniment to spicy food. Wine and other alcohol is not part of traditional Moroccan meals, but you can add a splash of vodka—lemon vodka is a good choice—to the spritzers for a great cocktail. MAKES 8 SERVINGS

1 cup sugar

1 cup water

½ cup freshly squeezed lemon juice

1 bottle (2 liters) club soda or plain sparkling water

1 bunch fresh mint, rinsed and dried

1 large lemon, thinly sliced and seeded

1. Combine the sugar, water, and lemon juice in a small saucepan. Bring to a boil over medium-high heat, stirring to help the sugar dissolve. Boil for 5 minutes, stirring occasionally, to form a smooth syrup. Set aside to cool.

2. Transfer the lemon syrup to a large glass pitcher and add half of the club soda.

3. Set aside 8 mint sprigs and 8 lemon slices for garnish. Pull the leaves from the remaining sprigs. Take the mint in small handfuls and twist to break the leaves so that the flavor will be released. Add the bruised mint and remaining lemon slices to the pitcher and stir well to mix. Refrigerate for at least 1 hour before serving and top off each glass with the remaining soda when serving.

4. Half-fill 8 tall glasses with ice and slip a mint sprig into each. Pour the lemon spritzer over the ice, garnish with a lemon slice, and serve.

MOROCCAN MINT TEA

This tea—usually poured from a pretty silver teapot into fancy decorated tea glasses—is usually served with a simple cookie or piece of candy. In Morocco, they usually use loose tea leaves, about ¼ cup would be the equivalent of the bags used here. Moroccans prefer quite a bit of sugar in their tea—that is what makes it so soothing. You may want to allow your guests to add their own sugar, but please don't use artificial sweeteners. To increase servings, add another tea bag and small handful of mint for every 2 cups of water. MAKES 6 SERVINGS

4 cups water

4 bags black tea (such as Ceylon or orange pekoe)

2 handfuls fresh mint leaves

1 tablespoon sugar

Bring the water to a boil in a medium saucepan. Put the tea bags in a teapot. Take the mint in small handfuls and twist to break the leaves so that the flavor will be released. Add the bruised mint to the teapot. Pour the hot water over the mint and tea, cover the pot, and steep for 3 to 4 minutes. Add the sugar and stir until fully dissolved. Pour the tea into individual tea glasses or cups and serve.

DAN MCCARTHY'S WINE NOTES

The cocktail nature here makes me think of Chardonnay for white and Pinot Noir for red, since they are such popular wines by the glass at cocktail hour. Both grapes are used in wines from many different regions; here I recommend you look for Oregon-made wines. When chocolate is on the dessert menu, port is always a favorite option. With this combination of desserts, including the fresh blueberries, a late bottled vintage port is the ideal sip. Seek out one with as much bottle age as possible.

GAME PLAN

Two Days Ahead

Make gazpacho and refrigerate

Make cheese crackers and store in airtight container

Make dough for onion tart and refrigerate

Make dough for tartlets and refrigerate

Make rub and wash for ribs

Make choux puffs and refrigerate

One Day Ahead

Make garlic butter for mussels and refrigerate

Caramelize onions for tart and refrigerate

Blanch asparagus, wrap in towels, and refrigerate

Make pots de crème in espresso cups or other small dishes and refrigerate

Marinate ribs and refrigerate

Make chocolate mousse for puffs

Make Champagne vinaigrette

Morning of

Make and bake blueberry tartlets, using 2-inch tartlet pans

Bake and grill ribs; refrigerate when cool

Toast pita wedges and store in airtight container; prepare cheese topping and refrigerate

One to Two Hours before Guests Arrive

Steam mussels and remove from shells, reserving shell halves for serving; when fully cool, fill shells with mussels and garlic butter, arrange on a rimmed tray, and refrigerate

Arrange meats and cheeses on platters, cover with plastic wrap, and refrigerate

Make Chantilly filling for puffs

Shortly before Serving

Arrange asparagus on platter and drizzle tops with vinaigrette

Bake mussels

Assemble and bake onion tart

Assemble pita bites

Reheat ribs, covered with foil, in a 275°F oven for about 30 minutes

Fill puffs

DÉCOR

With such a range of different foods, the cocktail fare itself becomes a significant part of the décor. While the central buffet is the show-stopping focus, make it easy for your guests to mingle and circulate by distributing other dishes in a few different spots around the room. I like to put the cheese crackers in small bowls and arrange them in different spots. You might have a platter with the gazpacho in shot glasses (or other small glasses) on the buffet and another near the bar area; likewise you can split up the pita bites in different locations. It's a good idea to pass the mussels on platters, while they're still warm from the oven, cooking and serving them in waves.

Be sure to provide plenty of plates (and no, they don't have to all match), so guests aren't too worried if they lose track of one. There will be another at the ready for them to use. Have plenty of colorful napkins, too, so people can eat with their fingers as they choose. For plates, I don't make them too small. Though this is nibbly finger food, I prefer using medium plates (7 to 8 inches) that allow guests to sample a number of items at the same time.

I store the white wine and any other cold beverages in a tub of ice, so guests can easily help themselves. A few flower petals sprinkled over the ice is always a hit.

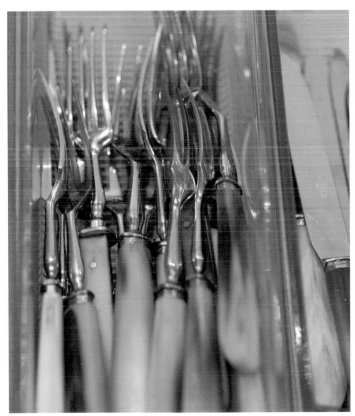

Dining Alfresco

As sunny days and warmer evenings set in, there is an insurmountable tug that draws us outside to eat on our decks, in our gardens, or at a nearby beach or park. It's a fun time to get creative with dining alfresco. All of these delicious dishes are perfect served at room temperature, ideal choices for no-fuss outdoor dining.

We have a great open-air dining room just outside the kitchen, which is covered, with a large fireplace and heat lamp for those cool Northwest evenings. It is a versatile spot we enjoy utilizing for many meals throughout the year. When the garden starts to burst, we may enjoy our pre-dinner snacks and a glass of wine while wandering through, sampling some of the fresh herbs and checking the development of the tomato plants. During the warmer afternoons we'll serve a full picnic in the garden, or pack up wonderful food and head to a friend's boat or beachfront.

If you'll be eating this meal on-the-go, transport the dressings for the corn salad and the coleslaw separately and toss the salads shortly before serving. This will help preserve the crisp bright flavor and texture of the vegetables. Everything else can be finished at home and transported ready to serve.

⌖ MENU ⌖

Pickled Shrimp with Capers (page 6)

Cheese Crackers (page 39)

Iced tea

Four-Star Fried Chicken (page 110)

Loaf of crusty bread

French Potato and Green Bean Salad with Tarragon (page 61)

Coleslaw with Lemon-Caper Dressing (page 64)

Roasted Corn Salad (page 53)

For a white wine, a Sancerre from the Loire Valley; for a red, a Côte du Rhône

Mother's Oatmeal Spice Cookies (page 189)

Clusters of crisp grapes

THIS MENU SERVES 8 GUESTS.

DAN MCCARTHY'S WINE NOTES

Dining in the open requires wines with big aromas. Try a Loire Valley Sancerre for a white selection; it is made from the Sauvignon Blanc grape and has a fully dry style that complements a wide variety of flavors. For a red option, a Côte du Rhône from France's Rhône Valley is perfect. The bold aroma of Grenache and Syrah grapes stands out in the evening air.

GAME PLAN

Two Days Ahead

Marinate shrimp and refrigerate

Make cheese crackers and store in airtight container

Make cookies and store in airtight container

One Day Ahead

Prepare corn salad ingredients, combine in a large bowl, and refrigerate; make dressing and store separately

Prepare coleslaw, storing dressing and vegetables separately

Brine chicken

Wash grapes and cut into clusters

One to Two Hours before Guests Arrive

Make potato salad and refrigerate

Fry chicken, leave out on baking sheet to cool, keep uncovered to preserve crispness

Make iced tea

Shortly before Serving

Toss corn salad with its dressing

Toss coleslaw with its dressing

DÉCOR

Eating outdoors calls for casual, fun décor and service. Provide interesting plastic plates or the stylish newer bamboo plates, colorful unbreakable glasses, and plenty of napkins for those fried-chicken fingers. If you're traveling to a park or the beach, be sure not to forget serving utensils, glasses, bottle openers—all the things you'll need. Bags and paper towels to use for cleanup are essential as well.

If you are eating on the deck or in the garden, arrange the dishes on platters to pass at the table family-style. You don't need good dishes, but do use colorful cloth napkins for a touch of panache. I have large wooden plates perfect for alfresco meals. Everything fits on one plate, so it is easy to sit on the ground or on a stool. Cover your tables with simple jars of seasonal flowers, fresh from the garden if you have them.

A Mardi Gras Feast

Years ago when Paul Prudhomme first opened his famous Cajun restaurant K-Paul's Louisiana Kitchen, I had an opportunity to visit New Orleans. I stood in line at his small restaurant in the French Quarter and waited patiently for a plate of gumbo; I will never forget it. Over the next few days, I took cooking classes to learn about creating the great dishes of Louisiana. It opened my eyes to a whole new array of spices, flavors, and energy that could only be found in this part of the country.

As the calendar leads up to Mardi Gras each year, heating up the streets of New Orleans, we are all caught up in the celebration. This menu will help you create an evening of great fun and lively conversation with memorable food served in a colorful style. The centerpiece gumbo is bold and flavorful; serve it in shallow soup bowls over beds of fluffy steamed rice. In the recipe for Spinach and Hearts of Palm Salad, you'll see that I recommend serving fried oysters as an optional accent on top of the flavorful salad. Here, instead, the oysters star as an appetizer, served with rémoulade. The salad is then served, oyster-free, as a fresh complement to the rich gumbo.

You can serve this as a seated dinner in several courses, though I tend to lean toward turning it into a grand buffet feast. It makes for a more dynamic, energy-filled evening that perfectly suits the mood and style of New Orleans. Crank up the jazz music and pass around those colorful beads (available at costume stores). Greet your guests with a glass of Planter's Punch when they arrive; it sets the party mood in style. This will be a night to remember.

¤ MENU ¤

Olive Pecan Bites (page 10)

Fried Oysters with Rémoulade (page 4)

Clam and Chive Dip with Pita Chips (page 17)

Salted roasted pecans

Planter's Punch (page 219)

Mardi Gras Gumbo (page 100)

Steamed white rice

Spinach and Hearts of Palm Salad (page 44)

Classic Cornbread (page 149) or Mini Corn Muffins with
Roasted Garlic and Fresh Herbs (page 136)

*Napa Valley or Sonoma County Sauvignon Blanc, or Syrah from
Washington State or California's Santa Ynez Valley*

Lemon Bread Pudding (page 166)

Late-harvest Sémillon from California

THIS MENU SERVES 8 GUESTS.

TECHNIQUES Here you will find a number of cooking techniques that are used frequently in this book's recipes.

Citrus: Peeling and Segmenting

Cut both ends from the fruit, just to the flesh. Set the fruit upright on a cutting board and use the knife to cut away the peel and pith, following the curve of the fruit. Try not to cut away too much of the flesh with the peel. Working over a medium bowl to catch the juice, hold the peeled fruit in your hand and slide the knife blade down one side of a section, cutting it from the membrane. Cut down the other side of the same section and let it fall into the bowl. (Pick out and discard any seeds as you go.) Continue for the remaining sections, turning the flaps of the membrane like the pages of a book. If the juice is also needed in the recipe, squeeze the juice from the membrane core into the bowl.

Eggs: Hard Cooking

We often think of these as "hard-boiled" eggs, but really they should be just gently simmered rather than boiled to prevent the whites from becoming tough. I love a little gadget called the Egg Rite timer, which when placed in the water indicates when the eggs are hard cooked. But it's still easy to do so without that little tool.

Place the eggs in a pan of cold water and set over medium-high heat. When the water just comes to a boil, immediately reduce the heat to medium and set a timer for 10 minutes. Decrease the heat to medium low if needed, to avoid too much bubble action. When done, drain the eggs and place them in a bowl with very cold water. (Quick cooling helps avoid overcooking and also helps make peeling easier.)

When it comes to chopping eggs, I often use the food processor to make easy work of the task. I first halve the peeled eggs, then pulse them a few times until the pieces are the size I need. Or, for a more delicate texture, I use the back of a spoon to press the hard-cooked egg—usually the white and yolk done separately—through a medium-mesh sieve to create a fine texture for sprinkling.

Garlic: Roasting

Set garlic cloves (or a whole head of garlic) on a piece of foil, drizzle 1 to 2 tablespoons of olive oil over, and wrap securely in the foil. Roast in a 375°F oven until tender, 20 to 30 minutes depending on how much garlic you're roasting. Let cool in the foil, then pinch the individual tender cloves from their skins. Some recipes call for the roasting oil, or you can save it to use in a vinaigrette or to toss with steamed vegetables.

You may need just a small amount of roasted garlic for a particular recipe, but why not go ahead and roast extra? It keeps well in the refrigerator, covered with a layer of olive oil for 2 weeks. It's delicious stirred into mashed potatoes, spread on toasted baguette slices for canapés (topped with mozzarella or goat cheese perhaps), tossed with pasta—any number of mouth-watering uses.

Nuts: Toasting

Toasting nuts helps deepen their flavor and bring out more of their crunchy character. Scatter nuts in a baking pan just large enough to hold them in an even layer. Toast in a 350°F oven until the nuts are lightly browned and aromatic, gently shaking the pan once or twice to ensure even toasting. Smaller nuts, such as slivered almonds or pine nuts, need just 4 to 6 minutes while larger nuts, like hazelnuts, may take 10 minutes or more. Be sure to keep an eye on the nuts: They can go quickly from "just right" to burnt and bitter; your nose will be as good an indicator as any as to when the nuts are nearly ready.

Hazelnuts also need to be skinned after roasting. Transfer them to a kitchen towel directly from the oven and loosely wrap in the towel. Let the nuts cool for a few minutes, then rub the towel over the nuts to help remove their papery skins.

If chopped toasted nuts are called for, be sure to toast the nuts whole, then chop. The smaller and varied sizes of chopped nuts make it very difficult to toast them evenly, as the tiniest bits are likely to burn before the larger pieces are toasted.

Peaches: Peeling

The technique for peeling peaches is the same as that for tomatoes (see right).

Peppers: Roasting, Peeling, and Seeding

Roasting chiles and bell peppers before using them in a recipe accomplishes a few things: it makes peeling much easier, softens the flesh, and brings out the sweet flavor of the peppers. Arrange whole peppers on a rimmed baking sheet and broil, turning occasionally to roast evenly, for 10 to 12 minutes, until the skin blackens. Place the peppers in a plastic or paper bag, securely seal, and set aside to cool. When cool enough to handle, peel away and discard the skin. Remove the cores and seeds and proceed as called for in the recipe.

Sesame Seeds: Toasting

The technique for toasting sesame seeds is the same as for spices (see below), but since sesame seeds are more oily, they can burn quickly. It's a good idea to toast them over medium-low heat for a longer time, stirring frequently.

Spices: Toasting

As with nuts, toasting spices helps develop their flavor and aroma. You can toast spices either in their whole or ground form; the smaller the size, the less time it will take. Place the spice(s) in a small dry skillet over medium heat and toast, stirring occasionally, until aromatic (in the case of some spices or seeds, you'll also notice the color turning to a toasty brown). Be quite careful to not allow spices to burn. Rather than leaving them in the skillet once toasted, transfer them to a small plate or bowl for quick cooling and to avoid overcooking in the pan's heat.

Tomatoes: Peeling and Seeding

In many recipes I don't bother with peeling tomatoes, particularly with summer's wonderful vine-ripe tomatoes. But if the tomato seems to have a particularly thick skin, or if the recipe will benefit from an extra-smooth texture devoid of skin pieces, I employ this simple technique: Bring a medium pan of water to a boil. Make a small "X" in the bottom of the tomato and gently lower it into the water with a slotted spoon. After 10 to 20 seconds, you should see the skin begin to split. Lift out the tomato and place in a bowl of cold water to stop the cooking. Drain and slip off the skin with your fingers. This same technique can be used for peaches, nectarines, and other firm-fleshed fruits with thin skins.

For recipes where the tomato will be served raw, I often prefer not to use this plunge-in-hot-water method. Instead, I use a serrated peeler, which is made with thin-skinned produce in mind. This peeler will also work for peeling peaches, plums, asparagus—any time you want to remove just a very thin layer of skin.

MY FAVORITE TOOLS

There are so many kitchen tools available that help us to be more efficient with our time or make easy work of a tricky task. This list contains the ten tools that I tend to reach for most often when I'm cooking, or the tools that do such a magnificent job—even if just on occasion—that I can't imagine not having them in my kitchen.

Bird's Beak Paring Knife

I just love this knife for small cutting tasks; the rounded blade and short length are perfect for trimming radishes, cutting wedges of grapefruit, or other jobs for small vegetables or pieces of fruit. The small size allows you to keep a firm grip in the palm of your hand.

Deep Fryer

When I deep-fry foods, I find it much easier to do so in a deep fryer rather than using a Dutch oven or other large pot. The newer generation of fryers are easy to clean, close tight while the food is frying to keep the smell to a minimum, and regulate temperature so you're assured of even cooking every time.

Fish Tweezers

It's a simple little tool, with broad edges to help grasp fish bones for the gentle tug to remove them. Your friends will thank you for the bone-free dining.

Garlic Press

There are so many styles of presses available now and all of them make quick work of mincing garlic. My favorite brand of press is Rösle, a bit pricey but worth the investment. The pressing action also releases the flavorful juices, so you get more intense garlic flavor more quickly.

Lime Juicer

The cupped form of this type of juicer is particularly suited to limes and small lemons, extracting a maximum of juice with a minimum of effort.

Shrimp Deveiner

Though some shrimp are now available pre-shelled and deveined, if you find yourself needing to devein a load of shrimp, this tool will be a great help. It slips between the shell and flesh, making a slit to help you easily lift out the dark vein.

Silicone Products

This category of kitchen products has been growing at an amazing pace in recent years. Silicone, being both heat-resistant and nonstick, is a wonder to cook with. My favorites in this category include silicone baking mats (incredibly versatile, good for everything from cookies to caramelized nuts); silicone spatulas (almost makes me willing to give up my wooden spoons, but not quite); and different types of baking pans (I really love the madeleine pans).

Small Mandoline

For smaller jobs when I don't want to pull out the V-slicer, I turn to this small hand-held slicer. It's perfect for radishes, fennel bulb, paper-thin onion slices for salad, and any number of small firm items from which you want thin shavings. It's incredibly handy to pull from the drawer for those quick jobs, with very little cleanup required.

Thermometer

A thermometer is an important tool to help assure the best results when deep frying. If the oil is not hot enough, the food will cook too slowly and absorb oil as it cooks. If the oil is too hot, the food will brown on the surface before the interior is cooked. (This is less an issue for small, quick-cooking oysters than for larger or denser items.) Allow the oil to reheat between batches as needed.

Some thermometers are made specifically with deep-frying in mind, though an instant-read thermometer may be used as well.

V-Slicer

This is a variation on the popular mandoline slicers, with the V shape guiding the food down the center for even slicing. Variable thickness options and attachments for crinkle-cutting or julienning are big pluses.

INDEX